The Miracle Maker

Murray Watts

Hodder & Stoughton
LONDON SYDNEY AUCKLAND

*This book is dedicated to Julie, Fionn and Toby
and in memory of Ruth*

*I am indebted to the vision and courage of Chris Grace;
the love and inspiration of Penelope Middelboe; and
many others including: Christabel Gingell, Sebastian
Born, Martin Lamb, Derek Hayes, Naomi Jones and
Cartŵn Cymru, Stanislav Sokolov and Christmas Films
Moscow, David Pileggi and Judith Longman.*

The version of Luke 1:32–5 on page 23 is influenced by
David Stern's translation, *The Jewish New Testament*, published
by Jewish New Testament Publications, Maryland, USA.

First published in Great Britain in 2000

10 9 8 7 6 5 4 3 2 1

British Library Cataloguing in Publication Data
A record for this book is available from the British Library

ISBN 0 340 73563 5

Typeset by Avon Dataset Ltd, Bidford-on-Avon, Warks

Printed and bound in Great Britain by Clays Ltd, St Ives plc

Hodder & Stoughton Ltd
A Division of Hodder Headline
338 Euston Road
London NW1 3BH

Prologue

I will set down everything I know. Memories do not arrange themselves obediently in order, and already I am thinking of a garden. It does not belong at the beginning nor is it at the end of my story, but it is there. A garden in the snow. It must have been two years later, after all that had happened, and I went back and it was covered in snow. Snowflakes wet my hair. I felt joy in that terrible place, because I had never seen snow.

This is how he surprises me, this is his way.

I was happy in the snow, but I was crying at the same time, or was it the ice on my face? There was nothing to fear any more, I knew that, and there was every reason to feel the happiness that I felt, but I could not banish the image of him going. He was leaving me and going into that place. I saw him and I have seen him, again and again, over so many years, vanishing into the darkness, leaving me.

I remember it as warm and dark the first time, so dark and the shine on leaves somehow, even though there was no moon, and his face turning. I remember what he said to me and it was something about that which called me back in the year of the snow.

There is deep snow here now, drifting up the palisades. I am no longer innocent of snow. I never dreamt of such a place or the wind gathering the geese over the endless greyness. I never imagined the cold and real snow. Snow that buries. I can see little and hear little, and this is to my advantage. I am so far from home now and even in what I must now call home I am lost in whiteness; so memory, even a disobedient memory, has a blank parchment unfolding across the world. I will write what I can now because I am ignorant of the Day. We are all blinded by our ignorance and dream of endless time. Isn't that so, even when he said there was no telling and that even he did not know?

You are like me, I'm sure; you dream.

1

I couldn't see. That was the first thing. There was a storm of dust at the South Gate, ox carts dragging huge blocks of white limestone, the shouting, cursing, whipping, the noise, screaming, it seemed, as if the whole of Galilee were in one place and shouting against the wind. My father's face was lost in all that smoke. I was sure I was going to choke to death. I couldn't see him for minutes, as we passed through the gates and everything was echoing and blowing around, although I could feel his hand so tight. He was holding on to me desperately, afraid I was about to be sucked into oblivion. Every time someone cursed, I could feel him wince. The shock of the whole place travelled down his arm, through his hand and into my fingers.

'I'm all right!' I must have said it hundreds of times. He didn't listen. Then I fell over, which gave him an excuse to pick me up. I was so thin, it was easy to sweep me up like that, absurdly and dramatically.

The smoke cleared and I could breathe again. I could see my father wiping his face. His sleeves were filthy and he was trying to hold himself and me, as if we were some kind of boat on a wild sea, churning with people. Any moment, we would sink and we would be lost for ever. I felt sorry for him, suddenly. I had never seen him so confused, not knowing which way to go or how to behave. In the synagogue in Capernaum, he was a

3

very important man; in Sepphoris he was nobody. He was just a man with a girl.

It was strange to watch him, curious. He was missing so much. I didn't think we had come to a bad place. There was the ox wagon trundling up a switchback street and the huge white blocks shifting all the time on the planks and the driver shouting and waving his hands furiously at his men who were dancing around, pushing, shoving everything into place, only to begin the whole routine again. It was comical. Chickens were running loose and some bald-headed man was trying to catch them in the draper's tent; there were traders arguing in every language. The legionaries were pacing the walls, gazing down indifferently. I saw women with painted faces laughing with soldiers in a doorway. I did not know this world. My father pulled me on, dusting me down all the time, as if the streets themselves were contaminated.

'I'm all right.'

He wasn't listening.

'Jairus! Jairus!' It was a relief to hear that voice. I could see the old man edging through the crowds.

'Cleopas?' My father's joy was almost pathetic.

'There you are, now . . . Now then!' He had such a deep way of saying 'now then', without meaning anything in particular.

'Now then, Tamar.' He was silent for a moment, but I read nothing into that silence. His face was shining with welcome.

Cleopas was my father's oldest friend, and the only person we knew in the city of Sepphoris.

'How can you live in such a place?'

Cleopas shrugged his shoulders. 'Living is a struggle. In the country or in the city.'

We walked on slowly. I was grateful for Cleopas and his shambling footsteps. There was no way my father could hurry him. The old man was our guide, and whenever my father sighed at something or exclaimed out loud – he was not a man to keep his thoughts to himself, but breathed them out with every look and gesture – he simply waved his hand a little impatiently, a half-wave, dismissing the whole world. All of my father's outrage. Such things were not important to him. Even the actors tumbling out of the crowd on their way to the theatre, leering all round us like mad creatures, scarcely earned a comment. 'Four thousand seats', he said, as if that explained everything. He said it without judgement. My father was not looking to the right or the left, he was walking on, holding me all the time, sometimes stroking my hair as if to put something in order. I remember he was very upset because I was laughing at a man with the most stupid mask, a bird's head with a huge beak and he was clucking and crowing all round me and dancing and flapping his arms. I wanted to see those actors so much and I suppose I went on about it, I kept on begging him. He shouted 'No!', which was not like him. He never shouted at me. He was such a good man, but on that day it was a heavy burden to have a father who was a good man.

'Just one look through the doors, I promise I won't go in.'

'Tamar,' he said, with such exquisite anguish. I knew I had failed him badly with that one question.

I don't know if it was that, or the dust, but I began to cough again. I didn't feel ill at all and I was angry with myself. It made him worse when I was like that, so I would try not to cough, I would keep swallowing hard, gulping, smiling. I was always smiling, I would sometimes laugh when I was coughing. I felt

5

fine and I couldn't bear that look of panic in his eyes, which fathers have when they are pretending to be strong.

'Come on,' he said, 'we're nearly there. A few more steps!'

'The doctor,' said Cleopas suddenly. He was the first one to mention why we had come to the city of Sepphoris. My father and I had not spoken about this all the way from Capernaum, not once on the mule ride, when I fainted in the sun, not even when stopping by the wells at Arbela. Not once across the whole of Bet Netofa had we said anything at all about doctors.

I could see a large oak-beamed crane, with multiple pulleys, slowly shifting a block of limestone from the ox-cart, towards a huge forest of planks and massive triple arches. There was a foreman, high up on walls, directing his men. Masons were carving patterns on to squared stones, so intricate I wanted to stop and gaze at their mystery. A workman was pulling a string taut along a foundation ditch and pegging it in tightly.

'The doctor', said Cleopas, 'lives by the new synagogue.'

He stopped, because there was something of significance at last. He waved, a strong clear wave.

'Now then.' He stood for a long time, in silence. I could hear the hammering and sawing, masons cutting and the white powder from the stone filled the air.

'This will be a light shining for us in Sepphoris.'

My father was looking all round. His eyes were restlessly searching the alley-ways behind us for the doctor's sign. Cleopas took his arm gently and moved him into the shadows. Their voices were low, but I could hear them.

'How is she now, my friend?'

'It comes. It goes . . . but each time the fever returns, it's worse.'

I could hear them, but I wasn't listening. There was a madwoman coming up the street. She was screaming about the emperor and spitting. Her face was odd, the kind of face you have to look at. Misshapen and beautiful. Her clothes were terribly dirty and torn. Everyone was laughing at her, as if she were one of the actors in a show, and she seemed to enjoy it. She was hurling insults at people and laughing. But then she would cry, softly, to the thin air.

Cleopas was reassuring my father.

'He is the best doctor we have in the city.'

'Cleopas, my friend . . .' My father couldn't finish whatever he was trying to say. I heard him clear his throat sharply and then he said, 'God is good.'

'Yes. Whatever happens. He is good.'

I glanced at them and they were embracing. Cleopas shambled off slowly into the crowd, back to his home on the north side. My father looked round at me hastily,

'All right?' he said.

'Yes,' I said, 'I'm all right.'

He turned slowly, with great deliberation, and walked into the doctor's.

I could hear hammering and I looked up, way up the scaffolding, and that was when I saw him.

There have been days when I have walked down the shoreline of the White Island and felt him near, in the soaking rain, when the mist and spray seem to hang in the night over the white breakers. I have seen him riding the darkness. I have touched him for one fraction of a second. I have heard him say, 'Don't be afraid'. All the stories I have ever heard from all the others become mine, they are borne in me each day and especially in the long, harsh nights here, so I cannot divide them from what I know and what I saw. What Cephas knew on Galilee, I know. What Miryam taught me, and the Physician, what they gave me cannot leave me and returns in dreams. The wind over Drumalban carries their words across this wilderness, and they are speaking to me again, beside the dying fires and underneath the stars where the crickets sang beside the boats at Magdala.

But this I saw for myself.

She was screaming so loudly and there was uproar in the streets. People were cheering and jostling her. She was putting on a fine performance.

'I said, *I said*, they were all, *all of you*, murderers, *thieves*, you think I don't see *you*. The Emperor *he told me*, I know!'

He had his back to me and pegs in his hand. He was riveting an oak panel in the great gilded doors and then, with his chisel, he was scooping out a channel of wood, turning it, twisting it around like the bend of a river in a deep valley. He stood back. I didn't see his face, but from the way he stood, so still, I knew he was happy. He bent down to pack his tools and then I saw the vine, flowing from the lintel. It was so lifelike you could have picked the grapes from the door and squeezed them.

The foreman and someone in rich clothes, the architect I think, were looking at him as he climbed down from the scaffolding, past all the cranes and pulleys and wagons. The foreman was shaking his head.

'You won't persuade him.'

'We pay good rates.'

'He's leaving today.'

'Today? I'll pay him double. What does he want?'

'Want? Who knows what he wants?' The foreman huffed, made some hopeless circle in the air. 'You see all that scaffolding? That's his. There's not a peg out of place, all the weights, the balances. There's not a crack in the whole structure. He'll have that down in an hour. And there you have it. The arch. Beautiful, precise.'

The madwoman lurched into the throng of builders, cursing under her breath. Suddenly, as if she had woken from a nightmare into a dream of paradise, she sighed and cried out 'Ohhh!', so loudly everyone turned. All the men on the building site were looking at her, leaning over wooden rails, they were laughing. I couldn't understand why. She was lost in the beauty of that place. 'Oh! Oh! Lovely!' She kept saying it, over and over, then one of the joiners began to imitate her. 'Lovely!' His voice was so harsh and his face looked so vicious, it frightened me. I didn't know why they hated her or everyone wanted to make fun of her as she swirled round and round sighing, pointing, but their catcalls 'Oh, lovely!' made her stop. An expression passed over her face. Like another woman, another being, it was a cruel and knowing smile that she gave back. 'Lovely', she said in a completely different voice, stroking the bare arm of one of the masons, and they shouted with laughter, they roared at her. The man was so taken aback, he almost fell over, but others were coming forward, holding out their hands, pleading, inviting her, calling, giggling like little children. I wanted to cry for her but I was afraid. I just stared and stared. She was going up to the architect himself. The overseer cracked his stick on the wall and screamed at the men, 'Back to work!' but they took little notice. They were transfixed as if they were watching some dangerous sport about to reach its climax. She was laughing, softly, stupidly, fondling the architect's robe – it was damask, so thick and rich, embroidered, it was shining and she was picking it up in her fingers like a little girl would take her father's cloak so innocently. She had that innocent smile now. 'You like nice things?' she said. The architect was stricken with horror and he could not speak. He muttered, tried to brush her off a little, she smiled up at him so strangely and then this great hand smashed her to the ground. Smashed her down like a mad dog into the dust. She was screaming, and I couldn't help myself beginning to cry now, because it was the worst thing I had ever seen. She was groaning on the floor, cursing, holding herself like a baby, rocking, her arms were flailing, whatever was wrong with her had taken on such force. And then she lay still, whimpering, and the men – the men were still laughing, some of them, I couldn't believe how they were laughing. The overseer raised his hand with the stick.

'Get out.' He said it with coldness, so quietly, and she just called out, 'Ohh, ohh, I–' and then nothing. Then weeping.

'*Out*–' he hurled the word across the whole city and put both his hands on the stick and prepared to smash it down.

Then this hand, a hand came from behind him and grabbed the stick and held it, frozen in the air.

'*No!*'

It was the carpenter.

There was a silence so deep, so instant, I did not breathe. I did not dare, no one dared move or shift a foot or clear their throat. We all looked and the overseer remained exactly as he was, his stick high in the air. He could not move for that moment, because I could see that he was in awe.

The man who had held that chisel and turned it to such beauty knelt down and held that woman's hand. He said nothing at all.

He dropped down slowly to the ground and knelt in the dust, on the broken stones beside her. She was lying there, moaning and mumbling. She began to sob with terror, such deep heart-rending sounds, like the sea dragging in a cave, something from so far inside. He looked at her, he looked at her then, in silence, for a long time. Perhaps it was only seconds. I remember it as an age. He took her hand. There was a gasp from someone. A stifled cry of disgust. He lifted her up and shifted the hair from her eyes.

'Tamar!' My father was shouting behind me, he was grabbing me away suddenly. I wanted to stay. I had to stay. He was almost hauling me in his panic.

'This is how it is in Sepphoris – in the holy place of the synagogue!'

What did he see but a builder holding the hand of a woman with a torn dress, touching her in the house of prayer?

He was shaking his head. He was taking me into the doctor's, but I was looking over my shoulder in tears.

'Father!' He wouldn't listen.

The last thing I saw was that woman walking away, through all the crowds. She looked over her shoulder as if to gain strength from the gaze that followed her all the way. The overseer was shouting loudly again, embarrassed, waving his stick aggressively to assert the authority he had forfeited, 'To work, to *work*!' This time, the men obeyed and the carpenter quietly returned to some task beside the scaffolding.

'You say he's from *Nazareth*?' said the architect, as if this were an absurd place for anyone to live.

'Yeah, yeah, Nazareth,' said the foreman, hardly listening. He was still staring at the carpenter's back.

'And he has other work?'

The doctor's door slammed. My father leant against it with his full weight. He breathed the cool air and said nothing. He took my hand and began to move down the tiled corridor.

'I *can* walk,' I said.

The doctor's house was a world of half-finished sentences.

'Is she—?'

'And does – um – ah, I see.'

'So there's no . . . mmm.'

'How often does, um – and would you say that was – ah, yes.'

I counted the bright jars along the shelves. Three hundred and twenty-two, I can remember that distinctly, but not what the doctor said. I can only remember the spaces between his words and the full silences and the way he would suddenly become very busy with something, a phial or some powder or something, as if he had suddenly got some bright idea which just as quickly deserted him. He would walk back to where I was lying and nod and keep rubbing the side of his face, and then return to his bottles, and then sit down and look at my father.

My father was in anguish. I couldn't bear the way he was trying to smile at me and say such stupid things, like 'It's cool in here.' 'It must be good to have a cool room like this.' 'The tiles are very ornate. Are they from Persia do you think?' As if

12

Persia were a very important place in our lives at that precise moment. 'Your mother would give so much to have a floor like this.' (My mother. She had looked so beautiful at the door when we left Capernaum and kissed me lightly, hardly touching me. I felt stronger for her presence, which seemed to go with me, especially the way she walked back into the house and did not watch us go. She was not interested in tiled floors.)

I must have looked half asleep, lying there, because they took the opportunity to go into a side room. I was dreaming, but of the world of Sepphoris outside, the white synagogue with its pillars and acanthus leaves and all the builders congregating there in the stillness. I could not stop thinking of the madwoman turning to look over her shoulder.

'Why should I deceive you?' That was all I heard from the sideroom. And then my father saying, 'Blessed be the Lord, the God of Israel.'

He came out. He put his hands under me. He was very quiet and gentle as he picked me up off the bed and held me. I always liked it when he did that, when he was not trying to take me anywhere or make me do anything, but just holding me to him. He put his face against mine for a long time.

At last, he took me out into the sunlight and set me down.

'What did the doctor say?' I said.

'We must return to Capernaum. You must rest.'

'I'm not tired.'

'No, no . . . We must thank God that you are not tired. Today.' His voice was very thick.

I told him that I felt perfectly all right. He wasn't listening. We walked down the alley-way towards the synagogue. He was breathing deeply, he seemed to be steeling himself to enter the

13

crowds. He waited, as if on the edge of a seething and violent torrent, as if we would drown in the flood of people. He stepped forward, one foot, his head bowed as if he was cast on the mercy of God. I clung on to him but he never looked at me, all the time his head was down, he was shaking it back and forward as if in some nightmare of his own.

'Never, never,' he kept saying. 'We should never—' and then breaking off, clutching at his head.

They came past in their hundreds, the workmen with their leather bags heading home at sundown, the mule drivers and ox wagons ferrying a last load of porphyry and slabs of green marble. An auctioneer was crying out somewhere, a slave was sold at a knock-down price. We passed actors again. They were drunk. A plump Roman official and his wife were sifting through heaps of linen on a stall beneath umbrellas.

'What has happened to the land? What has happened to the land?' My father was repeating the words like a prayer. It was like a strange psalm of his own composing. He was half-singing, half-weeping, sighing about our father Abraham, and every now and then he would cough in the dust and stop and ask me if I were all right. But he never looked at me. I was walking quietly, desperate not to do anything that would disturb him. I was determined to prove that I was well.

Sometimes I see the moment in the half-light of morning. I see him coming. The street is full and faces are floating past, thousands of people streaming and chattering past me. Then, with his bag in his hand swinging so casually, he is coming towards me. He is looking ahead towards the East Gate. He doesn't see me. He is a nobody in the crowd, one face. He could be anyone, there is nothing to mark him out at all. That's the strange thing.

I see this anywhere, in a house in Rome on the Appian way. On board ship, lying awake with the waves slapping the hull and the gulls screaming, always in the half-light, always dawn, he is coming. He doesn't turn and look. We're getting closer and I want to say something to my father about this, say 'That's him again', but I daren't or I can't, my mouth is so dry. I want him to look at me and acknowledge that I am there, but he is lost in the crowds for a moment, submerged, and I am convinced that I will never see him again.

Then he is right beside me, passing. I can see him, I'm looking up and my father is looking too, horrified. He is pulling me away. He recognises the man who touched the woman in the place of prayer and he says, 'We should never have come to this terrible city!' I am dragged onwards, and I turn back because I can't bear the agony and the loss. I have to turn back and see him go. I must see the man go.

And then he turns. He turns. He stops for one second. He is looking at me. He is gazing at me and people are pushing past him, onwards. The whole world is flowing through us, but he is utterly still.

The incident was scarcely more than a minute's interruption. My father pulled my hand as strongly as he dared – these things meant nothing. Some rough joiner who worked on the synagogue and kept the wrong company in a street full of actors. Everything was to be expected in Sepphoris. He called me on, with his special tone, 'Tamar!', that was mildly indulgent but concealed a warning not to stretch his patience.

The mules were ready. He shook the dust off both his feet, very carefully and methodically. I remember being very curious about that and questioning him, but he said nothing. We never entered that city again.

2

It was Miryam who comforted me on the night I stood outside the garden. She was the one who knew, she always knew more than everyone and so she said nothing for a long time. Her silences were offered like blessings. No moment with her was ever empty, and she took me back to her tent among the olive groves. All the pilgrims from the Galil were singing, you could see the fires across the hills burning in their thousands as if the stars had fallen to earth.

He had left me, it seemed finally, and walked into the darkness. But the pilgrims were ignorant and laughing.

'It's Pesach,' she said. 'They should laugh and sing.' Then she fell silent and she held my hand, and we gazed into the fire for hours.

She promised then that she would tell me something. It concerned a young girl in Nazareth who was not much older than me.

'One day', she said, 'I will tell you what that girl knows.'

Nazareth was an hour's walk from Sepphoris, by way of the aqueduct along the ridge. He walked past the slaves turning the water wheels with their huge wooden buckets dipping into the springs and carrying the long flow up to the cisterns of the acropolis. He walked away from the citadel of Herod Antipas, which they also called Autocratoris – the Emperor's city.

He climbed the cinder track from the tribute city with its extravagant marble to his home in the cliff-face of Nazareth.

There were other labourers wending their way up the narrow ridge. A thin file, some of them carrying lanterns in the fading light, and Yeshua son of Miryam was just one more joiner from the hill country, swinging his overloaded bag across his shoulder. The snows of Mount Hermon in the distant north had already sunk into the twilight, but the faint outline of Carmel towards the shores of the Mediterranean was tipped with fire. It was engulfed in the blueness as they walked on, chatting and laughing. The village was nearly dark by the time they arrived and the scattering chickens heralded their approach. Smoke drifted from an old chimney, built into the solid rock, and Yeshua bent low to enter the door of the thatched room which jutted from the limestone.

I will call him Yeshua for a little while longer, while Miryam's story still sings to me across the far outposts of an indifferent world. Here, he is neither Yeshua nor Jesus, but some eastern rumour. He is nameless. I once heard tell of a 'Chrestus from Palestine who was a troublemaker and caused an edict to be declared against the Jews in Rome' – I was reminded of this as a warning against superstitions which do not have a formal licence. I was warned not to speak of him on any account. So you will forgive me clinging to the name I first knew for a few moments longer, the name, whether Greek or Hebrew, which once known cannot be erased by edict.

As Miryam heard the sound of steps, she removed the cakes she had been baking and looked up. He was standing there as he always stood, saying nothing, breathing in the stillness. It was his way to say nothing for a long while, but the silence between them was different, fuller and, to both of them, painful. The unspoken words were lingering in the air, like the flecks of soot above the fire brightening and dying. Many times she began to say something and thought better of it.

They sat down to eat their meal as the silence prevailed and they looked at each other, for they had no need to avoid each other's gaze.

'What did you say?' She broke the silence suddenly, quite plainly.

'I said I had other work.'

'Your Father's . . . work.'

The way she said the word, held it on her tongue, spoke of her struggle and of her resolve. He did not offer a reply.

'You said that once so long ago.'

And her mind was already travelling, she was struggling through a throng of pilgrims against the flow.

'You remember,' he said.

'I remember everything', and even in the pain of the memory there was a brightness, that music, a touch of her laughter which had once so captivated Yosef in Nazareth. Now she was with her husband again and she was weaving through the people and he was calling out, 'Please, let us through, let us through in the name of all that's holy.' That was one of Yosef's phrases in desperation. She kept stopping and begging people, 'Have you seen him, my son, Yeshua? Is he with you? I thought he was with Reuben and Elisheva.' People were shaking their head, looking after them. 'The boy's gone missing.' Word travelled through the crowds and everyone was confident, 'The child is with his cousins. His aunts. His friends. Further up, back up, go back, Miryam', but she kept on fighting her way through, until neither of them said anything. The fear had overwhelmed them. They were at the end of the line and the jaunty laughing rabble was thinning into nothing. Jerusalem lay ahead, the water gate with traders striking their deals, shouts in the air and the braziers burning in the shadows.

For three days and nights they searched every quarter of Jerusalem for their child. Then Miryam woke up and grabbed Yosef. 'A courtyard', she said. They ran through the crowded forum. She could see the huge, dark tunnel beneath the Temple, they were rushing now, running with all their might, and Yosef was looking around frantically, unreasonably, into forgotten corners as if the boy would be lying there injured or dead, but Miryam ran straight into the whiteness of the marble precincts, across the court of the Gentiles. She ran into the colonnades, in and out of arches. And then she saw him, the boy, she saw his face through a forest of bright cloaks and embroidered girdles and a blue robe fringed with gold bells and pomegranates. The high priest was there himself, standing right in front of him, priests and Sadducees, lawyers, scribes were gathered round him. Some were sitting, others leaning against the pillars, all were listening or interrupting, debating. They were all nodding and murmuring, talking about the boy as if he had been unfolding the secrets of the scriptures to them. They seemed half-amused and half-disturbed by this child. Someone was asking who the boy's parents were, where was he from? And Miryam could no longer contain herself, but ran into the midst of them all.

'Oh my son!' she cried, 'Oh my son. Why have you done this to us?'

Yosef followed, whispering in this holy place but unable to conceal his anger and confusion. 'Running away like this! Do you know how we have worried, we have been through a thousand deaths from our fear!'

The boy looked at them, with a rebuke that stopped their breath. 'Why were you looking for me?' he said, 'Didn't you know where I'd be?' Yosef turned to Miryam with a hopeless gesture, no more than a raising of his eyebrows, as if to say, 'You explain, Miryam, explain the child!' But she was just staring at him. Yeshua looked at her and said, so softly but with such an unerring aim at her heart, 'I have to work at my father's business.'

That was the memory which burned in her heart until daybreak in Nazareth; she told me how it had come upon her like a wound, a freshly bleeding wound.

He lay on his bed and slept peacefully. She sat beside him, touched his brow softly, only for a moment and by way of farewell. She took her hand away.

A girl with tousled hair kneeling beside a huge stone pestle and mortar.

Her thoughts were pilgrims once again, only this time travelling to Nazareth, the dwellings hewn in the rock, the courtyards and chickens and rattling wattle fences, the same Nazareth, but a girl grinding corn, pounding in clouds of white flour.

There was flour on her robe and her hands. She stopped for a moment, scooping more flour into a dish. Somewhere a blackbird was singing, a full-throated song she remembered, tumbling, rising. Other birds were congregating in a jacaranda tree and the early morning light was filtering through deep blossom and dark branches. A tiny sunbird hovered at the mouth of a flower. It sipped with a long curving beak, the sunlight glowing on green and violet plumage. Collared doves murmured in the eaves and a chicken clucked, pecking at the fallen grain.

The blackbird spread its wings and flew to a bush beside her, its song thrilling in the clear morning air, and she smiled at the bird, gazed at it for quite some time. She was a girl with time to be still and to listen to the world, and she laughed and shook her head at the bird, which seemed to converse with her so intimately. She laughed out loud, picked up the pestle and pounded the grain. She pounded it now with her head down, both hands clutching the pestle, working furiously. Then she stopped for a second, brushed her hand across her face. The white cloud was dispersing as the birds sang. Their chorus seemed suddenly so far away, and she looked up and she saw the form of a man standing in the entrance of the courtyard. She gasped because she had not seen or heard anyone approaching and the figure was unfamiliar. He was very tall, taller even as the white cloud cleared, revealing the stranger in one breath. He stood right before her. She looked up into his face, but she could not see anything against the light. Then, as if a ray of sun had fallen across him in an instant, she saw an expression of such love and beauty, as he said:

'Shalom, Miryam!'

She was afraid, because the man bowed low, right down to the ground before her. He lay stretched out before her and then rose humbly to kneel beside her.

'Adonai', he said, 'is with you.' And when he said the name of the Lord God, his voice was like the sound of waters, running into a deep pool. 'You, Miryam, are the highly favoured one.'

Now she was trembling, she shook because she did not know the meaning of this saying or what this message could mean. She did not understand how such a greeting could be for her.

And the man, who was an angel sent from God called Gavri'el, spoke with great gentleness to her.

'Don't be afraid, Miryam, for you have found favour with God. You will conceive in your womb and you will give birth to a son, and you are to call him Yeshua. He will be great, he will be called the son of HaElyon. Adonai, the Lord your God, will give him the throne of his forefather David; and he will rule the house of Ya'akov for ever. His kingdom will never end.'

'How can this be,' she said, 'because I am still a virgin?'

The leaves were turning silver in the wind that blew from the ridge and from across the plains of Esdraelon, and her hair covered her eyes once more. The angel stood before her as he had appeared, by the gateway.

'With God,' he said, 'nothing is impossible.'

She looked at him and she began, slowly, very slightly to nod.

The angel was leaving and his voice was within her now, a whisper deep within, a music rising even as the figure vanished, 'Ruach HaKodesh,' it said, 'ruach!' 'The Holy Spirit will over-shadow you, the power of HaElyon will cover you, therefore the holy child born to you will be called the Son of God.'

Miryam knelt in the courtyard, beside the stone pestle and beneath the single jacaranda tree. She lifted her eyes up and she said:

'Here I am, the servant girl of the Lord!'

* * *

'Here I am.' She said it as she lay dying in that shuttered room in Ephesus, 'Let everything happen to me as you have said.' She was speaking to the angel as if he stood beside her bed. She was fourteen again.

I stayed with her a long time. She was peaceful and I remember some clattering procession was passing outside to the high temple, to the many-breasted Artemis of the Ephesians, and she did not turn or sigh or react at all to the howling songs and drums, for she was in Nazareth, and she took my hand weakly and said, 'I kept my promise.' She had kept faith with me, the girl who wept while the pilgrims sang.

We stayed at Cana that night my father and I left Sepphoris, in some old, messy caravanserai, and there was a soldier shouting all night. I don't know what about. The smell of the camels made me feel sick, that and the oil lamps, the wick was soaking in something horrible. My father kept fanning the air in our room with his cloak, it was the kind of silly and useless thing he would do obsessively, and I loved him for it. He sat down on my bed for a few minutes at one point, when the noise was getting to me, and he began to sing to me. It was some story and I can't remember it at all, what any of it was about, but he was making it up. Not very well. He kept stopping and saying, 'Have I sung that bit? What did I just sing?' It was some adventure of the Israelites, it was probably the girl with Naaman, the little maidservant, he was always doing that one. I was glad of the story and I did sleep that night.

My father was up early. Perhaps he had never slept at all. Dogs were fighting somewhere. It was very early and I could see him at the window. He was standing and he was trying to say

Barukh Atah Adonai. His arms were held high and I could see the sun beyond him and then he just fell on his knees. He was still for such a long time and I watched him, and I wanted to get up and put my arms round him but I felt ill.

We went by Nimra, through the low pass and into the Valley of the Doves. There was a spring at Mount Arbel and we stopped there and took water. It seemed to take for ever, but it was only a brief journey before we were on the Via Maris. Mercenaries from Gaul were on their way to the barracks at Capernaum and I could see my father was reluctant to travel with them, but they left us to ourselves. They seemed to respect our silence. I do not know if it was something about my father's face or the way I rode on the mule, lying into him wrapped against the sand, but they let us walk through and their eyes followed us. I could see them, just, there was a tiny space in the shawl around my head, and I suppose they could see these eyes looking at them as if I were some little creature. They did not sing or laugh as we passed through. At last we came by Gennesaret into Capernaum.

Our house is in the draper's street, which is the first paved street when you come up from the docks. A few years ago, it was still there, but I do not know who owns it now. It's an ordinary house, built of stone without mortar and plastered with clay and lime. There is a roof of reeds and sticks coated with thick clay against the rains, but what makes it different is the room on top. There were two chambers, and I slept in one of them. From the tiny window under the eaves or from the balcony outside, I could see into the street and across to the synagogue and quite far down.

My mother stood at the door. She didn't come running out

to me. She stood in the shadow and I couldn't see her face. I thought perhaps she would be smiling to see me, but I couldn't tell.

My father carried me in and laid me down beside the cushions. She brought water and a cloth and wiped the sand from my eyes. It was all in my hair.

I wanted to tell her so badly about everything I had seen in Sepphoris, but she was busying herself with wringing out the cloth and pulling the rug around me.

'She's shivering.'

'She's done well,' my father replied. 'It's been a difficult journey and she's been the best companion.'

'Look at her.'

'Yes.' He was distracted. He was standing by the window. Neither of them said anything of any consequence.

'Perhaps I should carry her up now.'

'No.' I said. 'No. I'll be all right now. Just give me a minute. I'll be all right now.'

'You're stubborn,' my mother said, and I felt better. I almost willed her to be angry with me. The silence between the two of them made me feel awkward and alone.

'I saw something,' I said. 'It was—'

'Am I to help her upstairs?' my father said, still talking as if I weren't in the room.

'It was in Sepphoris—'

'Sepphoris!' He shouted, exploded. He would have flung something to the floor but there was nothing to hand, only some flowers my mother had gathered in the fields.

'Sepphoris!'

26

'Jairus,' she said, 'can't you see! She's—'

'Yes, yes, I can see, of course.'

He walked into the courtyard. My mother led me upstairs, allowing me to walk slowly beside her. I was grateful for that.

I lay down on the bed and it felt good to be there, only the room was very hot. She sat there a long while and whenever I tried to tell her anything she said, 'Tomorrow'. I remember she paused the first time she said it, but then she said it very clearly, 'Tomorrow'.

She went downstairs softly although I was still awake, softly as if by some involuntary respect, like the soldiers, it was strange and it felt a little frightening to me. My father was still in the courtyard and she went out to him. I could hear their voices for a while on the night air, because she was shouting. She must have thought I couldn't hear them.

'Something, Jairus! Tell me something!'

'How can I tell you something? I can't tell you what I don't have myself. I don't have something.'

'Then what do you have?'

'I have a phial of . . .' He just trailed off and then he shouted, 'A phial! I have medicine!'

'What will it do?'

'Do you know what he said?' – my father's voice was shaking – 'He said . . . I said to him, "What will it do?" And he said, "Why should I deceive you?" '

There was silence. And then I could hear my mother weeping. She was weeping so angrily. She was banging her fists on something. She was so – it almost sounded like she was cursing. She was saying something I couldn't hear, and my father was

27

replying, 'You don't know what you're saying, Rachel. That you can't say.'

'Oh,' she said. 'Oh! Oh!' She said it like beating a hammer on the wall. 'Oh!' And then she was mumbling something. The door slammed. Then it opened and then it shut quietly. And I could hear them both in the room downstairs, but not a word of what they said. They were discussing me, I know. Talking about what to do and where to turn, I suppose. It was like floating up there, floating on some peculiar dream, because I could hear words and I could feel the anger and the sorrow, violent sorrow, and every now and then my mother pacing and it seemed just crying out nothing. It made me think again of the woman in the street, the madwoman just saying 'Oh'. And I felt so strange to think of my mother as if she were a demented soul but that's how she sounded for hours. I had not known her like this before.

'Rachel. Rachel. Rachel. God will—'

'God!'

My father was always trying to say something good. I could hear that, even though he was in the darkness too. He would always look for something good and that made it worse for my mother.

'Jairus!' She was pleading with him in some sort of angry sobbing moan, as if he were the source of all her pain. 'Jairus, oh, just leave me. Please, please.'

I was floating above these sounds and I felt quite well. I didn't feel hot at all. All I wanted was for tomorrow to come and then I would tell her everything.

Miryam held in her hand a jewelled casket, that night by the fire in Nazareth, and on it there were runes and symbols and a word she did not know. Perhaps it was only a pattern, but she fingered it as she had done over thirty years, wondered over it, turned it around in the firelight and studied the enamelled figures riding. They were always riding. The shepherds she had felt comfortable with, they belonged to her, she said. They were her people.

'He's here! He's here!' They burst in with such triumph, arguing and then hushing each other.

'He's here!'

'He's in here . . . I promise you . . . he's in the . . .' The old shepherd was overcome. He was coughing suddenly in his confusion. 'Oh, the baby,' he said. He just kept on saying it to himself, and then the little shepherd boy pushed through the others, shoving and pushing. He crawled through someone's legs and cried out:

'Aah, look at the baby, he's in the manger!'

She held him out and they took him, the old man first, with such delicacy, as if he had been rehearsing for a long while and was terrified to do something wrong.

'Like this. I held mine like this. You see? Experience, that's it.'

None of them could find words for what they had seen. One of them started on about glory and another about the people on earth. A whole garbled tale about angels in their thousands, 'thousands upon thousands' and peace to all people.

'On whom his favour rests,' said the thin one. 'I think I got that right.' He turned back to the others very uncertainly. 'It was favour, wasn't it?'

'Definitely "favour",' said the old one.

'Oh, oh, the little lad!' said the one with the wild hair. 'He's looking at me! At *me* . . .'

Then the little boy sidled up to her and whispered, 'We heard such music in heaven for this little child.'

I must have made a sound – perhaps I sighed at that – because she turned to me quite suddenly and she held my hand and said, 'You must be ready, for no one knows the Day.'

That was what she said, and the shadows were stealing across the room so far and I hadn't noticed, we were nearly in the twilight.

'I'll fetch light,' I said.

'Do you think I can judge between light and darkness?' she said.

There was one more thing.

It was the casket in the firelight, she kept talking of that. She said how she had turned it around and worn those symbols into a gleaming mirror. She could see her own face in the riding.

'Gold is for a king.' That was the first one, the Parthian lord. 'The riches of his glory.'

'Frankincense is for prayer, a fragrant offering to God.' The man with the Phrygian cap laid down his burden at the cradle. And then the Nubian warrior came forward, with the casket wrapped in a fleece, and he did not unravel it. He laid it down dumbly.

'Myrrh is for sorrow and the day of death,' said his Parthian companion. The Nubian signed in the air. 'A doorway,' said the magus with the folded cap. 'The doorway into life.'

The warrior said nothing and shook his spear and cast it on the earth, and then lay there weeping on the stones. He rose, silent as he had arrived, and departed. The others stayed for many hours and they rejoiced with her and with her husband.

Long after, by night, she unravelled the fleece. She held the casket in both hands and turned it, beside the fire, for the first of many times.

3

When Jesus left his mother Mary in Nazareth it was dawn. Yes, it is time. He was walking into the world by way of Jordan, and I must call him by the name you know.

I had heard many tales of the man by the river. Some of our people had been from Capernaum to hear him, and one year we had stayed at Aenon near Salim after Passover, and then we found him by chance at Nahal Kerit. They call it the holy ravine, because it was the place of Elijah the prophet. There were soldiers from the militia of Antipas, about fifty, and they were asking the wild man questions. He wasn't afraid.

Even when the temple guard came and they were throwing questions like rocks at him, he silenced them, and the men in white robes from Tiberias and Jerusalem, the sadducees, he walked right up to them and said things, sharp things. He was dripping wet. He had a goat skin and he shook it like an animal and the men looked at him with hatred. They didn't move, or brush the water off their cloaks and hats.

There were pilgrims with us who said he was a prophet. I don't remember what the man John said. He was standing far away in the green river, it was dark green, nearly black, and I thought the water was stagnant. It was like a dead pool in that place, but my father said the water was always moving underneath. The wild man was shouting something over and over, but all I can hear now is the arguing on the way back which went on for days and was still going on between my family and other families for some months.

There were followers of John in Capernaum and they believed he had been sent by God. My father thought he was dangerous and he made too many enemies.

'We need prophets, we need peace,' he said, 'that is our tragedy.'

'We have neither because of people like you,' someone said, and so the argument became insulting.

It was in that year that I became ill.

The mist was low over the green of Esdraelon, as Jesus walked up to the ridge. This time he was alone and even the first labourers were still wrapped in the comfort of darkness and lay beside the low embers of their fires. No one stirred or woke. Jesus did not turn round, to look back to his house, nor did Mary stand at the gate. They did not mark this farewell with words. She knew he was going to Jordan, to his kinsman John, the wild man who called the righteous men to strip themselves naked and wash themselves clean.

She understood nothing of this journey, why he had to begin here.

'Turn from your sins, turn back!' John threw the words to passing soldiers and priests, anyone who would catch them. A Pharisee, a well-known rabbi from Chorazin, stopped, questioning silently, as if to ask 'By what right do you say anything to me?'

'Turn from your evil ways.'

The man laughed and then, in the silence that followed, regretted his laughter. A fellow traveller stepped forward.

'How can we rid the nation of all its wickedness?' There were murmurs all around him, it was a good question from a holy man. John slapped his own chest with such force the blow echoed around the gorge.

'Start here,' he said, 'begin with your own heart.'

Sadducees were standing there with the temple guard, gazing coldly from the back of the crowd, keeping a considerable distance, but the wild man picked them out one by one.

'You brood of vipers! Show repentance in your actions! Don't think you can say, "Well, well, after all, Abraham is our father!" Don't smirk to yourselves as you bend low at the altar and bless yourselves, "Abraham! Abraham!" '

He gouged a stone from the mud, 'See here? Abraham!' He shouted, 'God can raise up children of Abraham from these stones!'

He hurled the rock into the water and waded after it.

'Repent! Drown your sins and live. Wash your soul in the sight of God!'

There were many who obeyed the desert prophet that day, not the priests and the levites or the scribes or the officials, but there were fishermen, and a merchant who astonished his fellows, and a soldier who ripped off his cuirass and helmet and stalked through the mud and begged God to forgive him.

The people were in fear of John, because he set hearts on fire and lifted their hopes for a coming kingdom, and because the man respected no one.

'I baptise with water!' He hurled into the sunlight a handful of drops showering like diamonds. 'Water,' he said, with a soft laugh, a curious teasing whisper, 'water.' He kept saying it and laughing. 'But there is one who is coming after me. There is one . . .'

He baptised many and said nothing more for a while.

Then he stood on the bank and lifted a sandal high in the air. 'I am not worthy to undo the strap on his sandal!'

The people, those who came every day to hear their prophet, were untroubled. The wild man was full of sayings and mysteries, sometimes his words scorched like the wind, whipped them, other days he tossed phrases and thoughts into the air like chaff and no one could grasp at his meaning.

'I have baptised you with water,' he said, 'but he will baptise you with the Holy Spirit and with fire.'

'Who are you?' One of the temple officials stepped up to John. 'We have to take an answer back to our masters.' John looked at him with an exaggerated sympathy that made a mule driver in the crowd of spectators spit with approval.

'Who am I?'

'Are you the Christ who is to come? We must have an answer.'

'You want to know?'

'We want to know if you think—'

'Really – you really want to know?'

John stood face to face with the questioner, staring into his eyes.

'Are you the Messiah?' the man said weakly.

There were many messiahs, many who talked of delivering Israel, they lived in caves in the hills, had their followers, had their day. John nodded, slowly, relishing the word.

'Messiah,' he said, and turned back through the crowds and wandered down through the sludge of the river. 'Oh, here's a man by the Jordan, who eats wild honey and lives in the desert and preaches and rants, and the poor starved fool dreams he is the Messiah!'

'Who are you then?' said a priest. 'It's the matter of our report for the appropriate authorities.'

'Am I God's chosen one to save all the people?' He turned round to the throng of people, so huge that men slid into the reeds to catch a glimpse of the crazed locust-eater. 'No!' he shouted, 'I am not your Messiah! Nor do I dream that I am anything but this, the voice – "the voice of one crying".'

Their faces were grey, still. There was deadness in their eyes as they shifted their gaze uneasily, mounted their horses and rode off. 'The voice of one crying in the desert,' said John, as if the wind could take his words and ferry them to whoever. 'Make way! Prepare a straight path for the Lord.'

The Sadducees and their party made their irregular path through the crowd as their horses turned through the straggle of latecomers and headed for Jerusalem. A man looked up at them as they passed, but they did not see him. He gazed at the clouds around the hoofs as the riders merged into the Jerusalem road.

John was already back in the river and his hands were on the shoulders of a bull-necked fisherman, massive, smiling, the sun on his huge forehead.

'Andrew,' said John quietly, 'I am baptising you now but—'

Andrew looked at him as the water streamed away from his face, but John was looking far up into the crowd, into the highest part, as a young man edged forward. He walked alone and he was scarcely noticed by the sweltering and chattering mass of people.

John held Andrew close. He was shaking and the fisherman

was puzzled. He smiled at the wild man, gripped his hand. John was shaking his head.

'Behold,' he said.

'What?' said Andrew. 'What is it, teacher?'

'Behold the lamb of God who takes away the sin of the world.'

He was down by the water now, he was entering. John was leaving Andrew and walking up to the man.

'No,' he said.

The man nodded slowly, with great deliberation.

John fell to his knees, the water sending a wave across his chest and his face.

'No.'

People were watching from the banks, more with curiosity than astonishment. The prophet was unpredictable. This was some dumb show of his own. They could hear nothing, but Andrew stood there in the river gazing. He could see that John was weeping.

'I should be baptised by you. Are you coming to me?'

'John,' the man said with strange insistence, quietly beyond all contradiction, 'John, when we were children we played by this river.'

'I remember.'

'Our mothers called and we ran to them. We followed them.' He put his hands on the side of John's arms as if to lift him high. 'Now there is another call. My father in heaven, and I must follow.'

Air was coursing down the valley, a cold air from the north, as John led the man into the deeper water. Andrew had trouble holding his cloak on the river-bank and pinned it into the mud with his foot. Robes and shawls tumbled past him with a life of their own, as if they were dragged into the boiling sky. People stumbled after them, snatching them, laughing, shouting. It was nothing unusual in that scorched place where bushes clung desperately to the crumbling, sliding river-bank.

But Andrew watched the figures alone in the Jordan. This was different. The man was leading John now, wading past him, and, suddenly, with one movement, he sank himself into the water and John was reaching out to him.

He is falling into the dark. He is sinking for ever and the darkness is touching him, clinging to his body like weed, he is so far down now. He can hear nothing and see nothing. Then the air travelling with him gurgles into life, bubbles of light explode in the blackness. He is breaking into the light. There is a voice, sounding in the far depths, but he cannot hear the words; then the light descending from the ceiling of the river breaks in, carves through the water as he rises to meet it, and it takes him, it captures him all around, light from far above and a bird flying. There is a dove for one moment, with outstretched wings as he breaks into the air, and only John can hear the voice too, which is singing from above and from below, 'You are my beloved son', a voice like the sound of the waters, a dark rumbling thunder of tenderness.

The man looked for a long time at John, and some of the crowd mumbled a few things, asked who he was, but no one seemed to know or guess what any of this meant. Their desert prophet was calling another sinner back to his God, purifying another soul. What did it matter? It was none of their business. They were waiting for John to stride on to the shore and harangue the rich or shock some old camel trader into a new bargain with life. They awaited the next barb against the Sadducees with enthusiasm, as the unknown visitor slowly walked away and, strangely, took a turn higher up the river and stepped across the sharp stones, then waded up the bank into the wilderness.

'Where's he going?' asked Andrew.

'War,' said John.

'He's going to war?'

John stared after the figure, which steadily vanished into the glare.

'War in the desert?' said Andrew. His teacher was testing him with riddles.

'There are battles which must be fought alone.'

John slapped Andrew hard on the back, smiled slightly and shouted, 'Come on.' The fisherman turned away from the emptiness of the desert, glad that the wild man was walking back into the cheering crowds, but something stirred deep within him, a mysterious fire. He knew it would not be the same now.

Forty days.

Mary spoke of it to no one. She knew, but some things she never told and perhaps never recalled. If this darkness was ever in her heart, then it was beyond forgetting but also beyond speaking. I never asked her. It was the Physician who told me, he had heard it from the Beloved Disciple who was once alone with Jesus for seven nights in the Judaean wilderness.

* * *

He was alone for forty days and forty nights without food and the devil came to him.

Rain skimming across the Jordan beneath a velvet sky, almost black. He is wading across shallow waters, stepping across sharp stones. He stumbles into the river, gets up and drives himself on. He is walking in the blinding sun and the dust is fingering the air around his feet, writing in the wind, and the steep crags rise all around him.

He prays at night beneath the vast sky. There are stars, an infinite number but no single light, nothing to guide. He is wandering in dark shadows beneath overhanging rocks and a voice seems to echo,

'This is my beloved son.'

'My beloved son.'

'If you are the beloved son.'

He turns and stares. A shadow seems to kiss his steps, but there is nothing, only the wind howling in caves. And then hot wind lashing him with sand, another day, many days later. The scouring through the bushes is like laughter—

'My beloved son.'

'If you are—!'

His face is drawn, his lips cracked like the steppes that reach into the haze. A scorpion dances with its mate, scurrying beneath a stone, and vultures wheel above a carcass. He is lying on the ground, his face in the dust, his fists clenched.

'My beloved son, the one whom I love.'

He is alone beneath the moon and a figure is following him. He turns round but there is only emptiness, the rush of air.

Suddenly a stone is rolling, bouncing and landing at his feet.

He picks it up. In the moonlight it almost looks like a loaf. He throws it to one side and it splinters on impact.

Noon, and he has collapsed by a stream and he lifts his hand to a desperate muddy trickle which he scoops into his mouth. A stone tumbles down a hill, trailing dust. It lands beside him. It looks like a freshly baked loaf. Suddenly, all the stones around him look as if they might be loaves. He is holding his stomach and his head is lowered down to the dust, scratched and bleeding from the sand. A soft, gentle voice speaks to him, calmly, reassuring, lilting.

'Command this stone to turn into a loaf of bread.'

He opens his eyes slowly.

'You have the power.'

The muddy trickle is becoming clear water, lying still, deep. A face shimmers from the depths, smiling lovingly:

'If you are the Son of God!'

He is sweating, struggling up on all fours, he stumbles, falls back. The stones before him, thousands of stones, are becoming loaves. People are appearing from the hills, running, eating, and he is standing among them, hundreds of people are calling his name. They are lifting him high, roaring his name. Suddenly he stands and shouts:

'It is written, "Man shall not live on bread alone".'

His voice echoes in the gulleys and caves and the crowd evaporates. A thorn branch juts into the sky and he is alone among the rocks and the shale which stretch out before him. He is climbing a great ridge alone, a tiny figure outlined against the burning sky.

But there are two figures. Close beside him, the shadow of a shadow, stalking.

The sun is setting, massive red, imperial splendour erupting into the ensigns of Rome and legions marching. All the armies of the world are ranged across the plain, the Emperor of China surrounded by his mandarins and his generals and thousands prostrating before him, the pyramids of Egypt and columns of warriors shouting, saluting. The ranks part, folding back, as a colossal statue is wheeled before him; it bears the laurel wreath, red and purple banners flow around its limbs and golden coins shower down bearing his own face, the statue's face, his face.

He is turning away, in agony and disgust, hiding his eyes, and the shadow is singing into his ear, 'Bow down before me and it will all be yours—'

'All yours!'

The subject peoples are infinite, the hands a forest through the world.

'It is written – "You shall worship the Lord your God, and no one else shall you serve! No one!" '

The statue shrinks into nothing.

He is standing alone beneath the stars. He kneels, he prays, his hands around his head, and in the dawn he is still there.

Now he rises, with pain, he sets one foot before another. Another. He stumbles up a steep hill, stops to rest, and as he moves on the double shadow returns. He is climbing on to the Mount of Olives and a dove seems to fly somewhere high over his head, a speck of white, and the words descending, half-breathed, 'You are my beloved son . . . my son.'

The brightness of the temple beckons.

'If you are the Son of God.'

The dove is gone. Suddenly, the ground drops away, he is on the pinnacle of the temple and gazing far down at people scurrying, specks of humanity. The world is tilting.

'Throw yourself down from here.'

Priests and Sadducees, the high priest, all the leaders, the devout, all are gathered, all gazing up to him.

'Prove who you are', the voice behind him is sweetly persuasive. He turns, and the figure is radiant, glorious, arms outstretched. 'For it is written in the scriptures that he has commanded his angels to take care of you. They will guard you, they will carry you up in their arms before you even hit your foot on a stone.'

He falls, he is hurtling through the air and brightness wraps him around, lifts him, the clouds boil and stream with light around his feet and the people are shouting,

'The Messiah!'

'The deliverer of Israel!'

'The chosen One of God!'

'No!'

He is standing on the pinnacle still, in the moonlight.

'No!'

The darkness recoils from him, curls into the blackness below.

'You shall not put your God to the test!'

His voice echoes around the Mount of Olives and across Gehenna.

He is alone on the hill, as the shadow leaves him, for now, sliding through the ancient olive groves.

There is warm sunlight on him. All around are flowers, white asphodel on thin stems, the dark blue of mountain lupins, the pink and blue of cornflowers and swathes of camomile, white and yellow, stretching through tall grasses.

That's how I want it to be for him, lying there after forty days and nights without food. Lying in the long grasses, on the hillside, by a stream.

I will lay him down in the grasses and the asphodels, let him lie there for a whole day sleeping. He was always able to sleep like that, suddenly and for a long time, so no one dared wake him, as if he hadn't slept for years. He could sleep in the midst of terrible noise and stay awake for nights when everyone was drowsy, even after one hour, just one hour, people would sleep all around him and he would watch. Then, another time, no one could sleep for one second and he would lie dreaming in the bottom of a boat.

I can see him in those fields, the meadow on the edge of Bethany which I know, the one which dips into the groves and where the blue seems to sail so lightly across the dark feathery grasses in between the trees, that velvet place.

It was Lazarus who found him, somewhere near the waters. Jesus was sitting up, he looked dusty, his robe torn and punished by the desert sand but his face was clean. He had washed himself and he looked quite well. He held out his hand and Lazarus sat down. Lazarus was laughing, not only out of surprise but because his sister Mary had kept on saying that Jesus had been down at the Jordan, she had heard his voice or seen someone like him in the crowd but never managed to reach him, and Martha had refused to believe her.

'They've been arguing for days. Days and days,' he said.

'Where are they – I'm longing to see them—'

'You'll start another argument.'

They walked on, up to the old farm, Lazarus with his arm

44

round his friend, chattering, innocent of the silence and the darkness which slowly and painfully lifted from his companion's mind.

They came to greet him, Mary running and falling into his arms, Martha smiling and dusting herself at the kitchen door, so hesitant, frowning at herself and her awkwardness, and then Lazarus running around, shouting to all his men, banging on a threshing sledge like a drum, making up poems like a king's herald. He was commanding a celebration for his greatest, most honourable friend. He was falling over himself absurdly, clowning with happiness.

I came to love Lazarus after the great day in Bethany, Lazarus' day, because of the way his laughter would suddenly tumble into silence. We spent many times walking alone and often, when he showed me things down on the farm or in the brook – he seemed to know every creature and every flower – we would say nothing to each other. He would just pick something up, very lightly, or point to it, stop me softly with a hand on my shoulder and put his finger to his lips. Then we would watch whatever it was, some insect or bird, or a fish like a stone in the shallows. We would watch for many minutes. Then walk on and Lazarus would talk to himself, I could see his lips moving, and then he would look at me and I would nod.

That day when Jesus came to the farm and spoke about the door, that was the beginning. He spoke about the door that would be opened.

I don't know how it happened, but Mary came to sit down at his feet with all the men, and this is what angered Martha. It wasn't just that Mary was avoiding the kitchen, it was something about the way she sat there, like a disciple of some rabbi. She sat there with the men – there was Reuben, the ox driver, and all the other farmhands, and Lazarus – and Mary. She planted herself at his feet. That's how it seemed to Martha. She was serving everyone, rushing backwards and forwards, doing the whole meal, and everyone else was listening, calling out, interrupting, she could hear them all. There was something important, something he was saying to them, but she didn't have time. She heard snatches, a comment, a laugh, and she kept thinking the laughter was at her. She came in once and Mary deliberately avoided her eyes, although Martha stood looking at her pointedly. Then she went back to the kitchen, slamming the door. No one looked up. She could have been in another house, serving another family.

'I don't understand,' Lazarus was leaning forward across the low table, 'Joseph died and left you a good set of tools, a workshop, custom, contact in the big cities!'

'I have new work now, Lazarus—'

Mary looked up shyly. It was the first time she had spoken.

'Is that what you mean by the kingdom?'

Reuben was completely baffled by all this talk, 'Yes, the kingdom of heaven! I mean, last time you came, you were just fixing the door!'

'Is the door still opening smoothly?' That was when Martha came in again and everyone laughed out loud, but not at her. She clutched her tray, her knuckles white. Jesus was still talking and even he didn't notice her.

'So,' he said, 'Do I need to mend the door again for you?'

Reuben was shaking his head vigorously, 'But I still don't—'

Martha couldn't stand any more of this at all.

'Don't you care?' she almost shouted at Jesus. 'Don't you care that my sister has left me to do everything?'

She hurled the cakes on to the table and Mary hung her head. She looked right away from Jesus and from everyone. She felt guilty. It was obvious that Martha was right. What was she doing there? She had no place.

'Oh Martha,' said Jesus.

Martha looked at him and then looked away. She could not take that stare. She was waiting for him to speak harshly to Mary.

'Martha,' he said, 'you're always hurrying around, so worried. You do so much for everyone else, but don't miss the most important thing for you.'

He took her hand. She was white and she was shaking, but he drew her near. 'Sit down here,' he said. 'Sit with us. And listen.'

And he guided her down to the place beside him, nearer even than Mary. She sat down. She found herself resting in spite of herself, her head against his side.

'Martha,' he said, and he said no more to her.

The lamps were flickering in the evening breeze and the cicada were welcoming the night. He talked for a long while, as if he were chatting about something so everyday, a matter in the family, news, gossip, so lightly. And from time to time he laid a hand on Martha's hair.

'I can still mend doors, but something new is happening now!'

'The kingdom?'

'Yes, the kingdom of heaven . . . a door into heaven. Knock, and that door will be opened.'

4

He sat down and opened his arms. He did it in one movement, spreading out his hands as if he were unrolling a cloth. I will never forget that. I could hardly see and at first I didn't recognise him. We were on the edge of a great crowd and walking past hurriedly. My mother was already anxious. 'It's too hot for the fields,' she said, 'we can't go walking when you're like this.'

'I need fresh air,' I said. 'I have to breathe.'

'This air . . . !' she said. 'None of us can breathe.'

'Just a few more minutes, we can walk a little further, can't we?'

'Child,' she said, 'child', and she held me to her, but she was looking at the sun. I knew she was afraid. My mother did everything to please me that she could, and she was battling between her fear and her love. She was standing there, unable to move, unable to think for a moment. She just threw her hands up, and stood there.

'Tamar, we must—'

Then I heard this voice, sailing down from the high ground, over all the heads and the squirming children who were clutching their mothers' hands and the people in the bright robes, the hundreds of people. The voice sailed, it wasn't a shout but it was like a song, a sing-song almost, as if he were teaching a poem.

>'Ask and it will be given to you
>Seek and you will find
>Knock and the door will be opened'

Ask, seek, knock, he repeated it, called it softly and then loudly. He punched the air with his hand, one, two, three. Ask and seek and knock and then, he said, and then . . . it will be given, you will find the door will be opened.

I didn't know the voice, because I hadn't heard it. I had never heard it before, and the man was so far away from me. There were people arguing near me, I think. It felt like arguing. When he said something about gifts, he threw his arms up and rained down with his fingers, and it made the children laugh. Gifts, he said. 'Your father in heaven longs to give you all good gifts.' Someone near us said, 'Why's he saying father, father in heaven?' I wanted to ask my mother but she was so agitated, she kept trying to coax me on, but I stood there as firmly as I could, I kept the pressure up on her hand. I was pulling hard.

'Let's stay.'

'I should never have brought you into the fields today.'

'This man is different from all the other rabbis.' That's what someone was saying, a rough man with bare arms folded.

'Different,' said another, with a sarcastic smile. 'You mean he preaches his own message rather than God's?' I recognised that man, he was one of the leaders of the synagogue and he came to our house sometimes. He was called Simon. My mother didn't want to speak to him, she was avoiding every reason to stay. She didn't listen to anything.

'Tamar', she was pulling me on now, but that was when I

crawled through the people, just one row of them, and I saw him. I saw him so clearly. It was him.

He was saying 'Come to me'.

That was the first time. The sound of his voice and then the face.

That's what I hear, the voice sailing across the heads, through all the people shifting around and the crying babies, the chatter, the shuffling stifling crowd, sometimes still and sometimes just rippling with laughter or people shouting questions. All that happening, but somehow I hear the words as if the whole world were empty. I can hear them against any storm and in the piling snow beside this leaking wall. In the silence I can hear them again, and if a thousand legions marched towards me screaming of war, I would hear them. There is nothing on earth that can block out those words, like a flute-song in the stillness of night.

'Come to me and listen.'

I ran back to my mother. 'It's him,' I whispered – I did not want to break the spell of that moment – 'the carpenter.'

'What?' she said – she was not hearing me at all. She was looking this way and that, looking for a space out, to walk out of the crowd which was growing so thickly around us.

'The man,' I said. 'It's him. The carpenter in Sepphoris!'

'Oh,' she said, caught for one moment, suddenly remembering the spate of words I had poured out on that morning, as soon as the sun had risen and flooded my room. I had stumbled out of bed, forgetting my weakness, and I had run and fallen on to her pillow beside her. I had told her everything, and she had listened in the dawn as if to a faraway tale. It really didn't make much sense, but because it was my tale she listened, she said 'Yes' and things like that, 'Yes, that must have been frightening' or 'Strange' or 'It was kind of him to rescue that poor woman'. She had half listened to the tumbling words and tried her best to pay attention, but I remember she kept mopping my head and saying, 'You'll stay in bed now, won't you?' And I was agreeing to anything, only I had to tell her.

So when I said, 'It's him – the man', she knew. And she tolerated me for a few more minutes, precious minutes, because I crawled back through someone's legs and I tried so hard to see. I could hardly see, but I could hear everything.

He sat down, in that one movement, with his hands stretched out, stretching out so wide, weaving in the air, 'Come then', he said, and all the children were moving forward, like they'd known this. They'd been here before, into the fields, and their parents had taken them to hear the man. My head was pounding. It was on fire, but I would not call my mother. Then she slipped in beside me, but I pushed her hand away. I didn't want her to drag me away now. She sighed, but she could see all the children gathering and it was very hard for her to deny me.

They were all around him now, there must have been about fifty or a hundred. He had a little boy on his knee and a girl leaning against his back and putting her arms around him. I felt fiercely jealous. I wanted to be up there, but I didn't dare move because my head was pounding so badly. I knew if I moved I would feel so ill and my mother would take me home.

'Come to me – and listen – and act on my words.'

'Act!' he said, to all the adults who were gazing at this storyteller from the hill country. Nobody really knew who he was. 'That's all,' he said. 'Don't just listen, act . . .'

51

'. . . if you do that,' the carpenter's voice sailed towards me, and we could all hear every word, 'then you will be like a very wise man who built his house on a rock.'

He took the boy off his knee, set him to one side, and the little girl. He sat them down carefully and looked at them sort of strictly, which made all the children in the front laugh. 'Listen,' he said, 'and act.' He hit the ground in front of him. He hit the rock hard.

'A wise man,' he said, then he stood up suddenly. 'But anyone who listens to what I say and does nothing about it is like a stupid man.' He made a face, and the children shouted. Everyone was edging forward. 'A stupid man who built his house on the sand.' He leant down, gathered up sand in his fist and then sprinkled it through the air, rubbed his hands and blew away the last grains from his palm.

People moved right in front of me and I was nearly crying.

'It's time to go home,' my mother said, as gently as she could, hoping to strike a deal now. 'No, no,' I said, and I was trying not to cry. 'No.' She sat down again for a little longer, only a few minutes. I couldn't see that face any more. None of those expressions. I couldn't watch his eyes, and they searched the whole crowd, as they had searched the street in Sepphoris, and then found me for a second. He had found me but I couldn't find him now. I knew that soon all the crowds, as they had in the street, would close round and take him away.

But I heard him in pictures.

I don't remember so much of what he said, but I can see this stupid man from the story and he is on the sand, a huge level bank of white sand. He is building, with lots of help, very fast. All these slaves were going backwards and forwards, plans folding and unfolding, and in a day this house rises on the sand. It's a villa with a portico and one of these long red-tiled roofs, and columns in front, it looks so fine. The stupid man is relaxing in the sun, on a broad pavement outside. He is drinking and lying back beside a river that flows so gently and beautifully past his garden.

The carpenter was saying something about 'deep foundations' and 'Don't take the easy way, take the hard way'. He was asking the children in front about that. I suppose he was asking what the hard way would be. I wanted to call out, but I knew I would not be heard and my throat was so dry. 'The hard way', he said, and he jumped high and landed hard. He stamped his feet on the rock and swung his hands. 'Dig deep, hack down, chip away. Go on! Hack into the rock! Be like that with my words, and dig them in deeper and deeper and deeper. Cut a trench in your heart for the truth!'

There were people saying things around me, I knew, bad things some of them, but others were hushing them angrily. 'Listen,' they said. 'Are you afraid to listen to a story?' The children were laughing and dancing around him as he built that house on the rock and I could hear them all thumping the ground, as if they were making music. I can see the house rising, so slowly. The wise man took for ever. He was pegging out lines, tying cords to stakes. He didn't spare any effort. The house was thick and strong, one level, broad and safe. Then the cloud came.

That was his fist again, I think, it must have been flying through the air or some gesture, but I couldn't see, only hear the children going 'Rain!' They were shouting rain. I forgot I was in that crowd, I was somewhere in the wild rains of spring, thunder

53

battling in the sky and the rain like knives, a million knives stabbing the earth. He took me into the storm and the battering wind. How is it I hear it now, I can hear it roaring as savagely as ever? I do not know how he made us believe we were being drenched and soaked to the skin, but his words flew around us and his arms waved and kept making sounds, huge sounds and small sounds, the tiniest, tiniest trickles which became a torrent shattering the desert calm. The river between those two houses burst, it blossomed suddenly into an ocean of raging foam, and the house on the sand wobbled, it creaked at every joint. The children were shouting again, because they could see the stupid man running up the stairs, banging shutters and nailing doors, but there were cracks erupting in the walls. The man was frantically dashing backwards and forwards with buckets, but then a whole wall peeled away, then another. The torrent surged through and all his possessions were carried off in the flood, and finally the man clung to a floorboard and floated away crying out, waving, disappearing. There was not one brick left or one board of the stupid man's house.

'Be ready,' he called out softly, over the heads once more, 'for the day when trouble comes and when terrible storms rage all around your life!'

We could all see the wise man. He was stepping out of his house. The door closed with a perfect click on the latch. He looked up at the sun which was appearing at last in the blackness. Every cloud scattered and the wise man sat down. He took out a drink and sipped it very slowly, by the river which had dwindled to a gentle, sluggish flow. It lapped past the foundations of the house, around them.

'Build your house on the rock!' he said.

Some people were leaving then, taking their chance. Simon was going, with some of his friends. I kept wondering what my father would say. I didn't know, and I didn't want to ask my mother. I just wanted to stay and listen. Most of the crowd were staying and more were arriving all the time.

'Come to me', I could hear him saying it again. What was he going to say now? What door opened with this song, the sing-song words?

My mother's hand came on my brow. She felt like ice.

'Oh,' she said. That terrible fear again, I could hear it, just, but I was drifting. I felt so strange and in some other land.

'Now you've caught the sun. Now the fever is coming.'

'Let me watch.' That's all I could say. I don't even know if my lips made a sound. 'I want to hear the man.'

'Come to me everyone who is thirsty!' That's what he was saying, I can remember now, all those 'come to me' words, 'come to me everyone who is hungry!'

I thought I saw his eyes for a moment. I thought I saw them.

'I want to stay!' I kept pulling my hand away, but I couldn't move it somehow. I must have been fainting in the heat.

'Whoever the father brings to me, I will never turn away.' Then he sang it again, 'Never, ever, never ever!' I remember it, and I wanted to run to him then. And hold him like the little girl, put my arms around him and hold him and stay with him. He would keep me. I knew he would keep me there. I would be all right.

My mother was shouting in my head, her fear was shouting at me, 'There are too many teachers in Galilee!'

She picked me up and I couldn't stop her, I couldn't say

anything. I was in her arms and she was carrying me away, so far away through the crowd. She was barging through, people were getting out of her way. She was stumbling and running with me back to Capernaum, and the crowds and the man vanished into the darkness that closed around me.

There were others watching, far up in the hills. One day I heard of this. We did not speak of it for many years, and Simon Peter would not name him. He once let slip, almost by chance, the 'one who was lost' and shuddered beside the fire and shook his head. Never did I hear him name the serious young man who came down from the hills at that time and joined the crowds. But John would speak of him from time to time. I heard him once, in his courtyard at Ephesus where the white clematis flowers, speak his name. There was melancholy in his voice when he said 'Judas', and love. He spoke of his friend. Something about that place in the twilight, that evening in the dank courtyard – it had been raining all day, all week – something came to him. He was in a cave and he was thinking of how it could have been for Judas.

A fire was throwing shadows on to the rough walls of the cave, and a man was stirring a pot of broth which spilt on to the flames, spitting wildly.

A young man was standing at the mouth of the hollow and looking down, far down to the crowds stretching down the hill and along the plains around Capernaum. One of his fellows, a coarse, handsome figure, walked up behind him and grabbed his sleeve.

'No!'

Judas did not turn but kept his gaze fixed.

'The people love him.'

Barabbas tugged his sleeve savagely and then let go.

'You're young, you've got . . .' He wandered round the cave, nodding slowly. He was selecting a word respectfully.

'Fine ideals, Judas.'

'Yes, his ideals are to have a house like Herod's courtiers, with baths and couches!'

Joram, one of four zealots who had joined Barabbas in the hills of the Galil, danced up to Judas with his knife, carving figures in the air, and Judas turned suddenly, violently. Barabbas grabbed the man's fist and shouted, 'Joram! We all want the same. We believe in the same God.'

Joram sat down beside the fire, where his silent companion stirred the broth, staring sullenly at the brambles that crackled and snapped in the flames.

'We fight together because we *believe*,' said Barabbas.

Then in the stillness, Judas said quietly, 'I believe.'

'What, Judas?'

He gazed down at the vast crowds, and it was possible to hear the hint of a voice, a single voice that rose with indecipherable words above the throng of people, and from time to time a cheer or applause would rise and then fall into the deepest, most troubling silence.

'What?' said Barabbas, dismissing the performance with a wave. 'That we should throw in our lot with an unknown rabbi from Nazareth?'

Judas half turned and the shadows leapt across his face, flickered like furious thoughts.

'They say he has powers from God.'

'Powers? What power can one man have against the might of Caesar?'

Judas looked down at the streams of people, tiny currents flowing across the emptiness, gathering around the solitary figure. 'What do they fear – what do kings and emperors fear?' he asked. His voice was hardening into resolve – he threw his hand forward – 'They fear the people when they rise up like one man, when they follow *one man*!'

In a fraction of a second, his mind was leaping, his thoughts tumbling over and over, he could see Jerusalem and the Antonia fortress, the legionaries traversing the long walls and the ensigns and the imperial insignia – and riding against them was the solitary figure, the man from Nazareth, on horseback, and cheering, cascading behind him were warriors, thousands of Galileans with staves and swords, and Judas was riding too, his sword dazzling in the air. Thousands were joining, streaming from the Mount of Olives with lamps and swords, and from the alleyways and courtyards, inside and outside the city, and then thunder bellowed as the walls cracked into pieces. He could see the commanders hurled from the turrets, and descend in fire.

'Dream of your Messiah, Judas,' Barabbas whispered softly into his ear. 'Dream.'

Judas walked away, down the hill, without turning for a backward glance. Joram stood in the mouth of the cave and shouted after him, 'Dream, Judas! Dream of your house with hot baths – and slave girls dancing!'

5

I woke up and the sweat was in my eyes. I don't know how long I'd been lying there, it could have been one or two days, but it was night. I could see the moon, it was balanced on the roof of the synagogue across the road, then it rose higher. I watched it rise for a long time. I couldn't speak and I don't think my mother knew I was awake. She was dabbing my forehead all the time, wiping it, wringing the cloth. She twisted the cloth in desperation, roughly, as if she could squeeze the fever out somehow, and she was trying to say something to my father. He was standing at the window. I could see his silhouette so clearly against the yellow light of the moon. He was doing that ritual again, as if he were alone in the world and no one was there or could see him or hear him.

'This is my fault,' he said, 'I have not lived a good life.'

He was whispering and then shaking his head, very slowly. My mother reached out her hand to him.

'Jairus.'

He wasn't listening. There was nobody there, only some terrible dark chamber and he was alone.

'Every day I stand before you and I beg . . . for mercy,' he said, and ran his fingers through his hair. 'I beg you,' he said. 'Please.'

Then he leant against the window, his head against the shutter. 'Please,' he said, so softly.

He was looking across at the beautiful building with the lamps burning and the basalt shining so darkly. There was moonlight on the capitals of the columns, casting shadows on the oak carvings of the door. He was looking for something, some light there. I wanted to speak to him so badly, and with all my strength I managed to say out loud, 'Father'. It was too hoarse and he didn't turn. My mother called to him.

'She's awake, she wants you.'

'Yes,' he said, so distantly, and turned, and I can see his face now. So lost in shadow against the light, but his eyes. His eyes were so full as he knelt down beside me. He kept looking at me as if he could hardly see me. As if I had left him and were somewhere else. Then he took my hair, ploughing it through his fingers, stroked it again and again.

'Tamar,' he said.

'When I'm better . . .'

'Yes,' he said, 'Yes', as if he would have given me anything in the world.

'Can I go outside again?'

He almost smiled at that, because it was so little, but it was all I wanted.

'Of course.'

Then he just turned away from me. He couldn't look at me or at my mother. 'Someday,' he said.

'I want to see that man . . . in the fields.'

My mother looked at him. There was fear in her eyes, I knew.

'I want to—'

'There are many things we want in this life.' His voice was strange and he was looking out of the window again. I pulled myself up and my mother gasped, she tried to lay me back down on the pillow, but I sat right up.

'You should have heard him – oh, the stories!'

'I have heard of . . . him . . . this . . . teacher.'

'Go to sleep now.' My mother did not want this conversation. She smoothed the pillow and took the opportunity to turn it around. It was sodden.

'I will go tomorrow! Mother will take me! We'll go, won't we?'

'Tamar.' He was struggling, and he wouldn't turn back towards me.

'We must not follow the people. We must follow God.'

'He talks of God,' I said, appealing to him, I was ready to try anything, 'Oh, you should just listen to him talking—'

'No!'

'So funny, so beautiful. You should listen.'

'No!' He was agitated, he was angry, but not with me. With himself and with the world. 'No! That man! I've heard . . . many bad reports of him . . . other leaders in the synagogue.' He kept shaking his head as he was talking, running his fingers through his hair as if he were feverish too, and he was looking across the road at the burning torches on the casement of the synagogue. He was drawing all the strength he could. 'We're all, we have to be so careful in these terrible times. Do you understand?'

He turned. He was pacing, caught in some battle which I knew nothing about, pacing up and down the room as if suddenly there were crowds of people to be talked to sternly. He did this when he had no idea what to say to me. He would address me as if I were a crowd of people, needing instruction.

'There are so many saying, "This way", or "That way", "God's way", "Follow this path!" Prophets, false teachers, deceiving the people and plotting war. Do you understand this? Do you understand, Tamar?'

My mother was signalling to him to seal his lips, shaking her head. She was mumbling 'Jairus' and whispering to me to say no more, to sleep now. Soon I would feel better, she promised, but I kept propping myself up on my elbow and following my father with wide eyes as he walked around and around.

'Father—'

'God's way, we must listen to God alone, God's way, his law, his life. I cannot, I cannot—' He was shouting suddenly and I felt the hot tears start into my eyes. Why was he shouting? Why couldn't he listen? I was trying to talk to him.

He swept away and sat down in the corner, throwing his hands up high.

'You see what has happened. What has happened now. You see! You see!'

Then he rose up sharply and walked out, down the stairs, out through the courtyard and across the street. I could hear him walking, and then the door of the synagogue opening, and shutting so heavily. It rang in the street. I just buried myself into the pillow, I couldn't stop crying then. I was angry with myself for crying, but I felt so powerless and the fever just hurled itself around in my head. I could see lights and then shapes and darkness, stars in the dark, like bits of the moon. Everything was banging. My mother just held me. She folded me in her arms and lay beside me and sang to me. That was good. It was so good to hear her soft singing like that, like a lullaby in my ear, like the distant waves lapping against the wharves. I felt all right after some minutes. I felt so quiet inside. I felt safe.

I knew where my father was. He was there in the synagogue. He was standing, I knew exactly what he was doing, he was standing before the menora. I could see him as I lay there, just standing in the dimness and the gold of that dark holiness. A figure, running a hand through his hair and begging in the silence. Pleading all alone, and above him, above the roofs, the wind was taking clouds across the moon, ragged strips scattered so high like leaves, floating out into eternity.

My mother left me there, dreaming in my bed. Of course, I heard her go, that deliberate, slow stepping she made when she didn't want to creak on the stairs. I heard her all right, but I was happy.

I waited for a long time, waited until my father returned. I heard them talking again far below. It seemed so far. They were talking tenderly, they were not arguing. I was glad of that. I knew he was holding my mother and she was weeping just a little, I could hear her, but she was not lifting her voice or shouting. She didn't walk around. They must have been just standing by the open door holding each other in the night.

I climbed slowly out of bed, with all the strength I could find, to move a fraction at a time in absolute silence. I did not want to stub my toe or trip up. I tiptoed across the old rugs on the floorboards and right up to the edge of the window, and there I looked up to the moon which had risen above Capernaum.

I could hear his voice. I could hear it then in the night, when no one disturbed the hush of the shadows, no door opened. I could hear him against the risen moon and see his face there. I dared to imagine his eyes looking at me alone, without any crowd or any other children hanging on to his robe, but looking so clearly at me. He was saying, 'Come to me.' I could hear it again and again. 'Everyone who is thirsty, hungry!' I reached out to the night air and I felt so light. He was saying 'Never'. He was just saying 'Never'. I remembered all that he had said, every word, and that he would never, ever turn anyone away.

The moon brought him to my bedroom and I cannot see it now, a cold disc above the sea on the freezing nights here, I cannot see the moon without hearing those words.

It must have been a day later that I saw the madwoman again.

'I come from *did you hear me* what I said I'm saying *a thousand people crying*, they all dead and gone, oh, oh, oh. Hands off me *murderers*, I'll kill you!'

She was in the crowds in the streets, just as she had been in Sepphoris, lost in all the people, sometimes pushed away viciously, sometimes laughed at. She didn't seem to mind anything. This was her life and she travelled from town to town. She traded with all she had, her twisted beauty and her child's voice. That was her favourite. There were so many.

Two soldiers were following her, I remember, and grabbing at her and laughing, then coughing and spitting. They were helpless with laughter. It was odd because I hadn't seen the soldiers laugh. They were always standing still somewhere, their eyes so narrow under the glaring sun on their helmets. They were usually down by the docks, keeping guard around the tax booths because there were so many fights. I wondered if the madwoman were following the carpenter, because I could see he had followers. There were quite a number of men with him and they had sat near him on the hill in the sunshine. There was Andrew, the brother of Simon the fisherman. Everyone knew he was one of the wild man's disciples and everything about Andrew seemed to fulfil my father's gloomiest thoughts about the people and their fickle lives. One day it was all 'John' and now it was 'the rabbi from the hill country'. I could see Andrew's big broad head bobbing around in the crowd. He was shouting and joking.

I couldn't see the carpenter, though. There were too many people.

She was screaming again, howling far down by the quayside. My mother stepped anxiously on to the balcony beside me and took my hand. I went back into the bedroom and I didn't argue with her. I was too tired and the crowds had flowed past me, carrying him onwards, way beyond. I could hear the shouts from the quayside, from where I lay in deep shadow – my bed was always in shadow, shutters slammed against the sun as if it would strike me dead with a single ray. I lay there, listening. There were shouts, catcalls, and something going on with the soldiers, because I heard more feet tramping past, and it was easy to distinguish them from our people shuffling and sliding down to the water's edge.

'It's all right, now,' my mother said, as if everything were fine so long as the world was at a safe distance. 'Is there anything you need?' I didn't move. I looked up at the ceiling. She went out gently and I was beginning to hate that respectful, that awful, caring, frightened calm that shrouded our whole house. I longed to be down by the slap of water on the granite stairway and watch the skiffs bash against the iron rings and hear the sharp crack of the ropes as they tightened against the flow. The madwoman's shrieks were music to me. I wanted to be with her, with them all.

Simon Peter was down there. He hadn't been home all night, I had been watching his doorway just down from the synagogue, and the women of the house had been looking out for him in the dawn. When it was a very long night it meant good or bad news. If he was out till this time of the morning, he'd be cursing an empty net. He used to get so angry sometimes, I could hear him shouting, kicking a stone or a pot against the door, hurling his scraping knife on to the cobbles. But he was kind to me. He took me out fishing once, one evening, on the sheer stillness and the mist of Galilee. The waters were black and I thought they were frightening, but he showed me how they tricked the fish.

The crowds kept pouring down towards the docks.

Simon Peter had no time for whatever it was, whatever this new excitement and chaos in the streets were heralding in Capernaum. He untangled his nets, cursing. He fed them through to James and John and they folded them carefully on the huge slabs of the wharf. They were empty for all to see, dripping in the sun and leaving their patchwork of stains.

The tax collectors were heading down towards him with their slates, ready to argue, and Simon Peter sucked in the air between his teeth noisily. He was ready for this dispute. They were convinced he was hiding fish somewhere, in one of the caves at Tagbha.

But they stopped half-way from the booth, because behind them the madwoman was screaming and tearing at the curtains. Soldiers were moving in. The bald-headed chief collector, Matthew, was recoiling.

'I only said – I only said—' he was burbling and striking some clay tablet in front of him. 'It's the law,' he said.

'Murderers, I know you!' she shouted. 'Hands off me, you want money! You want money!'

'You've crossed the border and you have to pay!'

She held a bag of coins in the air, howling and crying, 'Money, money!' She kept screaming, 'Oh, oh! You want money? *You want money!*'

Someone, some little official, tried to calm things. 'Leave this one. She's the madwoman from Magdala!'

'How much does she owe?'

'Nothing!'

A large fist smashed into the clay tablet and scattered the papers in the dust.

'Nothing and nor do we,' said Simon Peter. 'We caught nothing. No catch. No money!' and his friends James and John pressed close behind him, massive figures, a wall of flesh blocking out the sun. Matthew blinked at them. He was used to incidents in the booth. It was routine.

'We're not paying taxes for thin air!'

But Mary, the madwoman, was dancing around wildly, around and around. No one knew what she saw in her head, but it wasn't the docks or the booth or Matthew's sweating skin. The tax collector just shook himself as if to flick off some fly which was bringing disease from the rubbish tips.

'Get her out of here,' he said. 'Someone.'

They tried to hold her, but she was strong. Soldiers were moving in, in threes.

'I told the Emperor,' she said, 'Oh I told him about you. I told him – we know, we discussed it all in the royal – oh, oh!

Yes, the money! I have so much! I—' She was sobbing. Quite suddenly. And then she looked up at the huge soldiers, from where she was scrubbing around for her coins, miserable little bits of lead in the dirt, and she must have seen something so frightening, like monstrous faces or some nightmare twisting in the blackness of her mind, because the cry she gave stopped everyone still. It was a sound of such dread.

The soldiers were shocked for a moment. But they stood their ground. They took her away from the booths and crowds and dropped her somewhere down the shores, left her picking up stones in the shallows and laughing, piling them into her skirts, and giggling stupidly and then hurling them up, lining up each stone into little piles. Her money.

'I have money,' she said. 'Do you want money?'

Simon Peter was leaning over the table, in front of the tax collector. He would not move out of the booth.

'Look,' Matthew said, without raising his eyes, 'we have to keep records. It's the law. Comings and goings, border-crossings.'

'And is it the law,' said Simon Peter, 'for you to cheat and steal and line your own pockets? Is that the law? Traitor!'

A soldier unsheathed a sword. The blade scraped its warning. Simon Peter looked round and the hatred in his eyes leapt across the quay into the line of mercenaries, their leather scabbards and their bits of iron held up in a meaningless performance. His fury was unpredictable. One day he would simply fall on three of them, kill them all and be killed by a fourth. Those who knew him feared his temper.

Andrew was coming down, stepping innocently and smiling, into the uneasy silence. All the crowd were tumbling after him, children and women and herdsmen. Shops had emptied.

'Simon,' said Andrew, 'the man I told you about. He's here!'

'What?' Simon was unmoved.

'He's coming down to the shore.'

'So?'

High above the quayside, on the highest part of the sloping dock road, Jesus appeared, walking slowly, stopping every now and then. He talked to the children on the threshold of their houses, little ones playing in the dust, and the crowd piled into him and the followers all around him. He took his time, plenty of time. Then he moved on down, swiftly, purposefully.

'He is the one!' Andrew whispered urgently to Simon Peter, who had returned to his nets and was stacking them with savage precision.

'He is the one God has sent to save us!'

'You're mad. What can anyone do to save us from all this?'

Simon Peter jerked his head back, indicated the legionaries and the tax booths. All the militia of Herod Antipas, and the lists, the endless lists. The checklists of fish and costs and weights. The little accounting slates and the record books, and Matthew, peering from his curtains.

'We don't need more prophets!' He walked up to Andrew and threw the words into his face. 'We've got enough problems trying to eat.'

'James, John—', he jabbed his finger, 'tie up the boat and don't pay! Tie up the boat!'

Jesus walked towards him and the crowd followed him in droves, endlessly gathering all along the quay and up the road. Some climbed on to huge crates of amphorae, others up into balconies. Two or three tried to sit on the booths and were pushed off roughly, but they laughed. It was like a party. Everyone was expecting something, there was an air of joy and festivity, but Simon Peter shook his head. All this running to and fro. Andrew was always looking for some marvel. There was always a sign, always a message. Something was always about to happen in Andrew's world. His cheerful, hopeful face was maddening. 'Look—' he said, but Simon Peter interrupted with a furious, helpless groan.

'Andrew,' he said. And that was all he intended to say. But Jesus strode past him, across the rope he was holding and stepped over the gunwhale skilfully and sat down, in the prow of his boat.

'Hey – hey – what—'

'Push the boat out.'

'Push my – what is this?'

The crowd seethed down to the very edge of the stone kerb, and some sat down with their feet in the water.

'You want everyone else to come too?' said Jesus, looking at Simon Peter steadily, and the people behind him laughed.

'I don't want anyone. I don't want—' Simon mouthed the rest of his protest, lost it in the silence that was gathering expectantly as Jesus positioned himself in the boat, sat with his arms out. Everyone was listening now. This was the signal.

'Come on,' said Andrew, 'look, if you just sail out a little.'

Simon Peter found himself stepping into his own boat and casting off as if he were in a waking dream, one of those dreams where limbs refuse to obey the bidding of the mind. He was sure he was going to tie up his boat and eject anyone who got in his way. But instead he was snatching his nets standing on the gunwhale and feeding the rope through his hands and they were drifting out, just a little way, and then he was dutifully keeping the boat in check with his oar.

It seemed like most of Capernaum and many of the villages had gathered among the fishing pots and dragnets. Children were squinting in the sun. Simon Peter turned the boat to an angle and sat down, frowning at his own meekness. No one else took command of his boat. It wasn't happening.

'The kingdom of heaven,' said his guest. He stayed with the phrase for a long time. 'Kingdom,' he said. The children edged forward. They had heard stories from him about this. 'What's it like?' He threw a single hand up against the blueness of the sky. 'What do you think?' The man was musing, fetching a word from somewhere. 'The kingdom of heaven is like . . . it's like . . . a mustard seed.' He flattened his palm. He looked down at it. He inspected it thoroughly. 'You can't see it. It's so small. It's a speck of dust. It could blow away.'

He blew. And everyone watched the make-believe dust vanish into the sunlight.

'And yet,' he said, taking both hands, shoving them down deep, burying them into the boat and then lifting them up slowly, majestically, as he spoke, 'that tiny seed becomes the greatest tree of all, and all the birds in the air come and nest in its branches.'

Simon Peter was gazing up at the tangle of branches. He could see them, like a silhouette against the sun.

He shook himself out of this. He had better things to do than listen to stories.

But there were more. The people listened eagerly.

'Don't build up treasure on earth where thieves can break in suddenly.' He seized handfuls of air and hurled it above his head. He snatched at the sky, he stowed away the emptiness into bags, huge bags. 'Don't build up that kind of treasure where the moths,' his fingers fluttered now, fluttered into the bags which seemed to weigh the boat down, 'till swarms of moths eat up everything you own! Build up treasure in heaven, for where your treasure is . . .'

Simon Peter looked up again, slowly. He liked this talk of treasure. There were stacks of coins, his money, hoarded in the custom house, all the people's treasure stolen from them brutally. He could see the chief tax collector slip back behind his curtains at an opportune moment. He smiled grimly.

'Treasure,' said the teacher from the hills. 'What goes with treasure? Your heart. So if your treasure is in heaven, your heart will be there too and no one can take either away.'

He spoke for more than two hours, until the sun was scorching overhead. The people would have gladly stayed, pressing down to the waters in the heat, but he waved them to their homes. Some watched him long after he had fallen silent and lain down in the boat exhausted. Gradually, the quayside emptied of all except the soldiers. Simon Peter took up his oar and began to turn the craft back. He had spent too long listening to fine words and the heat was stirring his temper.

The carpenter yawned, and as if by way of an afterthought, mumbled to him:

'Push the boat further out.'

'Out?'

'Into the deep.'

'Why? What for?'

'Let your nets down for a catch, of course.'

This was too much. Simon Peter sighed, like a weary teacher

with a hopeless pupil. He waved his hands around, searching for something sensible to say in response to this obvious stupidity.

'No one catches fish during the day,' he began, very slowly. 'They hide. From the sunlight – right down in the depths.'

He looked over to Andrew for support, but there was none. He looked at the rabbi from Nazareth sitting in the prow, and then looked away. The man's gaze was so open, as if he had suggested the plainest thing in the world.

'But . . . if you insist.'

He sat down and took his oar. 'I'll let them down for you.' He felt this was generous. He sat back and rowed but under his breath he muttered, 'In the middle of the day.'

James and John followed, puzzled – but they assumed that Simon had some plan of his own, or they had to take the teacher to another town. They dipped their oars and kept within sight.

There was a splash as the net hit the bright water and sank, spreading through the clear depths into nothing. No one moved. Simon Peter raised his eyes to the sky, mastering his fury. 'We could be here for hours,' he said.

Andrew did not reply. He was watching something, far below, a glimpse of silver, as if the ripples of sunlight were scattering down into the water.

'We could be here for days,' Simon Peter said. He gripped his oar in its gate, held it tighter, as if the pressure would keep his lips sealed. He was ready to say something he would regret. The rabbi in his boat was staring ahead at the faint outline of the cliffs, high above the Decapolis, lost somewhere in thought. He was oblivious and plainly ignorant of the waters. All this was some mad whim and it was Andrew's fault. He would believe anything.

Andrew's mouth was open as he watched the nets filling with light.

'Ohh,' he said. 'Ohh . . .' He leant over and stared and shouted, 'Simon!'

Simon looked at him, darted him an angry glance, he was ready to slap him away with a word . . .

But then he saw them, there were hundreds, folding over each other, slipping, weaving light into threads of water, necklaces of drops, radiant in the air, flipping and fighting, diving, they were thrashing in some wild carnival of brilliance, like bags of jewels hurled scattering into coffers.

'What . . .' Simon was breathless. He was rising up.

'What . . . what is this?' He was leaping, falling over the side as he reached, half-blindly, in some trance, for the edge of the net.

'Pull,' said Andrew.

Simon Peter's arms felt weak. Their strength was vanishing. He pulled, but something was draining him. He was looking at the man in the prow who stood smiling, beckoning the other boat.

'James, John! Come on!'

Jesus leant over the side and grabbed the net and, with immense force, pulled.

'That's it.'

James and John pulled alongside. Trapping the haul, they seized the other side of the net and pulled what they could on to the soaking deck.

Andrew was laughing. Shouting with laughter.

There were hundreds, more than they had ever seen in two catches in two perfect nights. Two or three exceptional nights. Here, in the noonday, blistering heat, the entire shoal had risen to the surface as if it prayed for capture. They rowed to the shore. Simon, Andrew, and the sons of Zebedee. Two boats, rowing, and the shore seemed to reach them of its own accord. Simon Peter, dazed, was climbing out of the boat, waist deep in the water. He pulled the net and the multitude of fish behind him. But when he reached the shore, he left Andrew and James and John untangling and sorting their booty along the quayside before the astonished gaze of the officials and soldiers. He heard the murmurs and the shouts, comments flying through the air, jokes and exclamations. He heard but did not listen. He walked far down the wharf to where the stones are chipped and covered in weed. Beside broken baskets and rotting planks, he sat down and bent low, his head pressed into his knees.

It was a long time, it must have been an hour, before Jesus came to him. Simon Peter had not moved. His feet were deep in the water. He felt the figure behind him. He knew, already he knew well, who it was.

The man said nothing, but stood there, and Simon Peter turned.

'Lord,' he began. His voice was harsh as he tried to speak but couldn't.

'Lord,' he whispered. Then he shook his head.

'Lord, leave me because I am such a sinful man.'

He looked up but he could not see Jesus through his tears.

'Simon,' he said, 'don't be afraid.' He stretched out his hand and Simon rose up slowly to stand before him.

There was such laughter in his eyes and such pity.

'From today, I'm going to make you a fisher.' He nodded. 'I'll make you a fisher of men.'

Those were his words. I have heard them in many accents and from many followers of the Way, down long years. They became our prophecy and we shared them in bitterness and in hope. I can hear them as I write them, but the way they came, the shock of their birth, that I had from Simon Peter in the catacombs when I sat with him for the last time. When I sat beside him and he put his strong arm round me then, and he said, 'I haven't begun.' He said, 'I haven't learnt. One day', he said, 'I will let the nets down in the flaming sunlight and in the screaming mockery and before the stubborn silence of the world. I will let the nets down when they are least expected, and then I will begin to fish.' We all listened through the night, with the stampeding crowds above and the raging fires and the warm clay dropping, the spattering of rocks in the chamber. He asked me about my parents and if they still lived in the house, and I said I didn't know. And we talked of the docks and the piles of old crates, and we smelt Galilee in the moist air. I pretended to pick red anemones above the cave of the Severn Springs at Magadan and strew them at his feet and he laughed so tenderly, the old, hard, broken fisherman. The man who took me out at twilight and proudly showed a little child how to catch fish before dawn. The man who confessed his blindness and stupidity that night with tears, although I hung on every word and every oracle.

6

My father was silent that night, the first night of the crowds. All evening he sat there. I lay upstairs, but he didn't come to me and I felt it. It was rare for him not to sit beside me, sometimes for hours, and repeat some old familiar story, but my mother said he wasn't in the mood.

'I feel better, do I look any better?'

'A little better,' she said without conviction.

'He'll be happy if he sees me now.'

'He's busy.'

That meant trouble. There was some trouble, some worry vexing him. He was busy in his mind.

'Will he come up when he's not busy?'

'Tomorrow.'

That was final, I knew the tone. My mother stayed with me a long time. She didn't say anything about the madness of that day, all the people and the running to the docks and tales of boat and stories and miraculous catches, but I knew it was something to do with all that. My father had kept inside throughout, then he had been out somewhere, some talk with someone important in the synagogue, then he came back in. He was agitated and he sat down.

'Doesn't he have any friends to talk to when he's . . . busy?'

My mother looked at me, as if I were too knowing.

'He doesn't need friends when he's busy. He needs silence.'

I knew that Simon wasn't really a friend, Simon who was a good man and one of the Pharisees. He had sat in the school of rabbi Shammai, with my father, when they were young boys. They liked each other and trusted each other, and they spent so much time together over matters in the synagogue and in the school, but he was different in too many ways. He had powerful friends in Jerusalem and he was often travelling.

I knew my father had been talking to Simon and that on the way back he had seen a man on a horse arriving with servants, outside the courtyard of the house. It was the finest house in Capernaum and it had a tiled floor. Simon often had important guests, but my father had come back in and said something to my mother. He said, 'Why are they here?' She said, 'It doesn't matter. It doesn't concern us.'

'Everything concerns us now.'

'You're too worried about the world. Haven't we got enough heartache? Shall we find some more troubles?'

'You're being unreasonable.'

'It's the best way. You should be a bit more unreasonable.'

Then she came up to me, but she wouldn't answer my questions.

Simon was standing in his courtyard, beneath the vine. He was relieved at the stillness after the absurdities of the day. He had spent more than an hour with my father, and then a long time with Yacob and other leaders. They were undecided. Something would have to be done, but no one had a plan. They all hoped that the Nazarene, who was gathering too many troublemakers around him, would move on to another town and with any luck it would quickly become someone else's problem. It was certainly unfortunate that he was gathering huge crowds so near the garrison. That was very unfortunate, but was it deliberate? Herod would get to hear. There would have to be a delegation to Tiberias. They had to have some sort of plan, a rough strategy at least.

He was turning these thoughts around in his mind, grateful for the evening air which was heavy with scent and the moon which hung low over Galilee, a sight he enjoyed through the colonnaded walk. He had added that recently, and one of the legionary engineers had given helpful advice. There was time to sort things out about this crowd-pleasing teacher, at some leisure. He did not agonise like my father, he simply waited for opportune times and collected as much information as he could about what other people thought. He liked to do the right thing.

Simon was shocked by the sight of the man in the white robes, with the tall hat. He dusted himself down, nervously and pointlessly rearranged his robe. He shouted to his servants, 'Water! And some refreshment, hurry!' He stepped out of the shadows.

'Asher ben Azra.'

He greeted his visitor effusively. Ben Azra smiled, coolly.

'Simon.'

Simon called again to his servants, 'Figs – dates – cakes', he waved his hands once too often. Then he stopped at the entrance to the house. He bowed low, as if forgetting himself.

'An unexpected pleasure.'

The sadducee bowed slightly in return. There was silence.

'Um . . .'

Ben Azra stepped past him. 'There have been reports.'

'Ah . . .'

The servants attended to the visitor, took his robe and brought water and ointment for his feet. The whole chamber was filled with the perfume, as they wiped and towelled expertly and in reverential silence.

'Rumours. Disturbances.'

'No, I wouldn't say . . .'

'If this madness spreads to Jerusalem!'

There were sounds in the night, somewhere down by the custom house. Laughter, clapping, altogether too much noise for a border post. Simon looked out of the window, then looked back at Ben Azra hastily.

'You think this man Jesus from Nazareth is . . . mad?'

'He's more dangerous than John – and we had to deal with him.'

'Dealing', that was a word that Simon employed regularly. 'Dealing with situations', it was a useful, serviceable word. But suddenly there was venom in it.

'Deal with him?'

Simon had heard about the wild man, how they had sent fifty men for him. The temple guard had taken no risks and seized him at nightfall down among the reeds, where he had been fishing with his hands.

The prophet had been scavenging for food when men came beating him with clubs.

He was Herod's guest now in the fortress at Machaerus, in the darkness a hundred feet below the gardens that adorned the desert palace. He was in a stinking pit.

'What will happen to John now?'

Ben Azra walked across the intricate pattern of the cold blue floor, where leaves entwined birds with fabulous plumage, and he stood before a game with ivory pieces.

'Simon,' he said, 'you have all this. Your home, your servants, influence!'

There was a roar in the darkness, far down, some merry-making or group chanting by the quayside. The pupils never tired of their teacher.

'Do you want to see all you have worked for in your life lost in an uprising against Rome?' His hand smashed across the ivory draughts and scattered them into the darkness, sweeping the board clean. 'Do you want to be lynched by crowds, shouting about the kingdom of heaven on earth?'

Simon picked up a draught from the floor and clutched it.

Ben Azra sat down slowly and said nothing for a great while. They listened together to the echoing voices in the air, listened until they began to fade, to float in many directions and disperse in the darkness.

'I must prepare a report on this Jesus and take it back to Jerusalem.'

'Ah,' Simon nodded, 'ah yes, we must all be . . .'

But he looked out of the window, down to the colonnades and stared into the thickets.

The sun woke me. My mother had left one of the shutters open, only an inch or two, but it found me. I opened my eyes and they hurt so much. I closed them and the light was warm on my face, but my head felt so heavy. It was banging again. There were ringing sounds and lights, the same old things but coming and going, waves of light and sickness. I had to get up and get some air. I slid on to the floor and lay there, it was so cold and lovely. I just lay there and caught my breath and got as much strength together as I could. No one was stirring next door. I knew if my mother or father heard a single sound, one of them would run in. I hated the way they ran in and then sat on the bed pretending to be calm, as if everything were fine, and talked to me in that low, forced gentleness. 'How did you sleep?' 'Have you had the pains in the night?' 'Can you see?' 'What can you see?' I was tired of giving my reports. I just wanted to be alone and silent, in the sunshine.

I got up, very gently, because I felt all right if I could move a tiny bit at a time, because then there was no banging and no pain at all. I crawled, very very slowly, across the rug and got my hand on to the shutter. It felt like a triumph. I pulled it, and as soon as I did, I regretted it because the sun streamed all over my face and it burnt like needles. I put my head down, into the shadow, and stayed still. I was glad no one could see me or knew I was there. Someone was in the street, because I could hear a shuffle and then silence, then another shuffle. Long silences and then these scraping steps in the dust. The sun was rising above the hills of Chorazin and chasing the blue away and any minute the traders and the soldiers, all the bustle of the town, would burst on the silence. It always happened like that. I don't know why. It was never one, two, then a few, then a dozen people, it was never gradual. It was always this burst of noise and people. Some great cart clattering and drawing in its wake a crowd of merchants and shopkeepers. I lay there, curled beside the open shutter, in its shadow, and I could see out at an angle through the slats of the balcony, and there I saw him. He was a hooded figure and he was sitting a few alleys down the street, all hunched. It looked like he had crept in before the dawn and he was waiting, but he didn't want anyone at all to see him there. He was pulling things around him, some wood, anything he could, bits of cloth, and making himself into a pile. Even in the shadow he wanted to hide completely from the world. I kept looking at him, but he couldn't see me, and I felt as if we were two people in an empty town.

Then they came. The carpenter walked through the gates first. He must have been up the hills that night. He looked so tired and he walked slowly, but all round him his followers were clustering, asking him where he'd been, and Simon Peter was saying, 'You have to come to my house, you'll stay with me,' and he was nodding. People were flooding the street, heading towards him as if they'd all been waiting, up all night, talking about him, longing to see him, watching the dawn. I squeezed up as tight as I could beside the wall, in the darkest corner between the shutter and the rail. I could hear my parents talking but if they heard no sound from me, they would not come in, because they longed for me to sleep through the night and long into the morning. Some nights I woke up many times, and often I had nightmares and screamed with the sweating, so they were grateful for the silence. Soon they would come in, to make absolutely sure I was sleeping soundly.

I saw him in the deep shadow of the alley, shifting himself. He was listening to all the footsteps, his head to one side like an animal. I wondered if he were blind or there was something wrong, because I never saw his face or hands, just this shape moving, leaning into the sound. He was picking his moment. The people were coming up from the dock road and the carpenter was coming slowly down from the gates with Simon Peter and Andrew, James and John, and other faces I didn't know yet, but they were all smiling and talking loudly. Two waves were approaching and the huddle in the shadow twisted himself, got himself just into position, and suddenly – as the carpenter stepped past him – he leapt.

He stuck his hand out, one stump of a hand, and Jesus stopped.

The man coughed out something, I think it was 'Lord', because there was something very wrong with his voice. It rasped like a file.

'Lord.' Everyone stopped and backed off. The crowds were frozen for a second, which seemed like an age. I could see the man's arm, half of it was bare in the sunlight, and then his face peering from all these bandages. I could just see eyes and this horrible flaking. White patches. Half his face was gone.

Someone in the crowd shouted 'Leprosy!' and people scattered. 'Leprosy', it went back and people screamed warnings. The man just fell over. He just fell down at the feet of Jesus in a heap of rags, and his bell clattered to the ground and rang once. He was looking upwards, and he was grunting words, about 'cleanness', 'Make me', he said. 'You can make me.' He kept lying there, looking upwards.

Everyone was well back and I crawled right to the rails and put my head against them. I watched and nothing happened. The man was lying there, like a baby in his rags, and there was a huge, wide circle, way back down the street. The men around Jesus were far up by the gates. One of them was holding the doors open in readiness. They would have to lead him out, up to the colony in the hills. He had to go back.

Jesus stood there. He said nothing. Then he slowly reached out his hand. I thought he would wave at the man, wave him to

84

go on quietly, but then he did something so terrible. He touched the man.

Someone shrieked in horror, this wave went back through the crowd. I could hear my parents, their voices raised next door. They were wondering what on earth was happening so early in the morning and they were afraid it would frighten me. My father was getting dressed hurriedly.

Jesus bent down and he touched the man.

'I do want to,' he said. 'Be clean.'

The leper's face. He is looking down, he is studying his hand. He is lifting his other arm and counting his fingers. His face. He can hardly smile because he has forgotten how, he does not know he has lips again, to curl and to smile. But now he is smiling, his whole face is breaking into wreaths of smiles. He doesn't talk. He looks up at Jesus. He pulls back his hood, and he feels all over his face slowly. He feels his nose, his cheeks. Someone, some brave onlooker, takes one step forward. The man turns, but then the whole crowd gives way and scatters backwards. But he doesn't mind. There is this little child and he is wandering forward, away from his mother's hands and she panics and runs to him, but the carpenter is lifting his hand in a gentle command. She stops. The child wanders forward. She looks so desperately afraid, but the little boy comes right up to the leper and looks up at him and chuckles and says something. The leper is looking all round, as if for wisdom, what to do now, and he holds out both hands above the child's head, a little way above. There is a gasp and the mother cannot restrain herself, but someone shouts so clearly. 'He's healed! The leper! He's healed!' And the whole crowd start to murmur it, and the leper lays down his hands on to the little child's head, touches him and blesses him, and he is weeping. Jesus turns. He is turning.

I can see him, I can see him. He is turning. I am there. He knows I am there. I am in the shadows, I am hunched and hidden, but he knows. He is looking right into the shadow. I try to call him but I can't. I can't speak. I can't say anything. There are so many lights and the pain is ripping at my throat. He's going. The crowd are moving away now, they're flowing, somewhere. I'm standing up, holding the rails and my father is running into the bedroom, he is shouting in his fear, 'She's not here, she's not here!' My mother is coming: 'She'll be on the floor, she'll be beside the light, find her, find her.'

He stumbles on to the balcony and he is just saying over and over again, 'What are you doing, child? What are you doing, child? You must rest, rest!'

Rest!

'I want to see him – I want to—'

'No! No!'

'That man—'

'No,' he is half sobbing. 'It's nothing to do with us.'

'Everyone is going to Jesus, everyone, father, the whole town is going to him.'

My mother is sitting on the bed and staring at me, and smoothing my hair which is clinging around my neck. 'It's true,' she says.

'What's true?' he shouts.

'Everyone is going . . . to him . . . he has powers . . .'

'Powers from who?'

'We can just go and see.'

I am fainting in the dark. I can't see them now. I can just hear them and their voices rising, they are jumbling words together, into the banging in my head.

'Powers from who? Rachel! What powers?'

'Please!'

'How do we know this is not the work of the evil one?'

'Lost for ever.' I can hear my father's voice. 'We will be lost for ever,' he said.

It was many days before I was well enough to sit up and eat something. It was a morning after the rains, and they had come through the town like a scourge. The streets smelt fresh and there was almond blossom in the air, petals floating, I remember. I could focus on them. They had flown from one of the gardens higher up. I envied them. They could ride the wind.

My mother had come in to me. We had not spoken about that day, but I knew the whole town was full of stories. There had been a blind man too, and Simon Peter's mother-in-law, she had been cured of a fever in one night. I heard the chattering in the doorways, but my father had not come into my room for two days at least, or if he had, he had come by night.

My mother knew what I wanted and so she gave in to me. She lifted me and carried me on to the balcony, where I could stand and hold the rails. It made me feel so much better to stand against those rails and pretend I was strong. We saw such a crowd that day, there were hundreds down from Bethsaida and Chorazin. I saw Simon the Pharisee too, and Yacob and the tall man from Jerusalem, the visitor who had stayed for many days and walked silently through the streets at twilight with his companions. They had all gone into Simon Peter's house, because the carpenter was in there. He was in the centre of the big room and he was telling stories and teaching, and you could see people peering in at every window, hanging on to the stairs and sitting up on the roof listening. It was strange to see the Pharisees and their sadducee companion go in there, but the whole town was on fire with rumours and expectations, and the man spoke to anyone and everyone. He was fearless and said and did all that he chose.

My father would not go. At that time, he would not even listen to a word. He was studying the scriptures so late, until it hurt his eyes or the lamps burnt into wisps of blackness in the air. He was up early now, often before dawn, and he was praying at his window. My father was afraid for the nation.

We stood there on the balcony, just watching the crowds flow and flow, I suppose it was only for some minutes because my mother was strict with my time. She let me think I was out there for a long while, but it was rarely more than half an hour and never at noonday. We saw these men. They weren't from our town, but they were hurrying down the street as if they were going to be late. They were carrying, on this old mattress trussed up into a sling, a man. I hardly saw his face. He was turned to one side and he was groaning or complaining bitterly. He didn't want to be travelling anywhere, that was clear. He kept saying, 'It's no good. It's no good.'

But his friends were ignoring him. They couldn't care what he was saying. One of them said, 'Shut up', which made me laugh but not out loud. It seemed a bad thing to tell such a sick man to 'shut up' and yet I couldn't help agreeing with them. The man was complaining and shouting even, 'Die, die,' he said, 'I want to die!'

'Shut up.'

Even my mother smiled then.

'Look,' said the biggest man of the four friends – I suppose they were friends, because they were all talking to him like they knew him so well – 'We're going to take you, all right? So don't argue!'

'We'll take you to Jesus even if, even if . . .'

The darkest one of the four, a short swarthy man with big muscles, was looking around, darting around, surveying the whole building. It was so crowded, there was no way in. Every window, both doors, were jammed with people. They were half way down the street, and everyone was struggling to listen.

'Even if,' he said . . . then he looked right up to the roof, the thatched roof of Simon Peter's house where there were a few people lying stretched out and staring down. I suppose there must have been a few cracks in the mud or the reeds.

'Yes!' he said, and then he dragged the other three and the sling bed behind him.

'Come on!' They leapt up the stairs, almost threw him on to the roof and the spectators rolled away quickly. Soon, they were digging at the roof. I couldn't believe what I was seeing, because bits were beginning to tear off.

Inside, Jesus sat cross-legged in the middle. He was spreading his hands again and telling parables, and the children gathered nearer. Even the religious rulers were listening very carefully, studying each word. My mother said to me that people wanted to trap him. I didn't know what she meant, but when I asked her why Simon and the man in the robes had gone in, she just said, 'They have their own reasons.' She seemed to know something, but she was not judging them. She was in her own trap, as my father sat downstairs beside the courtyard window and stared out in silence at the rain which still dripped from the palms.

'How can you say to your brother, "Let me take that speck of dust out of your eye"?'

Jesus snatched a speck from the air and the children climbed forward to take a look. He showed them and put it in an eye, a figure he had dreamed from the air.

'Who are you to judge,' he said, looking over to Yacob and Simon and all of them, gathered in the corner, 'when you have a huge log in your own eye!' He stood up and stretched out his arms and carried the immense trunk and staggered and placed it into another figure made of thin air, and watched it go hurling through all the people and smack into the wall.

We could hear laughter from our balcony, and words floating, 'logs', 'beams', something about figs and thorns. There were many stories. The crowd kept repeating his words to each other, passing them down the street.

Simon sat there uncomfortably, shifting next to Ben Azra in the crush of people. The smell of bodies and the coarse laughter, especially from the window behind him where the tax collectors and the soldiers' women were bunched up, made him feel dirty. Even that grotesque little man, Matthew, was there, slipping in somehow unnoticed or, for once, ignored by the crowd, who were transfixed. They couldn't care about anything for those few moments. They saw nothing but the teacher from Nazareth and the wide world he spun in the air.

'I hope we're not too proud to learn something from a younger man,' Yacob said softly, warningly to Simon. Yacob was a good, quiet man, a learned man.

'This man has no respect for anyone,' said Simon, half as a question, testing the opinion of others around him. Ben Azra looked up at the window behind them, clogged with its rabble of faces.

'Oh, he has plenty of respect,' he said, 'for thieves and vagabonds.' He turned to Simon, but his words were drowned by falling turf. A clod of earth fell into a water jar.

Simon Peter struggled forward. 'Hey,' he was shouting, 'what's going—', but everyone was staring at the huge square of sky which had suddenly appeared, and the four rough faces peering down. Jesus laughed and threw his hands up, waving.

'Friends! Welcome!'

Simon Peter was shaking his head: 'My roof, my roof! My poor . . . roof.' His voice trailed off pathetically. No one was listening. He just stared at the mounds of turf and grasses scattered everywhere. People were dusting themselves.

'Come down,' said Jesus, 'there's plenty of room.'

They lowered the man down, as gently as they could, but the mattress swayed backwards and forwards. At last it settled on the floor, scudding along the stones a little way. It stopped at the feet of Jesus.

The man just lay there. He was utterly still except for his face, which was moving all the time. His eyes were rolling and expressions of anger and desperation twisted his brow and his mouth.

'It's no good, no good.' He kept repeating it, with determination, sometimes spitting the words out. 'Let me die!' He was furious with his friends who met his gaze calmly from the roof. They said nothing, just looked down like four children who had succeeded in their prank. They were smiling, accomplices.

Jesus knelt down to him and touched him very lightly on the forehead.

'My friend,' he said.

Everyone leant forward, but nothing happened. The man lay there and with all his strength turned his face slightly away from Jesus and stared into the dark corner of the room.

'My friend . . . your sins are forgiven you.'

A shudder went through the whole crowd, a movement which passed outside and down the street. It was as if a cold fear had suddenly gripped them. One of the Pharisees stood up to go, mumbling; others looked down hard at the floor. They knew they had heard blasphemy.

Ben Azra did not speak but his glance at Simon was eloquent. It had an air of finality. He shrugged, the tiniest flicker, as if to say 'You see where this leads'.

Jesus stood up, very slowly, after a long silence in which no one had spoken a word.

'So many questions,' he said, shielding his eyes from the brightness.

'Questions.'

No one looked up.

'Let me ask *you* a question,' he said, and he stared straight at the line from Yacob to Simon. 'Which is it easier to say, "Your sins are forgiven you" ' – he tossed the words away as if they were insignificant, a breath – 'or "get up and walk!"?'

He shouted it like a command to the man, but again nothing happened. The crowd were baffled. They expected something, but not this strange duel in the silence. Ben Azra sat absolutely still, as Simon shifted for a moment. The smell of sweating bodies stifled him. Everyone was leaning in, waiting for something, some clever word or story from the teacher's repertoire.

'But to prove to you that the Son of Man has the power on earth to forgive sins,' he turned to the man and said softly, as if this were nothing, 'I command you, pick up your bed and walk.'

The man obeyed.

He sat up, to his own astonishment. He sat up straight. He put his hands down on the floor beside him and pushed himself up. He stood up. He looked round, he looked up at the roof where his friends were half falling through, their mouths open, he wheeled round. He looked at the line of Pharisees and rulers, and then wheeled around again, and looked at the rabble of smiling, speechless, gawping faces in the window. He said, 'Ha!' Just that, 'Ha', like one breath, one new beautiful deep breath from down in his lungs, and then it rose again, this time into laughter, one breath after another. He was roaring with laughter.

'Glory be . . .' He shouted, seizing his mat, rolling it up in one movement, hurling it into the blue sky, where his friends caught it and shouted 'Yes!' 'Yes,' he echoed them, 'yes . . . glory be to God. Oh glory to God.' 'It's impossible', someone said in the very front of the crowded room. 'It's impossible . . .'

'Yes,' he slapped their hand, 'yes but it's true.' He leapt over some children, lying there amazed, beginning to laugh and point at the extraordinary man dancing. He leapt through the door into the harsh beating sun and flung his arms in the air. 'Impossible,' he shouted, 'and true.'

We heard him first, just the shout. 'It's true, it's true.' Then he appeared, he was laughing and running, spinning, leaping up. My mother turned to me. She didn't know who it was at first, couldn't make it out. But then we saw the men on the roof, all four of them, screaming and waving, 'It's true', they shouted after him. 'Oh,' he kept saying, tumbling up the street. 'Oh, glory be to God. I've been healed!' It was like a three- or four-year-old dancing. He couldn't dance, he didn't know how, so he made it all up. It was like the newest dance in the world, something so different, it was strange and glorious, and he was singing, sort of, a homemade song. A healing song. He was parading in front of everyone. All the anger and bitterness was like some cloud, evaporating in the hot sun, far far away, forgotten and floating into oblivion. He raced through Capernaum. People were staring and then running after him, trying to chase and capture some of his wild happiness. His friends came down from the roof and they were talking to all the people, the crowd surging all around them, asking if it were true. Was this man truly paralysed and condemned to his bed for twenty years, had they witnessed this, did they know him, did they believe it was a miracle before their very eyes, and they kept saying, 'Yes, yes', they said 'yes' to everything.

My mother stared. She stared long into the empty streets. Long after he had gone and his friends had joined him on the road to Chorazin. She stared into the emptiness and up at Simon Peter, mending his roof, patching in the dusk. Stopping every now and then and sighing. And then saying something out loud, shaking his head. Piling on the clay and slapping it together, mending into the night.

She didn't talk to me or answer my questions. She just held me, very close. She said, 'Don't talk, don't waste anything on words. Save your breath. Keep yourself' – and then she wept suddenly – 'you must keep yourself. Strong. Don't talk. You've been too long in the sun again.'

'Talk to father, now. You must talk.'

'What I have seen . . . I have seen, but . . .', then she broke off and begged me to say nothing to her, and to say nothing to my father. To look to God. To look to the Holy One of Israel, not at the crowds, but at the way of God.

I didn't know what to say to her. I wanted to comfort her. It was so peculiar that day. I wanted to do anything to make it right for her. She was wounded inside and she was crying deep down, she was shaking, but not making any sound. Just holding me tightly, softly begging me not to speak. 'What I have seen,' she said – but she did not know what she had seen. That was her pain.

Now I know. I know in the wild, barren places. I know, as light fails and the snow heaves into mountains of oblivion, as the driving snow takes all shape and all distinction from the earth, I know that she was in utter terror. She had seen the most joyful thing, an impossible, absurd, terrifying newness, and it did not belong in the world where she had been born. It was shattering all the barriers of her life. When others were laughing in the streets and when the man was dancing, she was weeping uncontrollably in the stillness of her heart. I wish I could take her now, after all the years, and soothe away the pain of that evening with one kiss. She is so far from me, so lost to me now, but on this wind I can hear her moaning in the night, in her sleep. I can feel her sorrow as my father lay on the cold stone floor below, in abject silence and in such desolation, after Simon came to our house that night.

He had gone home with Ben Azra, Yacob, Joel and the others,

and they had talked for a long time. They had talked long into the night.

I must have slept for a while, but I woke when he arrived. He stood at the door and knocked and it was some minutes before my father answered, although I knew he was awake. He had been sitting down there, and he never seemed to doze when he was reading. He read the scriptures with such intensity. His face looked beautiful to me when the lamplight reflected in his eyes and on his cheeks. He was lost in the world of the prophets, somewhere on Mount Carmel or on Horeb, or else he was sitting in a dungeon with Jeremiah. I looked at him, secretly sometimes, and I could see his mind walking. He was always walking somewhere, walking through the Torah, spreading his tent in the wilderness. He seemed to spend his life waiting on God, and although my father was not handsome, his face would become beautiful even in despair. There was something about the waiting and the silence, something he knew within in those times.

I knew he was awake, but he did not want to answer the door. That day in Capernaum, my father had craved solitude. Now, at night, at last he had the silence back and there were no threatening, calling crowds, no demands and no problems ringing on the stones of every street. There was silence and the perfumed blossom still floating against the blackness.

At last he got up and went to the door and pulled it open with a jolt. It banged and echoed in the fragile quietness. His voice was so weary.

'Simon.'

'Can we . . . talk?'

'Why shouldn't friends talk even at this hour?' My father was always so polite. He said what he wanted to say, but he was skilful with his courtesies. Simon walked around the room for a long while and said little. Eventually, he spoke, blurting out what they already knew, but with a sharp edge of fear.

'The whole town talks of nothing but Jesus.'

'They say he is a good man.'

'A good man,' Simon came back with sudden violence, 'who is breaking God's holy law!'

My father paced the room for a while. He said nothing. He paced, and tapped on the table for a while, and then paced again.

'What law?' he said. 'What law is he breaking?'

Simon stared into the lamplight on the table. Then he looked out through the window, across to the synagogue, where the lamps burned in the darkness.

'If we took a sick man,' he said, as if dreaming up an idea as he spoke, 'into the synagogue on the Sabbath . . .'

'On the Sabbath?'

'Would he heal him?'

My father laughed, almost. Spluttered the suggestion quickly aside. 'No, he will not break the Sabbath law. He will rest. He will worship God and heal on some other day – unless he is a madman.'

'Or a devil,' said Simon.

He walked towards the door and opened it for himself. My father said nothing. There was a horrible, dark emptiness in the silence now, which had been filled with prayer and solace only a few minutes before. The lamp guttered in the breeze.

'Jairus,' Simon said quietly, 'the ruler of the synagogue must speak out against this evil.'

My father shut the door and lay down upon the stone floor that night, and did not come up to me even though I was coughing.

No one spoke about Simon coming in the night. I woke up to find my mother next to me. She was drenched with my sweat and both her arms were around me. I couldn't speak because my mouth was so dry and I had to point for the water. She kept pouring it on me, over my face, into my throat. It tasted like fire. The only cool was the sound of the pigeon on the balcony. He had been murmuring for a long time, burbling like a stream and I blessed him for visiting me. It was the Sabbath eve.

All day my father walked around the house and said nothing. My mother did not ask him about Simon. She quietly baked the hallot and prepared the table. I did not know if I would be able to come down, so I was saving my strength. I was terribly afraid of lying in my bed, alone, while father recited the kiddush. It seemed like I was losing everything, even the freedom to breathe in another room. I listened to them coming and going. Outside, the streets were very quiet, because the carpenter was up in the hills and the crowds had gone out to him. There were people from all over the Galil and far beyond. Everyone was with him, everyone in the world.

I couldn't cry. I could hardly move. I did not know what was happening to my legs and arms, but they were so heavy. I could not even roll out of bed on to the cold floor. My pigeon had gone, and there was nothing to distract me from the emptiness of that room. All I could hear was Simon saying things, mad wicked things, but I knew he wasn't mad or wicked, and I was dreaming. He was knocking at the door in my dreams. He was bursting through with such hatred and I was shouting, 'Why? Why?' And my father was furiously angry, and he was afraid and kept holding me down and begging me to keep quiet. I must not speak. I must say nothing. My mother was throwing herself around and she was cutting herself. There was blood. I woke up, screaming and screaming for her, but my voice made no sound. It just crackled. She was there, she was sloshing water across me again and stroking me. 'You're dreaming again,' she said. 'It's all right.' I kept saying, 'No, no', but she nodded. 'You're all right. You're here. You're in your room and I'm here. In a little while, I'll carry you down.' I was so grateful, so happy for one moment. I knew they wouldn't leave me alone.

My father came into the room and he stopped for a minute beside my bed. He was just looking down at me and his face was so serious and it was so full of love. He knelt down, without saying a word, and pushed his hands under me and lifted me into his arms. I said 'Father', he said 'Yes'. That's all. He couldn't say anything else. But he carried me so gently and with such precision, as if he wanted me to float down those stairs, as if he was desperate to make sure that no jolt or stumble could send the pains stabbing through my body. I feared those pains. I just prayed that they wouldn't come. He carried me down and set me in a chair which he had filled with a fleece and some cushions. He tucked me into the chair, put a shawl around me, and one over my head. I looked at him all the time. I didn't want to take my eyes off him. Then my mother came behind me, with her arms out and she lit the Sabbath lights. Oh, those lights, little flames, they were like suns burning in the night. I looked into them, and beyond them at my father. I could see them in his eyes. He was lifting his hands up. He was leaning forward, across to me, but he was being so careful not to touch me too hard, to let his fingers alight on my head like birds, ready to fly away. He said, and it was so soft I could hardly hear him, but I knew every word so well, 'God make you as Sarah, Rebekah, Rachel and Leah. The Lord bless you and keep you. The Lord make his face to shine upon you and be gracious unto you, may the Lord lift up the light of his countenance upon you and give you his peace.' I couldn't see my mother, but I could feel her. She was trembling behind me. I felt such peace, and such a strange joy, although I knew she was weeping and that she was terribly afraid. 'Jairus,' she said, but she didn't say anything else. I don't know if she signalled or what she did, but my father went on quickly. He said the kiddush over the wine. He told how God had completed all his work and rested. He rested. My father kept saying it again, praying for rest, because he could not rest. He was working, his mind was working and running backwards and forwards with such desperation, and so he sang the word to himself as a prayer. He was commanding his soul to rest. I kept watching him and wishing he could be at peace. I knew he could not.

He laid his hands over the cup, which was silvered bronze, it was very old. He had had it from his father and his grandfather. There were patterns on it, dark and light in the flashing candles, weaving a journey round the rim. He fingered it lightly, held it up and drank. We all drank wine. That was enough. My mother's hands were round me. This time, she lifted me up and gave me to him. I felt such pain. I wanted to scream out, but I made myself keep silent. I did it for God on the Sabbath day. My mother knew I was in agony, but she did not say anything to comfort me, because she was afraid. It was as if, by not mentioning anything, we could all be safe again as we once were.

My father took me up to the bed and laid me down. He said another blessing. He turned and left. My mother sat down, and sang to me an old rhyme. It was not from the scriptures, it was a lullaby. Some old forgotten rhyme. She had sung it when I was a baby. I managed to take her hand and it made us both feel better. We stayed like that for a long time, in the shadow, listening to my father walking and walking, all around the courtyard.

In the morning, the shofar sounded high above the roofs, a long plaintive sound calling, a deep beauty, as if the synagogue were high in the hills of another world. All the people walked through the streets. I could hear them chattering excitedly. The word had gone around that the teacher from Nazareth would speak today.

I couldn't move from where I was and I was finding it difficult to hear, because my ears were blocking up all the time. The sheets were sticking to me and I could see my whole body like an outline, like one of those Roman sculptures in the forum at Sepphoris. I was lying like a block of marble, and I tried to imagine myself freezing cold like stone. My mother stood at the balcony and she told me that the rabbi from Nazareth had gone in and all his followers, and she gasped because there were some going into the synagogue who never came in. The chief tax collector had walked in with his head bowed, alone. Simon had gone in with Ben Azra and his servants, and Yacob, Joel, then some people from the villages who looked very poor, there were women and men pouring in, and there were some women that my mother just shook her head at. She said nothing but 'those women . . .', 'those people'. She turned to me and said, 'The whole world is in the synagogue.' There were soldiers in the streets too, just a few, keeping well back. They normally avoided the Sabbath very carefully but the garrison was taking no chances. There were so many people and anything could happen. They kept in the shadows out of respect and did not flinch even to brush off a fly.

My father sat in the place of authority, beside the great chair and near the desk where the Torah was kept beneath its linen mantle. Everyone in Capernaum looked up to him, because he weighed his words so carefully. He was a man of the greatest caution, so no one was surprised that the ruler of the synagogue had kept himself to himself. He was not a man to follow the crowds and, if he were the last person in Capernaum to meet the rabbi from Nazareth, there was nothing strange or remarkable in this. It was typical of his prudence. My father gained respect by his silences.

He welcomed Jesus to the place of honour. The teacher walked slowly towards the ornate chair and turned, facing all the people. He gazed at them all, until some became restless and began to cough. It was as if he knew every single person in that building by name. At last, his eyes lighted upon a man with a deformed arm who was sitting beside Simon and Yacob. The man was looking down, almost furtively. He was ashamed of his affliction, and he tried to hide the ugliness within his robe. Jesus was looking at him intently and the man felt the gaze as if it were light burning into his face – he looked up, and then away suddenly. He was so afraid. He knew that the whole synagogue was now staring at him. Jesus waved with one hand, curling his fingers. 'Come,' he said.

The man would not move. Simon prodded him, but he shook his head fearfully.

'Come and stand here.'

He looked up, and again he met the eyes commanding him.

'Go on,' said Simon, whispering to him, 'do what the . . . master says.'

The man was in terrible conflict. Somehow he knew that he was caught up in a game, or felt that he was in a cage, an animal to be prodded forward, a bear lumbering into an arena to wild shouting and children cheering. He had not wanted to come into the synagogue but men had found him at the gates and brought him there, wise men who said he should listen to God today. Simon the Pharisee had welcomed him and shown him disturbing courtesy. He had smiled, taken him so thoughtfully, and led him to a seat before the reading desk. Now he must stand in front of the leering mass of people and walk up to the 'master'.

The man got up, very slowly, and did not look behind him. The hairs rose on the back of his neck. He knew that hundreds were gazing, pursuing him, across the cold floor. He stood before the teacher, who nodded.

'It's all right, just come and stand beside me.' He stopped. The teacher sat down, in the great chair. His hands circled each other, then clapped together as if he were drawing an idea suddenly from the emptiness. 'Let me ask you all a question,' he said.

'Question.' He repeated it, in the way the crowds had come to know. 'Just a thought,' he said, and smiled slightly, deliberated with his hands. Wove something from the air again.

'Hmm . . . lawful,' he said.

There was a long pause, and the man just stood there, but he found himself strangely at ease. He was standing beside the teacher. He was not in front of him, and this debate was nothing to do with him. He felt protected, wrapped by the considered silences and thoughts which were flowing all around him.

'Lawful . . .'

Jesus looked at Simon and Ben Azra, Lamech and others who sat, staring solemnly. My father watched from his chair, intrigued and uneasy. There was a bad feeling in the synagogue, something bad in the way this strange performance was captivating the crowd, who leaned forward and peered over each other. He wondered if the teacher would read something from the scriptures. He longed for something familiar which he could grasp tightly in his mind, the old, sacred ritual.

'Is it lawful to do good on the Sabbath day?'

Jesus folded his hands and waited a long time, but there was no answer, no hint of a reply, only a darkness in the silence as men, the wise men, returned his gaze.

'Or is it lawful—', he curled his hand in the air, like a leaf floating from the sky, as if the truth were falling softly from somewhere above the painted ceiling, 'to do harm?'

'Is it lawful to do harm on the Sabbath?' He was blunt and ferocious suddenly. He wheeled round to all the people. 'Is someone allowed to save life or to destroy it?'

He stood up, clenching his fists. There was rage and there was compassion in his face, as he said softly, 'Stretch out your hand.'

The man looked at Jesus. He did not dare disobey, but the shame was consuming him. He stared all around him, then back to Jesus. Then he looked down at the floor, and with all his courage, with every spark of life left to him, he pulled – pulled out the withered arm from its hiding place. He pulled out the old twisted tree root of a limb from its shelter in the bunched folds of his robe. Stuck it out full length. He was ready for the sighs of disgust and the gasps, or the sickening silence, the sympathy that crushed without a word. He was ready. He held out everything, all the long years and the misery and the secrecy. He held out his arm, stretched out the fingers, and looked up at the vault above. He waited, without looking, to see what parable, what lesson must be taught.

Then he heard the whispers, like a breeze in a forest. Breath drawing, and someone saying, 'You see – he has healed on the Sabbath!' He looked down. His arm was stretched out before him, like a newborn baby, like a life that belonged to him but was separate. He looked at it in bewilderment. He did not move it but stroked it with his other hand, felt the blood coursing and the warmth, and sensed the strength. He looked up at Jesus, half in fear. He was trembling, and then he looked down again. He flexed his fingers, each finger in turn. He bent his arm at the elbow. He raised it and pushed his new fingers through his hair. He wept. He hugged himself. He did not run or dance, he just stood there before the whole synagogue, holding himself, clutching himself. Tears were falling down his cheeks and on to his shawl. He was shaking his head, but Jesus was nodding gently. He didn't notice the roar, now, of voices. The whole place was erupting in a chaos of fury. The Sadducees, Ben Azra, Lamech and others, and the party with Simon, even Yacob, were throwing their hands up, wildly shaking their heads.

'He has broken the Sabbath law!'

Simon turned to my father, with an odd delight on his face –

it was a face scarcely belonging to him. 'You see!' he said, and shouted it loudly so Ben Azra and the others would hear too. 'You see. He has healed on the Sabbath. The *Sabbath*.'

But my father was staring. He was staring at the man, who stretched out his arm again in childlike wonder. My father did not hear the voices around him. He simply looked. Simon walked up behind him. 'He has healed on the Sabbath.'

'He has healed . . .' my father said.

I could hear the wild arguments and the shouting, and then people pouring out of the synagogue, carrying their arguments down the streets. I did not know why they were all shouting and carrying on, but it was a long time before my father returned home. That night he sat downstairs with my mother, and they too carried the arguments and the confusion long into the night. He was struggling, he was wrestling with something so deep and I could hear him hit the table and then walk, and then sit and then rise up again, and she would plead, she would plead so long and hard. And then it would go quiet, and it would seem almost tender in the silence. I could hear her saying, 'Please', sweetly reasoning. She was trying all the reasons she could find. He was listening, but then he would sigh or groan, or shout 'No!' They lay in bed until dawn, and they were still battling.

'He has healed', I heard him say so many times. 'Healed. But why on the Sabbath?' he would shout in desperation. Then he would calm down and it was as if his mind were travelling again.

'He stretched out his hand . . . it was like . . . it was like new. As if there had never been any disease . . . like new!'

My mother was becoming angry.

'Can it be wrong to do good?' she whispered.

'That's what Jesus said, but . . .' Then my father leapt out of bed. 'He has broken the Sabbath commandment . . .'

'No.'

'Broken . . . he cannot be . . . from God.'

My mother stumbled after him and seized him at the door, she was clinging to him furiously. 'If we could just take her to him . . . in secret!'

'No . . . no. There can be no secrets between a man and his God!'

'Jairus, please . . . Jairus.'

My father cried out and banged the wall, 'No!'

7

They did not sleep together that night. My mother lay in her room. I think she was on the floor, where he had pushed her away and left her sobbing. She just lay down all the night and moaned and wept. She no longer cared what I heard. I did not cough, I forced myself to stay quiet. I knew if I called them they would be overwhelmed. My father sat on the steps below. I could hear him, I knew he was weeping in his own way. After a long while, he came up and he thought I was asleep. He just knelt beside my bed and touched my hair. Then he couldn't speak. After many minutes, he begged God softly for mercy and said, 'Even though the vines do not yield or the fig tree bear fruit . . .' and then something I don't remember, and he buried his head in my sheet for so long.

I did not move or open my eyes.

I kept thinking of the carpenter. I wanted him to come to me now. It was time. I knew he would come. He would come when he was ready, when he decided. He did everything he chose. The streets were quiet and I wanted to hear him. I wanted to hear him walking alone through the darkness, and he would stand beneath the balcony. That's what he would do. He would just stand there and call to me and I would get up. I would walk to him and kneel down and put my hand through the railings and he would take it in his. He would hold it so tight and he would say, 'Be well, now.' And no one would know, my father, my mother, no official or leader or wise man would come between us or say anything against him. He would just look at me and take my hand. I knew he would take my right hand. That bit I knew. I believed it. And this was how I could endure the terrible nights, and especially the grief of my mother.

My father went back down to the fire below, which was burning into nothing, and lay down there. I do not know if he heard the howling that came through the streets of Capernaum that night. It was the most chilling, deadly sound, and it was in wild harmony with all the hatred and fury of the day. It was as if all the rage and confusion had collected into one poor being. She hurled herself down the streets and crashed into walls, cutting herself. I heard her from far off down by the docks, and then running, falling, and then laughing and hooting like some strange bird. I knew who it was and I hid under my sheet. I didn't want that sound in my head. I longed for someone to comfort me but no one came. My mother was sleeping deeply, as if the grief had taken pity on her and plunged her into oblivion. I could hear her deep sighing. My father was silent. He did not pace and I knew he must be lying by the fire. He would not come up to me now for fear of waking me.

Mary was screaming to the blackness, 'I see you!'

She was laughing and then crying. Then the rains came. They burst from above and my shutters swung back and forwards. The rain drummed. It pitted the ground and soon there were rivers running down the channels, flowing down towards the wharf. I kept thinking of her soaking, twirling around in the storm. I knew she was like a little child and she had no idea how to look after herself, but no one could approach her when she was like this. She was strong and vicious.

'I see you! Ah!' She was shouting so knowingly, at nothing. It was the last I heard from her, her voice drowned in the cascading water. Her screams were just washed into the night. 'Ah, ah, I see you. He told me! I see . . .'

Then running streams, just gurgling and swilling. She must have run out of the gates. She often went there. She was often on the rubbish tips at night, sometime she lit fires there. Sometimes she just scavenged like a dog. Then, days later, she would be down at the soldiers' barracks, and she would look so beautiful and so dead. She would have scratches on her face and she would be lying there, gazing up at the sky, her clothes all torn.

She was gone now and I was grateful, although I felt sad for her. The rain kept coming, then it lightened a little. I could hear the water dripping off our roof on to the wooden slats of the balcony, a regular splashing. I could listen to that sound for hours. Sometimes I counted my way through the whole night like this when I couldn't sleep and the clouds unburdened themselves over the town.

I listened to each fallen drop and imagined they were notes in a song, music for my dreams. I felt so ill I knew I wouldn't sleep. The banging had come again and I couldn't move or call out. Then I heard a different sound between the splashes. It sounded like steps. One step, then another. Someone was walking through the street but so very slowly, wandering, one step at a time. Listening to the night air. Listening to those screams far away, that nobody else could hear now, on the rubbish tips and by the graves.

I knew who it was.

I longed for him to stop. I begged for him to stop at my

house. I was lying there and I was frozen so hard, so heavy and the night lay upon me like a huge rock. I couldn't move or shift it. I couldn't call out. I could just hear those footfalls. I could see him in my mind, walking, and I knew he was near. I whispered, without sound, 'Come now', but the footsteps went away. I heard them going out towards the gates, and then the rain fell in a fury. There was thunder. The whole sky seemed to empy, as all the heat of the day broke its bonds. There was roaring and the wind hurling. My shutters banged. He was gone.

She was waist-deep in all the filth, slithering and falling. All her voices were clamouring, they wanted to be heard. The sweet, sighing small voice, the pretty seductive one, 'Ohh,' she was singing out, 'ohh, I know!' She was laughing, like tinkling bells, and then another, a menacing shout, a rending animal wail overwhelmed her, 'Son of the Most High!' She screamed herself hoarse. 'I know you! I know you!' It hurled her down, rolling into bricks and pots. The water streamed across her face, which was blackened with silt. She was laughing quietly, singing, then she leapt. She clawed the night. 'Jesus Son of the Most High God! We know who you are!' Anger raged and ripped out of her. She wept and clutched herself. The rage threw her like a doll into the stench of the sewage. She lay there, and then the little one came back, the voice imploring, 'Ohh', the gentle deceitful twisted smile, 'You can have me,' she said, 'I know who you are, I know and I know!' She hugged herself, stroked herself, rolling and buckling and then flailing into the thunder, flinging her arms up and wrenching at the clouds. 'I know who you are!'

He was standing right above her, he was looking down,

reaching down. His hands were touching her fingers, and she snatched them away with a scream as if she had been stabbed in her eyes. She was clutching her eyes, burying herself down into the dark filth. 'No, no . . .' He slid down beside her and knelt in the filthy water and put out his arms again. 'Mary,' he said, in a whisper. The voices retched, they tore at her. They hated the word, the sound of her name. They threw her bellowing and cursing, scratching, 'Jesus Son of the Most High God! We know *you*!'

'*Come out of her*!'

His hand swept across the huge darkness hanging. His hand stayed above her, then fell slowly on to her head. He held her head.

'Mary.'

She collapsed, folded into a ball at his feet and lay there whimpering. She opened her eyes. She saw him. He was right before her, and he was looking at her. She held his foot with her hand, timidly, and he knelt down. She put both her arms around his waist and he lifted her up to face him. The water streamed down them, between them. It fell from his hair and his face on to hers, and the dripping streams of mud coursed from her dress down on to his robe. He held her to himself as she wept, and folded his arms around her.

'Mary,' he said.

'Mary.' She repeated it, as if it were a new name.

His disciples found him in the morning, sitting on the rubbish tip, and Mary sitting at his feet. He was talking to her but they could not hear what he was saying. All they saw was the sunlight, the dawn turning the filth into fire. They saw the figures silhouetted in the radiance. Gradually, they realised that he was with a woman.

They held back, shocked and unable to speak. As the shadows slipped from the figures, they recognised the woman from Magdala. They did not dare utter a word to her, as Jesus lifted her up and sent her on her way. She walked straight through the men without fear. She walked in graceful silence. They watched her go, through the gates and into the town.

His followers gathered all day in the fields, there must have been fifty or a hundred who had spent many weeks listening to him and watching everything he did, sometimes joyfully and sometimes in perplexed silence. There were moments when no one dared ask him 'Why?' or 'What does this mean?' There had been arguments about the Sabbath and some of the teachers in the school, including one of the most respected Pharisees, had pronounced that there was no commandment against healing on the day which God has blessed. Others warned against the man who invented his own laws and did everything to suit himself. Now he was seen publicly with the worst woman in the district. He was consorting with evil.

All this was on the day he chose the twelve. The day they watched him in silence and did not dare ask any questions.

He walked slowly through the men sitting there and every now and then he would stop. He smiled when he came to Simon the fisherman. Perhaps it was the way the huge gruff man sat so meekly and awkwardly. He was just sitting there, hunched up, his hands clasping his knees and his brow tortured into long furrows.

'I shall call you Peter!' He was laughing and others were joining him, as Simon creased up his eyes.

'The rock!'

'Rock?'

'Yes, I'm going to build on you.'

Then he turned to Andrew. He swung his arm across his shoulders, two workmen together, the great squat balding fisherman and the tall builder from Nazareth. 'Andrew . . . you will be my apostle too. My messenger!'

'James and John. The sons of thunder!'

And so he went on, plucking names from the sky, creating new men. 'Philip, Bartholomew, James, Simon.' Then he stopped and spoke very quietly. 'Judas – you too. You will be one of the twelve.' Everyone was pleased with that. Judas was well-liked. He was clever, a courageous man.

'Thaddaeus.' Gradually, he was completing his round, and then he turned back suddenly as if with an afterthought. There was a young man sitting under a bush. He was lost in thought, his eyes without focus.

'Thomas.' The man didn't move. He didn't hear.

'Thomas.' Still he stared away. All this was about other people, but Jesus was standing beside him and waiting patiently. It was as if his own name came floating down through his mind and settled like a leaf on a pond. 'Thomas,' he repeated emptily.

'Yes,' said the teacher.

'Me . . . ?'

'Yes . . . you, Thomas.'

'You really mean . . . me . . . ?' He got up quickly, like a man shaken from sleep and suddenly remembering something important. 'Me?'

Jesus was already walking down the hill, towards Capernaum.

Thomas followed with the others. He was bewildered, dazed and chosen.

'One more,' said Jesus.

They walked in silence and came to the docks, and Jesus walked on towards the custom house.

'Master,' Simon Peter seized his arm. 'This is not a good place.'

'One more.'

'Master – the boat – the boat's ready – we'll find a quiet bay, I know the best place for us.'

Jesus walked on, through the soldiers and towards the booth with the curtains.

'Don't stay around here. We'll go down the coast. We'll talk, we'll eat!'

'Master!' Judas ran in front of him. 'This is an evil place!'

Jesus held up his hand and all his disciples stepped back.

'One more,' he said.

He peered through the curtains where Matthew was sitting. The chief tax collector was scratching out a calculation. He rubbed at the slate, flicked a fly away in the sweltering heat. He shook his head, still looking down at his desk and the scattering of coins. Everything, the lists and the sealing rings, the parchments and slates, the stacks of coins, buzzed and shimmered into whiteness. He wiped his sleeve across his sweating face and then he looked up.

He saw the man staring at him and he was afraid.

His throat went dry and he tried to cover his table with both arms. He felt strange and sick. He looked away, but he could not move. He found himself turning, slowly and inevitably, back to meet those eyes.

'Matthew.'

'Yes . . . ?'

'Matthew, you must leave.'

'Yes . . .'

The others were whispering in horror, far back from the booth. Someone muttered 'Traitor.' Jesus stepped out and behind him came the chief tax collector, shuffling, trembling with confusion. The disciples stared, and the voice of their master rang out with anger and sorrow, down the docks, across the waters, 'Follow me!'

My mother sat with me for many days. Perhaps it was only a few. They all merged, and the nights seemed hotter than the days, the daylight darker than the night. I could hardly see her face. My eyes were sticking together. She sat there and I heard her rubbing her hands together sometimes or hugging herself, rocking and humming. I was floating again, and she must have thought I was asleep for some of the time, but sleep did not come easily.

One morning, she just got up and went out. I heard the door of the courtyard clang.

What made her do it, I don't know, but she defied my father and went out secretly into the crowds. It was the day when Cleopas was coming and perhaps the thought of the old man gave her strength. He would say 'Now then' and mean nothing by it, and everyone would calm down.

All she wanted was a glimpse. She had no plans to defy my father. She would not speak to Jesus or come near him, but if she could watch a little, hear a little, then perhaps she could understand. Maybe she would find some patience in her heart with all this arguing and confusion among the teachers in

Capernaum. She had no patience with them at all, and she knew that she was wrong.

There were some who believed that even to associate with Jesus would contaminate the soul.

She heard his voice clearly, even though he was a long way above her on the ridge. There were hundreds there and no one noticed her. They were mainly from the villages and she felt comfortable among strangers. She would only stay for a few minutes, long enough to be gathering flowers, not so long that she would arouse suspicion and make my father look a fool.

'How happy are those who hunger and thirst for goodness, for you shall be filled!'

His voice sailed in the air and brought with it a yearning. One word and it seemed she was longing for something she could never have. She was longing for happiness. Every word seemed to carry with it the same fragrance. There was happiness in that throng of ragged people and their lined faces, their shabby cloaks and wilful children playing and shouting. There was a beauty in the midst of all the misery and the sunken eyes of the old. She looked round, as if guilty. She needed to find some condemnation for this rabbi with his mixture of good and evil, light and dark. She needed to shut her heart, if she could, shut out the pain of longing. She was longing for him, longing for him to come down to her, and it frightened her so badly. Now she was imagining the crowds parting and he would run towards her and say, 'It's all right, I know. I know everything in your heart. Don't be afraid.'

She was shaking herself, angry with herself. She turned to go, because there had to be some sorcery in the man, something wrong that would ensnare all these people and trick her into believing anything. He had healed, but men said he had healed by the power of the devil. He kept company with the madwoman, and everyone knew she was the plaything of demons. But now the woman from Magdala was sitting up there, very near him, right beside him.

My mother crept into the crowd a little higher up. It was true. The woman was there, and she was sitting so quietly. She was ordinary, an ordinary woman. She was beautiful in the sunlight, but no more beautiful than a hundred young women in the crowd with their children. She was sane.

'How happy are you who are weeping now, for you shall laugh.'

The way he said weeping. The way he said that word. My mother looked down, down at the ground to hide her tears. How did he know? How did he know so much about weeping, like that? Again, she wanted to run, but she couldn't. She had to listen, and to move a little further up. Was this the evil in him, was it true that he could possess people?

'We will be lost for ever!' My father had said it. He said it once, so desperately, and he believed that we could be lost. All lost. She knew it was terribly wrong to be in this crowd, but why was it wrong? What was wrong? Her being here, or her staying at home and watching her child in agony?

'Bless my baby – hold him in your arms!' A woman, a rough-looking sort, was fighting her way through the crowd. 'Bless my baby.' She was desperate for him to touch her little one, and there were men circling her, the disciples were coming down fast. 'Pray for him—', but they interrupted her sharply.

'He's busy!'

'He hasn't got time—'

Another woman, two women, lifted up their babies. They all

wanted a blessing now. One of the disciples, a serious and stern-looking young man, shouted, 'Take your children home!'

That was when the carpenter stopped suddenly, in the middle of what he was saying. He stopped and he rose in anger. He came leaping down through the crowd and people scattered.

'No!' He was shouting. 'No, Thomas, Thaddaeus, *no*!'

He was right above her, and he was taking the little one, the tiniest one in his arms.

'Don't forbid them! Let the little ones come to me.'

He was taking another in his arms and then kneeling to the little toddlers who were clutching at his robes. He was surrounded by all their chattering faces. He was setting one down, picking up another. He was wrapping his arms round them, blessing every single one.

The disciples were shocked and overcome. They wanted to protect their master but he had driven them away . . .

'The kingdom of heaven is full,' he said, full – the word flew from his mouth, flew across the crowds, 'full of children like these!'

Then he looked over the heads of the mothers, who were so proud, so thrilled at that moment. He looked over their heads and straight into my mother's eyes.

'Bring the children to me,' he said.

There were hundreds around her, but he spoke to her. She knew he had spoken, even though he was still quite some way from her.

He had looked into her at that moment, and then she knew.

He is looking and time is standing still. I can't see him anymore, not like that, not like she saw him then, but he is looking into this night. Through this blizzard. He is walking across shifting seas. He is coming across the empty whiteness. He knows where I am, and he recognises the hanging ice on the wooden eaves of this desolate place. He is looking for me, and I know that he can see whatever he chooses. He can see me in this night.

She came running. She came running into the courtyard where Simon and Cleopas were greeting each other, and where my father had scarcely noticed her absence. She burst into them, as if gathering flowers in the fields or buying food from the market had suddenly turned her mind. They had no idea why she was jabbering.

'What is it – Rachel? Rachel?'

She could not catch her breath. She stood there, as if winded, and then she blurted out, 'Take . . . take her.'

'What?'

'We must take her to him . . .'

'What are you saying?'

'We must take her to Jesus.'

In the silence she saw Cleopas. She reached out for him, falling into his arms, 'Ohh, Cleopas—'

'Now then, Rachel,' he said.

'You must tell him!'

Cleopas looked at my father, who looked at Simon. He freed himself gently from my mother and asked her, very directly and quietly, 'How is she?'

'She is dying!'

My mother shouted the word, the forbidden word, and my father leapt forward – as if he could stop her saying more. He did not want to hear the truth. She was shaking.

'*No!*' he said, and he hushed himself suddenly. 'No, she is not *dying*, Rachel!'

He knew he was lying to himself, the man who longed to see the light of God in every corner of his being, he was lying to himself, to his friends. He was not lying on purpose, not wilfully, but he could not bear to hear the word. He did not want to hear that word. Not dying. If he spoke it, somehow it would happen. It would happen quickly. If he could just go on believing – in what he didn't know – in the mercy of God, in more time, in another day, then perhaps it would all stop. The nightmare would be over. Nothing was impossible. He looked at Cleopas and there was a silence. A look of such immediate love and sympathy, but of harsh reality. There was always reality in his lined face, something about him that put a stop to every little subterfuge. He was a dangerous kind of friend.

'Cleopas . . .'

But the old man said nothing.

Jairus looked at Simon, who wrung his hands. The man was struggling, torn by duty and by influences beyond his control. He coughed. He did not want to be the arbiter of life and death, but there were things happening. Things that were wrong and deeply dangerous. He knew that this Jesus affair would end in bloodshed in Galilee.

My father kept looking, appealing. My mother walked up to him, right up to him and said, 'Are you so afraid of them? Have they got such a hold over your life?'

'God is my life! Not . . . man! Not any man!'

'And your daughter . . . what is she? In your *life*?'

The word stung him into silence and he looked down at the cobbles, shaking his head. He was quivering with anger, not with her but with himself. How had it come to this? How had he brought his family into utter confusion? Cleopas coughed. He rubbed his hands slowly, chafing his old blotched hands very slowly.

'I think we should listen to this Jesus,' he said.

My father and Simon looked at him in astonishment. The man was known for his wisdom. He had been famous for his learning and everyone spoke well of him. Was Cleopas too seduced by the crowds and the sorcery?

'No one ever lost their souls by listening to a liar,' he said. 'Only by believing him and following! But if he speaks the truth—'

'The truth?' Simon was scornful.

'My friend.' The man's meekness was intimidating. 'We have nothing to fear from God, do we?'

'No, no.' Simon was blustering. It was true there were divisions over the Sabbath incident and there were factions, even among the learned. He was busily collecting his thoughts. 'No,' he said, 'er, we must question this Jesus further.'

Ben Azra and his men were away in the hills, gathering information. He was assessing the influence of the Nazarene and listening for any rumours of rebellion. There was time in Capernaum for a little harmless investigation, and if Simon could present a more united front on his return there would be credit in that.

'We must see how he defends himself.'

'Yes,' my mother looked hard into his eyes, 'you must listen.'

'Why should the people think their leaders do not listen?' Simon held his hand wide open. 'I will invite Jesus and his . . .

band of followers to my home, and we'll see whether he really is God's prophet!'

Simon's tone added to the turbulence in my father's heart.

He scarcely heard his old friend Cleopas, who put a hand on his shoulder and said, 'Now then, Jairus.'

I heard none of this. All I could hear was buzzing. Voices were like insects circling in my head, swarms of them, picking their way in, fluttering between my ears. I kept longing for something simple and clear. One word or sound which I could distinguish. My mother's touch was all I felt, her hand so cold. Incredibly cold on my neck. She must have said things, but I didn't hear. I did not know she had been in the fields or that she had seen the carpenter herself. I did not know the raging worry inside her now, because my father had agreed to the feast at Simon's with such a tormented look at her – like a man drowning in a sea of confusion. I did not know that she was losing me by the hour. I was hardly speaking and hardly waking any more.

Darkness. I remember that, but not the darkness you would expect. A darkness that was so full of colour, muddy colours, as if I were at the bottom of a river. Something was dragging at me. There was no pain. There was darkness that came and went in waves and in many forms. It was never quiet in there. It was always banging like clashing rocks, hitting and hitting together. It was a furious, constant sound and I just wanted to be quiet again. I was calling out for some silence. If only everyone in the world would be absolutely still and there would be no foot on a floorboard and no door banging, and no mumbling in the streets. If only people would stop shouting or talking, not even whispering, if only everyone would just stand in silence and let the waves settle to flatness. If only there were nothing anymore, no sound or light, I wouldn't mind, but the screaming dark, the swimming night that was falling without stopping, always falling like a horrible twilight that refused to become black and starless – it was slowly deliberately smothering me, so that I couldn't shout. I could not tell anyone. There was no one, I was calling and there was no one anywhere in the world.

Simon prepared his feast with great care. He paid minute attention to detail. The perfumed bowls were awaiting his rich guests, merchants from Caesarea, a Sadducee from Tiberias – a distant relative who had accepted the invitation out of curiosity. The rabbi from Nazareth excited curiosity. There were reluctant guests, like my father, and other teachers of the law from Bethsaida and Magdala. They were all greeted with ceremony, with drums and flutes and footwashing and the scattering of petals.

The table bore goblets of blown glass and the wide plates of terra sigillata which Simon had received as a gift from Ostia, the port of Rome. Some traveller who had been seeking influence in the tetrarchy had delivered them for favours, and Simon was a discreet broker of influence. He knew people. He took care to listen, and his reputation for hospitality had spread to the borders. He was on familiar terms with the commander of the garrison. He was trusted on every side, and it was a costly and subtle affair maintaining such a status. Honeyed sweet meats and spiced wines, and the rare red glaze from Ostia, the imported delicacies from the Cyprian markets, they were all essentials in the curious economy of his existence. He ate very simply when alone.

My father did not dislike Simon, and I suspect that he pitied him in some way. They had gone down different paths, once so close. Once they were free in the world and spoke of their passion for justice and for holiness. They were eminent pupils, in their humble way, and their teachers had expected great things. Time had altered little for my father. Simon had experimented with righteousness, found new definitions of survival and accommodation. He was still regarded as an upright man, but most spoke of him as a fortunate man. His life had become complicated.

Simon had no children. He believed he was in danger of losing everything, when in reality he had nothing to lose. Right up to the end, Simon never inquired about my health. He thought it better to leave such matters in the hands of the Almighty.

The lute playing was his own inspiration for the occasion. It added so much refinement and relaxation to the tension of that day. He controlled the minstrels and gave them secret signals when to play.

It was a remarkable achievement that Jesus had so readily agreed to the invitation. He was well-known for his love of wine – he had flagrantly drunk the health of the chief tax collector in a party that had lasted for several days – he was all too ready to eat and drink in the wrong company. He had never, before, sat down with the ruler of the synagogue or the teachers or the honourable assembly of elders. Many thought he would refuse, such was the bizarre nature of the man's behaviour.

But he had said yes. The servants had come back to the house and announced that Jesus would come with all his twelve disciples, which seemed a shocking liberty, but Simon had taken it as an opportunity to demonstrate his open-hearted hospitality. He had a reputation. Let them all come.

Now they were there, hunched together at a separate table, and they were eating noisily. They had been led in by a separate door, away from the atrium. It would have been a mistake to mix the guests indiscriminately – unfair on both sides.

They were whispering constantly and staring furtively, some almost in contempt, others in bewilderment at the array of men in their elaborate robes, their fringes and purple filigree from Tyre, their poise and elegance, as they reclined the Roman way with their left arms on the table and their feet outstretched. Servants clustered around them and catered to their whims, but only visited the other table to refill the glasses perfunctorily.

'Why are we here?' Simon Peter was shaking his head at Andrew and hardly lowering his voice. 'They don't want us here.'

'I've no idea, but let's eat.'

Andrew always had a straightforward answer. This was not an occasion for reflection. That could come later, after the final course.

My father sat next to Cleopas and was close to leaving. He was disgusted with himself for coming, what could this absurd performance achieve? Simon's whole world was suddenly like a pit of darkness to him. He was troubled at his own weakness. He could think of nothing but my mother, sitting on my bed, bent low, humming and moaning. He could see the shutters and the desperate, interminable shade of that room. He could see me lying, as if I were in some other country, as if I had already travelled far away and I was only a shadow left behind. He was sweating. He looked over to Jesus, who said nothing. The rabbi kept a forbidding silence, and my father was drawn to that. But it was useless, there was nothing to be said. He was in between two worlds meeting, and neither held any hope. Whichever way he looked, whether it was to the rabble of fishermen gorging themselves, with their silent and darkly musing teacher, or whether it was to the haughty and loudly discoursing merchants, full of their own schemes and opinions, the sadducee with his over-emphasis on every word, his heavy opinionated stupidity – whichever way he looked, he saw folly. And he saw his own utter folly.

'This was not wise, Cleopas.' The old man said nothing. He did not flinch at the rebuke. It had been his intervention which had spurred Simon on to meet and listen – listen to the man who now sat at his table in complete silence.

Jesus.

Who was this man, and why, why, had he agreed to come?

There was something so wrong with everything, with the whole state of things. It was as if the conquerors had not only robbed them of their land and their freedom, but of their souls. The Romans had marched into the promised land and ripped out the promise and the heart, leaving them all to their childish dreams and murderous futile uprisings, or to false messiahs and sorcerers, travelling exorcists and healers who would sweep the whole population down to hell.

'Not wise.' Cleopas repeated the words softly.

'What will this achieve?' my father said. 'It will make fools of us.'

Cleopas looked at Andrew, plucking dates furiously, and then at Lamech the Sadducee wafting his hand, punctuating the silence with some long-winded, heavily emphasised observation about life.

'Fools,' said Cleopas. 'In that case we'll be in good company.'

My father shifted, to go. He intended to leave quietly. He would slip out the side door and return home and seal himself within our house. He hated banquets and, at the best of times, shunned the crowds. Now he craved his silence again. He was pining for the darkness and his lamp burning and the roll of the scriptures, with the sound of the wind outside. He was longing for a place where he could endure the pain that was eating away at his heart. He was shouting out, inside, as if he were paralysed and could say nothing or move anywhere. As if he were like me, and he were lying in impenetrable darkness. He was holding me in his mind. He was lifting me up and cradling me.

'No,' said Cleopas, 'stay.'

Then Lamech spoke.

'Master . . .' he said.

Simon waved at the musicians, a discreet flick of his fingers behind his head. They stopped, and the music seemed to hang for a moment and the smell of the food lingered. Even the disciples stopped eating and looked up. Something would happen now, they knew.

'Master . . . we are honoured by your presence at . . . our humble feast.' Lamech opened both hands and then clasped them together. He looked up at the fretted ceiling. 'Although,' he continued, 'we hear . . . you prefer to keep company in another part of town.'

The man beside him, with a damask collar, leant forward.

'Yes, master, we realise you would rather be eating with tax collectors and sinners. Why is that?'

Jesus did not look at them, but drank some wine slowly. He

put the goblet down, picked up a honeyed pastry, toyed with it, broke off a piece and ate it.

'Those who are well don't need a doctor,' he said. 'Just those who are sick.'

My father sat back a little.

The mention of illness.

He was breathing deeply. Cleopas put a hand on his shoulder without looking round and stilled him.

'I haven't come for the sake of good people.' Jesus looked across the line of guests, his eyes passed across them, measured them, their goodness.

'I haven't come to call good people to repentance,' he said. 'Just sinners.'

He broke off a cluster of grapes and ate them thoughtfully, relished them individually.

The guests were whispering among themselves, preparing a question. Simon glanced over to the musicians and one of the minstrels took up a bow, but he shook his head slightly. The situation was still under control.

Lamech took a breath. He took time, elaborately. He had a good question, but as he opened his mouth . . .

There were shouts. Simon stood up. He looked round, flustered, ashamed.

He excused himself, muttered about servants . . .

The shouting was coming from the courtyard. It was quite violent.

'No, no!'

'You can't come in here!'

'Get her out!'

She was running, nimbly, evading their hands. She knew

how to run. She had had years of practice, she dodged through colonnades and they stumbled after her. One servant fell down on the doorstep. She leapt over him. Simon stood at the entrance to the hall but she swept past him, he clutched out.

'How – dare—'

But he was helpless. He turned after her, suddenly stupid and undignified. He beckoned furiously.

'Please,' he said, desperately trying to observe decorum. 'This way.' His servants gathered round her, but she stood there quite unafraid. It was as if she didn't see them, she was blind to everyone in the room except him.

Jesus lifted his hand and the servants drew back.

He waved his hand, again, and the servants drew way back to the walls.

The woman walked to him.

There was a gasp because the men at the feast now recognised her. It was Mary, but her hair was washed, and her dress was clean.

She knelt down. She knelt down beside him and she took his foot. She held it timidly. He looked at her.

My father saw him. He saw him look. He felt the look at that woman in his whole body. It ran through him.

He had never known such a thing and he sat there, afraid to breathe.

The stillness in the room was something he had never known, even in all the years of his solitude in the long winter nights.

She took his other foot and stroked it. She looked up at him and the tears stood in her eyes. They shone. She shook her head, shook the hair loose, and her tears streamed down her face. She was crying and crying, but not sobbing. She was holding both his feet and wetting them with her tears. She was wiping them, around and around. Her tears were falling all down her face and on to her hands. She spread the water on to him. She rubbed her hands around his feet and soothed him.

All the time he was looking.

He saw no one else in the world.

That was what my father saw.

She embraced him, his ankles, in perfect humility, sweeping her dark hair around him like a silken towel. Then she took a jar from her side, from a purse slung round her waist. An alabaster jar with an onyx stopper.

It was the most expensive, most beautifully crafted object in the whole room, and she cracked the seal.

She broke it over his feet. The ointment poured like water, all of it, all over his feet and on to the floor. Then she spread her hair across the marble and wiped it up, and drew it across his feet again.

The smell of that perfume was so rich, it reached into the courtyard. It hung above the heads of all the men, who were outraged at this crime, the waste of this wealth and the woman who had won it with her own wild body.

The madwoman from Magdala.

He looked at her and he did not see their faces.

He held her to him, as she sat there, and tears came in his eyes.

My father saw them. He saw what he had not understood before. He saw for himself what I had seen outside the synagogue in Sepphoris. He saw how the carpenter protected her, how he saved her. How no one could do anything to hurt her in his presence.

He saw how the whole world was banished in one moment and how there was only the two of them. This was her moment. He saw it and he was deeply troubled, because he knew this could not be evil. This could not be sin. But he did not know what to do.

Simon was behind him, and said to him harshly, 'If this man were a prophet, he would know what sort of woman is touching him!' Others nodded their approval. It was clear to many of them what they had witnessed. When Jesus touched her hair and smoothed it down, Simon could not help himself but called out again, 'She is a sinner!' Then he sat down in despair. He looked round at his many guests and they returned his gaze. He shrugged his shoulders. He was ready to apologise, but how could he accept responsibility for this? Such an attack on all human decency. On goodness.

Jesus held her for a while, then he spoke without turning.

'Simon, I have something to say to you.'

There was silence. Simon returned his gaze with all the calm he could muster.

'There was once a man who had two debtors, one who owed him a huge sum of money. Five hundred denarii! The other – fifty! But neither of them could pay up, so he forgave them. So which of these two men will love their master the most?'

Simon sighed audibly. It was one of the rabbi's traps. He was known for them.

'Well, the one who was forgiven the most, I suppose.'

'Your judgement is correct.' He said the word judgement with emphasis. He looked at Simon seated among his friends, beside my father, beside Lamech and the merchants and the teachers.

'Judgement.' That was the other thing, that word. My father

felt, suddenly, that he had been sitting in judgement all his life, but in reality he did not know how to judge even his own life.

Now he did not know anything, and it was possible that the man was not evil. But he might be dangerous, yet . . .

The way he was with the woman.

It was something beyond judgement. It was beyond goodness, and beyond evil.

It was something completely outside all that he had ever known.

'Do you see this woman?'

Simon nodded, forced like a child to play some game. Everyone could see the woman.

'Do you see her?' said Jesus, and the answer was not so clear. It was doubtful if anyone in the room, all the disciples, the guests and servants, whether anyone saw her at all.

He had a way of looking and seeing everything.

He spent time then, looking at her, then looking back at the men all around, meeting their hostile gaze. 'I came into your house,' he said to Simon, 'you gave me no water for my feet, but she has wet my feet with her tears and wiped them with her hair. You gave me no kiss, but she has not stopped kissing my feet. You didn't anoint me with oil, but she has poured out this ointment, all over me, all this fragrance, all over me.'

He took her by the hand. 'This woman has been set free from so much, that's why she loves so much! But the man who has been released from hardly anything, will return . . . hardly anything.'

He lifted her up.

She stood there in silence before him, so still and so confident. She stood there straight and beautiful, her hair reeking of Arabia and the spice gardens of India.

'All your sins are forgiven now,' he said.

And then the men around, the others around Simon, stood up too, because they had seen and heard enough blasphemy.

'He's saying it again!'

'Forgiveness—'

My father put his head in his hands, because he did not know what to think. He buried his head and all the thoughts whirled around and voices shouted within, as if he were afflicted by the woman's madness, as if the demons had found a new home.

'Go in peace.'

She went. She walked through the throng of servants, who fell back. No one dared come near her. She vanished through the arcade of roses into the quiet of the garden. Her footsteps sounded on the brick pathway. Then there was silence and the chafing of a lone cricket. The warm air was moist, and the perfume still lingered in the humid room, a cool heavy aroma like a thousand flowers crushed beneath their feet.

After Jesus and his disciples left, my father sat there with Simon, and Cleopas and men whom he had considered wise, righteous men. Simon was agitated and paced around the hall.

'Now we know,' he said. 'We know for sure. We *know*.' He kept saying it, to comfort himself, to produce order from the chaos of his banquet. He picked up a fallen lute.

At last Cleopas said, wearily, 'What . . . do we know?'

Simon wheeled round to my father and pointed, shouting in spite of himself, 'You saw him on the Sabbath. You . . . you saw what he did!'

My father replied, ignoring his own misgivings and as if in

some dream, 'He . . . did good on the Sabbath.'

'Good. You saw that "woman". Is she good?'

'He has . . . power.'

'Yes, because he is in league with the devil!' One of the Pharisees from Magdala struck the table.

Phineas stood up. He was a gentle and respected teacher in the district and my father held him in great regard.

'So then,' said Phineas, with unexpected finality, 'anyone following Jesus is an enemy of God.'

8

I heard my father running. His footsteps were so far away, but I knew it was him. He always landed heavily on his left foot. He was running as hard as he could. The door in the courtyard banged so hard, twice, as if he had fallen against it or fallen over himself. He stumbled up the stairs.

He was breathing so quickly. My mother was holding my hand, like anchoring a boat. I was slipping away. The darkness was dragging at me and most of the time I was deep down. I was so far down. But then I heard him running.

He burst into the room and fell at my bedside. I felt his weight, all his weight, but I couldn't wake up. I couldn't climb up the dark. I was in a cave. Water was dripping everywhere, streaming down walls I couldn't see. I could feel this horrible damp, this penetrating cold in my heart.

He spoke. I didn't make out the words.

It was him, though. He was squeezing my hand, and my mother said something to him. He spoke again. A word, I don't know what, I think it was 'Tamar'. I think that's all it was. But it came down to me, where I was and it drew me. I felt myself coming to him, slowly, but I couldn't see him.

'Father.' He didn't hear. I tried to say it again and again, and then he did.

'Yes,' he said, 'I'm here.'

My mother sighed. She held me with both her hands now.

I said to him, 'Am I going to die?' He made a sound, a groan. He said, 'No . . . no!'

Then my mother. I remember her voice, so light and trembling. She was so full of fear and she didn't want to speak. She was trembling all over and she couldn't stop herself mumbling, 'Jesus.'

'She keeps saying his name . . . Jesus.'

She had never said it before.

The name.

I spoke it out loud to my father. He leant down because he could hardly hear me, he was watching my lips. They were blue. My face was like wax. I couldn't open my eyes to see him and I so much wanted to look at him, at his lovely, sad face. I wanted to see him even though I knew he was tortured with all his thoughts. I wanted him to hear me clearly.

I said, 'Take me to Jesus.'

He let go of my hand. He stood up. The voice was ringing in his mind so loudly – 'Anyone who follows Jesus is an enemy of God!'

And he shouted 'No!'

I cried out. My mother wept. She clung to him, and he shouted with all his force, 'No!'

He walked to the door. He said, 'No . . . I will not listen to them . . . I will go. I will go to Jesus!'

My mother fell down beside me, she was so shocked. 'You will . . . ?'

He was already going, and I was slipping down. I was falling so far. I could hear his words, he was calling out to me, 'I will go, and you will be healed by his power . . . by the power of God!'

He was running.

I let myself fall. I felt that nothing mattered any more. He had spoken the name. He was going. I could hear him in the street, it was the last thing I heard, those uneven footsteps disappearing. There were people shouting somewhere, but I couldn't make out any more. I knew that everything would be all right.

The crowds were shocked and parted before him.

'It's Jairus.'

No one had ever seen him run. No one had seen him stumble and push down the street and struggle through dense crowds, no one ever.

'It's the leader of the synagogue.'

He was desperately making his way through Capernaum, through the blocked streets. People stared.

He could see, in the far distance, the face of Jesus – he was talking to someone. He called out, but the noise was too great. He pushed on as hard as he could. It was impossible to run further. He begged his way through.

'Make way for Jairus,' someone shouted, and the crowd folded back.

He was in sight. Jesus was standing alone, turning. He was turning. He could see him now. He could see the man running, half-stumbling, and then falling.

My father fell down at the feet of Jesus.

The whole crowd, the whole town of Capernaum seemed to fall silent. The disciples stared. No one could believe this. It was Jairus. He was in the dust. He was weeping. He was looking up to Jesus.

'Master . . .' he said. There was a gasp. Jesus looked down at him for a long while.

'My little girl . . .'

He couldn't speak. He was overwhelmed, and Jesus took his hand. He helped him to stand up. He took command of himself again, slowly, with great difficulty.

'She is dying . . .'

Everyone watched him, holding out his hands and trying to speak, to catch the words. 'Please,' he said. 'If you come now . . . to my house . . . and lay your hands on her, she will be healed.'

He had asked.

No one moved. A bird fluttered somewhere, high up. No one coughed even. They waited, they could not believe that the ruler of the synagogue had come to Jesus and fallen on his face before him, and called him 'Master'.

'Yes, I will,' said Jesus, 'I will come.'

My father tried to say 'thank you', but the words stayed in his throat. He nodded. He began to walk with Jesus, side by side, and he was pointing desperately.

She was watching me and she heard the rasping breaths, the long dragging and then the short return, the gulping and rattling. She was all alone. She looked out of the window and the crowds were so far away and she could see nothing. She cried out loud and called on God, but there was no one coming. There was no one anywhere near. My father had gone. He wasn't there with her and she was begging him to come back, because she knew something so terrible was happening to me, so final, and she couldn't wake me, she couldn't reach me any more. My hand was frozen, and it was limp.

My father was urging Jesus on through the crowd, as fast as he could.

'A little way further.'

Why didn't they give way? Why didn't they all move back? But there were simply too many people, a thronging world crammed into back streets. Jesus walked so slowly.

Then he stopped.

He stopped in the middle of the baker's street, just near the corner. So near, almost within sight of the house. He stopped. He looked round.

'Who touched me?' he said.

My father took him by the arm, 'Master,' he said. 'Please—'

But he stood there looking and everyone went very quiet. Simon Peter came forward. 'Lord,' he said, he was smiling and shrugging, 'Lord, everyone is touching you! Look at the crowds!'

'I know someone touched me! Who touched me?'

The whole crowd shifted back, fearfully. No one spoke up. Jesus stood there, alone in the dusty street and my father stood as near as he dared. He was desperately wanting to take him by the hand and pull him onwards.

'Master . . .'

Jesus looked deep into the crowds. 'I felt the power go out of me,' he said.

After a long while, something moved. Something shuffled. People looked round and made some room. It was a woman, a little woman. She was quaking, and looking about her. She came out into the open, as if she were in fear of her life.

She was covered with dust. She had been crawling. She had made her way through all the legs of the people, past all the

140

children, through the disciples, and she had reached him. She had reached out secretly and grasped for one instant the fringe on his garment.

'It was me, Lord,' she said.

Then she looked round again, as if she were afraid of someone coming up behind her and hauling her away to prison.

Jesus lifted his hand a little, to still her fear.

'I was bleeding. Inside me, so many years . . . the doctors did nothing.' She began to weep. She shook her head. The years came upon her. She just shook her head at the memories that stirred, the years of living alone and hiding from reproach. Her bleeding had made her an outcast. 'I was afraid to come to you before all the people, so I . . . just wanted . . . to . . . I wanted to touch.'

Her knees gave and she fell down, sobbing – but he caught her. He held her with both hands and lifted her back on to her feet.

'Daughter,' he said.

She looked at him like the tiniest child, looked right up to him. She was so earnest. Her eyes were wide open at that word.

He nodded. 'My daughter, your faith has made you well. Go in peace.'

She turned round, and without a backward glance, she walked into the crowd.

It was Cleopas who found my mother. She was lying on the stairs and she had torn her clothes. She was lying as if reaching up to my room, and she was howling and sobbing. He stooped down to her and took her hand. She turned her face to him and in that instant he knew that I was dead. The old man began to

141

weep, there on the stairs. He looked into my mother's eyes and he saw her complete hopelessness. He squeezed her hand. She lay down again and began beating the stairs. Her shouting and screaming carried into the street where people stopped and stared. Cleopas climbed past her very slowly and softly and entered my room, and there he saw me.

I was lying with one arm hanging out of the bed. My head was turned upwards and my eyes were open. My shoulders were bruised because my mother had been hugging me and clinging to me, shaking me so hard. I was already quite cold. The old man came to my bedside and he didn't touch me. He stood there and he tried to utter a prayer, but he could not. He took the sheet and pulled it over my body. He said it was like pulling the night down for ever over the world. He said that he sat on the floor and the sorrow for his friends had been worse than he ever imagined. He had expected my death, but he had not expected to fall into the darkness so suddenly. It was a sorrow he had never known, although he was old and had lost many he loved. He stood up, after several minutes, and tore his robe down the seam. My mother looked at him again, and again he tore it. He came to her and tried to take her hand, but she grabbed it away and curled into the wall. She pressed herself against the wall, screaming.

'Where is he?' he said softly.

She shook her head violently.

'Has he gone to the synagogue?'

My mother muttered something.

The old man shook his head and put his hand on her shoulder. 'Where is Jairus?'

She cried out 'Jesus', but half the sound was lost in the

howling rage. She kept burbling the name until it meant nothing. It became a horrible empty craziness.

Cleopas nodded.

'Have you . . . seen her, seen her?' she said.

'Yes, yes, Rachel,' he said. 'I've seen her.'

'Ohh. Have you seen her?'

'She's at peace,' he said.

'No, no, no, there can be no peace,' she howled, 'no peace, no peace, Cleopas. She isn't at peace. There is no peace.' She was sliding down the stairs, banging her head. He stopped her gently.

'Peace will come,' he said.

'No, no, never.' She sat on the floor. 'It will never come.'

The old man gazed at her and could not find anything to say. He shook his head and felt the darkness all around him. He had never felt such dark, and he felt that he too was dying. They were all shrouded now. There would be no peace.

He walked slowly away from her and looked one last time at the woman moaning and hugging her legs and then suddenly hurling shouts, sounds, strange gulping sounds, like screams without breath. He turned through the courtyard and into the street. There were many neighbours gathered. They looked up at my window. They had grown used to me sitting there or calling down to them over the months. My mother and father had received so much love. Everyone wanted me to be well and no one dared mention the word 'illness' or 'dying', although everyone in Capernaum knew.

Cleopas walked through them and said nothing, and they began to weep. A group of about ten of our neighbours sat on the threshold and began to cry and beat themselves. They tore their clothes but they did not dare enter our house, where they could hear my mother. She was walking round and round the room below and she sounded like an animal that was bleeding to death.

The crowd were thronging round Jesus again. They knew nothing of this. People called out to him from every street corner, there was always someone begging for attention. Children came forward and waved at him. Shopkeepers were coming out of their stalls. My father was terrified that there would be another interruption.

'Please, Master,' he said, 'please hurry.'

Jesus walked on, always at the same pace, slow, but moving. He was not looking to the right or the left.

'Master—' My father turned, he was pointing to our house at the far end of the street. 'Here,' he said, but then he saw Cleopas.

He saw the old man walking purposefully towards him. He wasn't shambling in his usual way. He was walking so steadily towards him, and people were stepping back.

Cleopas stopped.

'Jairus,' he said, and my father called out 'No.' He sank down. He saw everything on his friend's face. He saw his robe flapping around him, the strands of cloth trailing in the dirt.

'Don't . . . don't trouble the teacher any more,' he said.

My father turned to look at Jesus, then back at the old man. Cleopas held his hands out as firmly as he could, but he was engulfed in sorrow. When he saw my father's face, he shook his head. He just kept shaking it and saying, 'Jairus'. He held his hands out wide, questioning. They were trembling.

My father said nothing. Nothing around him existed at that

moment. The crowds had gone, melted into the air. The streets, the shopkeepers, even the sound of wailing that was riding over the heads towards him, the harrowing cries, all this he could not hear. There was the most terrible and deadly silence that wrapped him. He could not move.

And in that place, all he could hear was a voice which spoke to him and said,

'Don't be afraid. Believe.'

He looked up and now he saw the face of Jesus, looking at him, straight at him, and gradually the people were appearing again, the world was assembling around him. Cleopas was still standing there, his hands out and the tears on his cheeks.

'She will be well,' said Jesus.

'She's dead,' said Cleopas, very distinctly. He was afraid for his friend, but my father nodded, very very slowly. He had understood.

When they came to the house, there were many weeping and crying out, and the whole crowd was taken by the grief and it seemed to flow through mothers and children. Weeping rent the air, screams and sobs. Everyone was shaking.

'*Stop!*' Jesus shouted out. People were shocked, they were outraged at his harshness. 'Stop all this crying!'

They stared at him as if he were a madman. 'She's not dead,' he said, 'she's just . . . fallen asleep.'

Now they knew he was mad or cruel.

My father did not react. He did not think it strange or wrong for Jesus to say these things. He thought nothing, except that he wanted to come to my bedside. He wanted to kneel down and hold me in his arms. He wanted Jesus to stand beside me, although everything was too late. He wanted it for my sake, because I had wanted it, and he had failed me. He had denied me. He was shaking his head, unable to speak.

He walked up the stairs, and he saw my mother standing at the top. She stood there against the light. She was like a figure in a dream. He hardly dared touch her. She was quiet now, and she stood aside. She stood all by herself at the balcony as my father fell down at my bedside. He pulled back the sheet. He looked at me and my eyes were still open. He shut them. He looked round at Jesus, and he saw such sorrow. He saw all his own sorrow there. He held out his hand and then, thinking better of it, just turned back to me. He put his head against mine like he always did, softly, so closely, and he picked me up. He sat on the bed with me in his arms. He rocked me there, for a long time, and Jesus watched. Then he laid me down, straight out on the bed. He was overcome with violent sobs, but my mother did not come to him. She could not. She was frozen in her own world, and she was colder than my body lying there.

I did not know what had happened. I did not know anything. I knew I was falling. Falling, although there was nowhere further to go.

I am falling. There is no place above me or below me, so there is nowhere I am going, but I am still moving. There is no one to hold me. I cannot hear anything, or see or feel. I cannot taste the dark, but it is inside me, inside my mouth. It has come into me. I am falling so fast, and the spinning darkness is unravelling me. I am calling but I do not make a sound.

Falling and then holding, stopping. I am stopping now. I am

146

lying somewhere. I am lying down. I cannot move. I am so still. I can hear . . .

a breath. A breath of sound, a voice, it is so so distant. It is calling. I can hear words, 'girl' I can hear. I can hear the word 'girl'. Someone is saying, 'little girl'. It is a man's voice. It is falling down, down towards me, that voice, and it is so deep. It is coming down beside me, so I can hear all it says. I know the voice.

'Little girl, it's time . . .'

It is his voice. It is singing, I know how it can sing over the crowds and how it can ride the waves. I do not doubt. I know. I am trying to say something, but I cannot. It is all around me, and it echoes like a song in the shaft of a well. Deep ringing around the endless stones.

'Little girl, it's time now for you to get up.'

I can see light. I can see this light so far, and then immediately it is all around me. I can see burning light. I can see his face. He is there. He is leaning over me and looking at me. I can see him. It is him, and he is smiling and I can feel his touch on my hand. My right hand. He is holding my right hand and lifting me.

'Tamar.'

I sat up. I sat up quite suddenly, and I said to him, 'You came.'
  And he said, 'Yes, I've come. I'm here, I'm here.'

I was holding him and he was holding me.

And the whole room was silent. I saw all the faces, I saw my father and I saw my mother. They could not open their mouths. I saw Peter and James and John, standing beside the doorway. They were afraid. They were trembling so badly. I saw Cleopas, he was peering through them and holding his hand to his face. That poor man, he was about to faint on the ground.

Jesus was holding me and he was laughing. Laughing. And I began to laugh.

'Feed her,' he said to my parents, 'give her something to eat. The girl's hungry.'

'Food,' my mother murmured the word in all its absurdity. 'Food,' she said, 'we must get—' and then she ran to me. She held out her arms as if afraid to take me, as if I had to give her permission. She was afraid, but she was crying. She was saying 'Little girl', like an echo. And my father said it too. He said 'My little girl'. 'Yes, it's me,' I said, almost crossly. And they began almost to laugh and almost cry. They were holding me, touching me and feeling the warmth. I was so warm to them, I remember that, but I hardly looked at them.

I was looking at him. 'You came.'

He said nothing now, but he sat on the bed with me and then pushed me softly with his hand, as if to push me into the world. I sprang up and I ran into the people at the door. There jumped back. They were still frightened. I ran down the stairs. It was good. I was running. I came into the courtyard and there was such a shout. The whole crowd stirred and fell back. There were people screaming, and some running. It was funny. I ran into the street and I just shouted, 'I'm all right.' I danced down the street, like the man in his crazy made-up dance. Only I could dance. I was good at dancing and I did my best one. I swirled and I did the feet, the movements, it was a beautiful dance down the road. I jumped and sang. I shouted 'I'm all right.' People were cheering, they were running after me. Other children were coming to me and touching me. A tiny boy touched my arm to see if it were really me. He thought I was a dream, a dancing dream that had leapt into his garden.

I ran everywhere, round, down to the docks. I saw the water. I felt the water. I cupped my hands and threw it over myself. I ran back up the road and all the crowd were singing. They were singing praises. An old song, such an ancient, flowing, lifting song, about gates and the king of Israel.

I will never forget Cleopas on that balcony. He was singing. He didn't care about the world. My father and my mother were at the door of the courtyard. They were waiting for me, as if they had lost me for an eternity. They ran to meet me and held me. They both held each other. My father tried to lift me up, but I shook my head. I told him sternly that I could walk. I kissed him. He was crying and crying so freely. He knelt there in the dust, on hard stones, and he thanked the God of heaven, the God of all the earth.

Jesus came up to him and stood silently.

My father looked up. What I saw in those eyes, in my father's gaze, what I saw was such brokenness. I saw a man who was begging forgiveness. And Jesus put his hand on him, so quietly, and nobody heard him but me. I heard him say,

'Your sins are forgiven, Jairus. Go in peace.'

That night, Jesus walked alone in the mountains. He went far from Capernaum. He went into the upper region, where it was bitterly cold under the stars, up on the highest ridge. It was many hours before Simon Peter and Andrew found him. They knew where he went, when he was in the greatest anguish.

He had been lying on the earth for a long time.

They came to him and told him what they had heard from merchants arriving in the town that evening.

'Master,' Andrew said, 'we have heard . . . from Jerusalem.' He looked at Simon Peter. The two men hardly dared to speak. These were evil rumours on a day of rejoicing.

The crowds had been roaming through the streets for hours. No one would go to bed, all sat up late and talked of everything that had happened. They talked about my father, how he had thrown himself down at the feet of the carpenter, before the crowds. They talked of their shock, they talked of Simon and Yacob and Phineas, how they had shaken their heads and bolted their doors, how the wise men of the town had pretended to see nothing. They talked of me, dancing in the streets, and everyone argued that they had spoken to me first, in person.

They talked and laughed, but Simon Peter overheard two merchants talking with soldiers near the garrison. He later found them in the inn and they told him what they knew.

'Master,' said Simon Peter, 'it's John.'

Andrew was whispering, in tears.

'Herod has killed John.'

They left their master alone and walked back in the thick darkness, down through the meadows which filled the air with the scent of lilies. They walked in silence, beside the black waters of Galilee lapping and surging around the rocks. They did not exchange a word.

Jesus lay on the earth. He had not stood up to greet his

friends or turned to look at them. He said nothing when they spoke. After they had gone, a long while after, he lay down and beat the ground with his hands.

'Father,' he said. He said it many times, 'Father'. He wept for John, for his cousin, John.

9

'Yes, the death of John . . .' Herod Antipas twirled a necklace of amber and gold in his fingers and crushed the beads into a ball. He grated them together in his fist. He was an educated man, and the frescos all around on the theme of wisdom bore testimony to his refinement. But he was superstitious. He believed in ghosts.

Mention of the name of John in his presence was a dangerous gamble. The wild man still stalked his mind somewhere, raving down forgotten corridors. John had spoken against Herod's marriage and he was still speaking, raging away about adulterers and judgement in heaven. If only John had kept himself sensibly to religion and his little theme of hypocrisy. If only he had kept shouting down in that filthy river about the temple and the priests who were in the pocket of their Roman masters, that was a harmless preoccupation. The people enjoyed his performances. But now the priests and Sadducees were queuing up in Tiberias. They wanted some other wild man silenced.

Ben Azra looked at the king with a disturbing, mocking gravity. Herod hated people to stare at him in that relentless way. He flinched and looked upwards.

'Yes, the death of John was . . . unfortunate.'

'But necessary, my Lord Herod. A warning to the people.'

'To warn them of what?'

'Disobeying their rulers. Destroying your kingdom.'

'You do have a talent for easing my conscience.' Herod stretched out the beads in his hand and pulled them taut. He looked at Ben Azra and his companion with contempt. 'But one dead prophet is clearly not enough for you?'

Phineas stepped forward. He bowed slightly. The reproach stung him, for he had accompanied Ben Azra uneasily. He had decided, after weeks of consideration, to make known the fears of many good men in Galilee.

'There is far greater danger here,' he said quietly. Herod returned his gaze for one moment then flinched again, craned his neck as if studying the huge cornices with their plaster vines and painted fruits.

'You say this Jesus can perform the impossible?'

'Oh he can perform', Ben Azra clasped his hands, 'powerful illusions, Majesty.'

'Powerful illusions.' Herod toyed with the phrase like the beads, stretching it out, then wheeled round at the two men, startling them, flinging his hands around the vast chamber, 'Well, isn't all human power an illusion?'

'Not the kingship granted to Herod.' Phineas spoke with confidence. He was learning this art. Herod shook his head, smiling.

'You really are encouraging to a vulnerable soul. Oh, if only Caesar was as sympathetic as you' – then he smashed his fist on the claw of his chair and rose, screaming into the darkness – 'but if I *fail to govern my people!*' He sat down. He looked around him, over his shoulder, up into the vaults, he snared the beads between his fingers, 'What will happen?' – he was murmuring to himself, the men were nothing to him, paltry trouble-makers from the synagogues and the temple, but they were tormenting him now, their vile presence and their ill-disguised threats.

'If Pilate sends back reports to Rome,' Herod was rehearsing the scene. He knew the ways of the Senate. 'If this Jesus goes on . . . and on . . . performing such extraordinary tricks . . .' The necklace snapped in his hands and the beads cascaded on to the marble, echoing and bouncing into the shadows. He roared after them, into the darkness,

'Where *will it end*?'

It ended in fire. When the Circus Maximus burned. When the Palatine burned and we were running, in the terror and the endless burrows, the footsteps, the children crying. It ended when the temple fell and the standards rose over the ashes, when all Jerusalem was weeping, when all the gilt dripped in the heat and the sanctuary was opened to the sky. It ended when fire was matched with fire.

I came here with the smell of fire on my clothes. It can never be washed out. All the way across the waves and through the straits, even when I saw the island in the mists, when it loomed and it was whiter than I had dreamed and so much colder that day, I could still smell fire. All the rains and the snows of the years have not dampened the smell of destruction.

The end.

So many ways of ending, and then discovering a forgotten way through smoke and through death.

There are deaths all around me here and, before the snows came, I walked among them. I was given that privilege, among the tombs and the garden of victory. I gathered myrtle and the violet lavender, but I did not rest them on the graves. I carried them in my arms, into the darkness.

I have stood by the inscriptions and the statues, the winged gods. The fading lines: 'To the holy goddess Fortuna Conservatrix, the hymn of Marcus Aurelius Salvius, tribune of the first cohort of the Spaniards who willingly and deservedly fulfilled his vows.' 'To the holy goddess Minerva, Flavius Severinus, the tribune.' 'To Jupiter, best and greatest, Gaius Arrius Domitianus, centurion of the Twentieth Legion Valeria Victrix who gladly and willingly fulfilled his vow.' I have stood in the onset of the winds, in the first falling flakes of the year, and fulfilled my vow. I have turned from the shrines and the emperor's niche in the aedes where the candles burn like sulphur.

Where the fire burns, and I can still hear the screams of children and the dying, praying fathers. I have taken these deaths with me.

I have taken my own.

I have taken courage from one death and I see him coming again. I can hear him in this darkness, one more time. His voice is so far away, but he is singing. He sings in the darkness and that is how I know him, I will always know that voice.

The dwellers on the ends of the earth know him, we know him. We will not forsake him.

They want me to say I do not know him, to renounce the name. I was warned about the edict and I did not comply. I spoke his name wherever I could, at Caerleon I spoke it, and at Inchtutil, beyond the Brigantes and far beyond the Tay. I spoke his name wherever I could and to whoever I could. And I will call it now, into the driving wind, into the night. I will sing out in the wild blackness what I know. When all else is gone, when nothing is left to me but a nameless grave without a tribute and with no garlands, I will rejoice in the snow sweeping over me. I do not fear dying again.

I fear only losing him. That is when I call, in my sleep, when he is turning and going into the crowds and I am calling and he cannot hear. When he turns to go into the garden, on that day, when I was holding him and begging him, when I knew from the look on his face that he was bleeding so badly in his heart and I could not hold on to him, when he turns in my dreams and is lost. I wake up weeping and clutching at the pillow.

I wake up in the night, and then I remember. I remember Simon Peter, sinking into the blackness, how he saw him. How he saw him coming.

How he knew it was him, even in the midst of the storm.

He came walking but at first they did not see him. They were too busy bailing out the water. They were in fear of their lives. Peter said it was the worst storm he had ever known, a vicious squall that had suddenly erupted into a mad conflict of waves and dark. They were in danger of sinking. Everyone worked. They were shipping more than they could lift out in the buckets, but they slaved and said nothing.

Then Peter saw it.

'Look—'

'What is it?' John couldn't see anything, the spray was driving into his eyes and stung.

'Over there—'

It was a light. The tiniest light. It was sharpening.

'We must be near land.'

But they weren't, they were way out in the middle. They were nowhere near land.

The light was coming. Andrew called out, 'What is . . . it . . . ?' He couldn't hide his fear. Peter grabbed his arm. 'I don't know.'

The light was growing, forming. It was shaping into a figure and it was moving through the dark. Thomas screamed out then, 'It's a ghost!' But Peter held him back.

'Wait, wait!'

'It's a ghost!'

They were all shouting, and Matthew sat in the boat holding his head and begging, 'Oh God have mercy, have mercy!'

The figure was standing there. It came to a halt on the waves, quite some way from them. Just standing there, waiting in the dark.

The light.

Simon Peter stood up. He had great courage. All the others just sat and hid in the bows, but he stood. Very slowly. He tried to stand up against the wind.

'Who . . . are . . . you?' he said.

Then the voice. Then the note on the waves. It was so quiet, strangely quiet and clear in the storm.

'Don't be afraid, Simon Peter . . . it's me.'

Peter looked back to the others and none of them moved. They knew. But they didn't dare move, not one of them. No one spoke.

'You, Lord?' said Peter.

The figure just stood there, quite still. It wasn't moving at all, not moving with the waves or in the wind. The cloak did not move, as if it were standing in complete calm.

'Lord, if it is you, then tell me to come across the water.'

The figure laughed. He laughed in his way, a rippling laughter as if he were so pleased, so delighted with something. There was such love in that sound. If ever I heard it, it made me so happy.

Peter heard it in the raging night. He heard the laugh hanging softly, lingering in his mind. He knew very well it was Jesus, but he was afraid.

'Come on then,' said the figure, and held out his hand.

Peter took one foot and placed it on the gunwhale. Andrew grabbed him and tried to stop him. What if this was a dream, a demonic nightmare? But Peter shook off his brother roughly. 'No,' he said, 'it is . . . it is him! It's him!'

He swung his foot off into the freezing waves and they held. He called out. He was shouting to the others, but no one followed him. He put both feet on to the water. He stood there and they all watched him. They watched the huge fisherman balancing like a child on a narrow wall, his arms flailing around. He was laughing for a moment, because he knew it was so impossible. Then he just put a foot out, far out, and put it down squarely on to the water. He put the other one after it, and he was standing looking at the figure, who beckoned.

'Come.'

He began to walk, as if he were learning something new. A new art. A baby on the floor, standing up so proudly for the first time. His arms hovered in the air, but he didn't need to balance. He began to walk, very slowly, as if he were on dry ground. He began to walk normally.

The boat was behind him, some way behind, and the wind was whipping at his face. The spray leapt across his eyes, suddenly he couldn't see. He couldn't see anything at all. He looked down. He looked at the waters, the murky blackness, lapping around his feet, it was up to his ankles. It was rising up and he was sinking, and now the night was claiming him.

'Lord,' he shouted.

He was drowning. His head was going under. He could see nothing but black, there was night around him for ever. He was in the freezing dark.

And he heard the voice.

'Simon.'

It was deep inside him, inside the night and the water pouring into his lungs as he drowned.

'Simon.'

A hand pulled him, took him with great force and pulled him into the air. He rose, the waters sliding from his back and his hair and his beard, raining down him, and he stood again on the waves, coughing. He was right in front of Jesus, who was holding him around both shoulders.

'Oh, Simon.'

He was shaking his head, slowly shaking it, but just sighing softly at his friend.

'You have so little faith.'

Little. He said it with such passion. As if little would never do, for Simon Peter.

'Why did you doubt?' he said.

The boat was up against them, they were right beside it. Jesus led Peter into the safety where all the others cowered. He slapped him on the back. He hugged him. He was so proud of him, but he would not let Simon be satisfied with so little.

He would weep and talk of his little faith. We let him speak and did not contradict him, whenever he was by the fires or in the last days. Sometimes he could not speak of anything. It was painful, as if the memory of some things abolished all he had ever done. He carried with him a wound. I so wanted to hold him and tell him that he had done everything, everything that he could. I did not say so. He would not accept anyone's comfort. On such days, in such nights, he would just look into fires. Especially the fires in the braziers. Once I was with him at dawn and I heard the cock crowing. He leapt up and ran and he hid. I found him, with John and Mary and the others, we found him lying on a rock somewhere and the tears stained his face like blood. I will never forget that crowing which came before the first brightness like the cruellest shrieking, like the nightmares that come, still come for us all.

We only live in the half-light. Some days, some years, we see the light. We are blessed then, but we descend into the dark and we must carry that too.

The disciples did not know what kind of man could do this. What man could walk on water. Something about that, even beyond the healings, took them to the edge of their lives, of all they had ever dreamt. They went with him into the mountains, toward Mount Tabor.

There were crosses there and many bodies, the shadow of a rebellion, and the imperial standards flapping above the smell of rotting flesh. There were birds of prey feasting, all along the road. He stood still and gathered his disciples and asked them, 'Who do people say I am?'

Andrew spoke first. 'They're all saying you're a prophet.'

'But who do you say I am?'

That was when Simon Peter spoke. He did not know where the words came from, but they rose up from the depths, he sang them out into the hills, 'You are the Christ, the son of God.'

Jesus held him, held him for many minutes, their faces close together.

'O Simon,' he said. 'O son of John.'

He was filled with joy. He turned to all the others and said, 'No man could have told you this, only my father in heaven. You *are* Peter, the rock! I will build my church on this rock and the powers of death will never overcome it!'

Soldiers were arriving in the far distance, with carts, and they were levering the bodies down. Some they stabbed with lances, others they smashed the legs. Some they prised off, limp, and flung them like rubbish on to the cracked boards. The horses moved off and the disciples made their camp at the foot of the mountains. No one spoke of the smell of death.

Their master was troubled and wandered into the darkness, beneath a thorn bush. He snapped twigs in his hand, held them, and let the spikes fall into the long grasses. There was a sharp wind and the disciples huddled round the flames, and Simon looked anxiously for Jesus, who did not come. He sat beneath the thorn bush, leaning against it, and he watched the shadows of the men moving around the flames, whispering like children. He stood up, after a long while, and he came to them, sat down in utter weariness. They handed him something to eat, but he did not eat.

'You must tell no one,' he said.

'No one?' Simon looked at him, his eyes burning in the firelight.

'Tell no one that he is the Messiah?' said Judas, turning to

Andrew and Thomas, who stared at Jesus. He had lowered his eyes to the ground. Judas put his arms up to say more, to protest – now they knew. Now this was their time. The Messiah had come to deliver the land.

'The Son of Man must . . .'

Jesus prodded the fire with a stick, stirred the burning twigs where the sap boiled and dripped into the heart of the flames. He threw the stick into the fire and stood up. His hands covered his face, he held them there for a long time, as if thinking, working out something impossible. He gained strength suddenly and spoke.

'The Son of Man must suffer,' he said.

They looked up at him, bewildered. They had not heard or understood. It was some parable of his making, he would tell them the meaning.

'Suffer many things', he went on, flatly. There was no feeling in his voice, and they were disturbed. They had not seen him or heard him in this way before.

'And be rejected by the elders and the chief priests and the scribes. I will be killed.'

Simon Peter stood up. He looked down at the others, their wild looks and their shifting eyes. Every man looked to another for a word, for some hook for their thoughts.

'No,' he said, 'no—'

Jesus went on, without changing his voice, without lowering or lifting it, he went on, delivering his words away from them into the darkness.

'But I will be raised again on the third day.'

Simon Peter seized his arm.

'No, no,' he shouted, 'this will never happen to you! Never!'

Jesus turned and his look sent Peter backwards, made him stumble.

'Get behind me, Satan,' he said.

Peter collapsed, he fell down with his head in his hands, buried his head. He was in violent confusion. The love seemed to drain from him, all the love that had filled his mind and his heart bled into the ground. He shook his head. He muttered to himself. His face was burning with anger and shame – he had spoken wrongly, but he did not know. No one knew what to say, what this was. This dream of dark which had come upon him, like a cloak.

The pain shot through his voice as Jesus said 'Get behind me' – because he wanted, he wanted so badly to hear those words, to seize on a hopeless comfort. He wanted to take his friend's false hope and kiss it and bind it to his heart, and so he raged against the spirit.

The shadow that still stalked and came offering kingdoms.

He knelt down beside Peter and said, 'You are thinking as a man again.'

Then he walked away into the grove, he stayed long in the shadow of the trees. He walked among them until the moon came.

At dawn, he took Simon Peter, James and John up the mountain. There were flakes falling, a few solitary flakes of snow against the blue, and then they came. They came down fast. As they walked higher, the snow shrouded and hid them. They walked up into the cold region, high above the ridges, where the sun on the whiteness hurt their eyes.

They were up there so long, the others became restless and afraid. A whole day passed.

When they came down, Peter and James and John could not speak. They had seen something. Whatever they had seen, it was too fearful, or too far beyond their lives, for them to know what had happened to them.

It was John who told me, and he would not tell me more than this, that they had seen the glory that was to be.

He told me down in the harbour at Ephesus, before I left for Rome, when I was afraid. He sat with me, on crates of fish and pots of linseed oil, he sat with me and took me up to a mountain. He told me how the snow was dull and the white glare became grey. How the bright sky became darkened and the sun eclipsed. He told me how they had hidden in a cave in terror from the burning glory. They had heard a voice saying 'Beloved', saying it so deeply and so truly, it shook the earth, but they could not make out anything else. Or if they did, he would not say. He would not or could not, because that quiet man who prayed in the nights for the people of the empire, that silent man was choked with tears then. All he could say to me, as I left him, was 'Glory, we have seen his glory'.

When I sailed with all of them, and he was on the quayside, I could still see him there for such a long way. I could see the figure on the end of the wharf as we turned beyond the stones and the beacons. I could see him, both hands high in the air. I heard his voice – I dreamt I heard it – following me as surely as the gulls gathered in the wake of the vessel. I heard him say 'Glory'.

When they came down from the mountain in silence together,

Jesus came first. He came a long way before the three, who held back. They held back for some distance, hardly daring follow him.

The others rose up, Judas leapt up, Thomas, Andrew, they were all greeting him, as if somehow the dawn would burn up the terrors of their night, their confusions and the talk and the smell of death. He stood there before them, so warm and so familiar, his hands out to them. Suddenly, they were glad like children, talking of nothing, putting out the fire, grabbing their bags and their cloaks.

'It's time,' he said, when they were all gathered.

'Time,' said Simon Peter, still dreaming, still sitting in a cave among the snows.

'Are you ready?' he said softly, and they nodded.

'The hour has come.'

He walked on alone, far down the slopes, alone, and they followed.

'What does he mean?' said Thomas. 'He says it like . . . like something terrible is going to happen – what hour?'

'Don't worry' – Andrew had no intention of returning to the evening's troubled silences around the fire and the grim mood which had robbed him of sleep until the third watch – 'we'll all travel down, we'll share the Passover feast in Jerusalem, we'll come back. Like we do every year!'

Judas snorted, as if Andrew were an imbecile.

'You don't understand. This is the moment! When the kingdom of heaven will come on earth. There'll be freedom – we'll win a great victory over the Romans!'

'The kingdom of heaven – now?' Philip was catching up with him, Judas was so full of energy and life and vision. 'Now?'

'Yes, yes, Philip, now!'

The men ran down the old track, down to the villages, they marched together singing, all the long way back to Capernaum where the pilgrims were gathering in their thousands.

For the first time, I was not afraid of the crowds around him. I knew I could find him. I could run like all the other children, I could crawl under the donkeys, I could slip between the fat merchants and their baskets. When I saw him at last, everyone was thronging around him, some were singing and cheering and the children were everywhere. I was not jealous. I just watched from the circle around him, watched him love them, touch their heads, say something to a little girl who ran off laughing. I saw him lift up a boy who was too big to be lifted and who struggled and chuckled, in the competition to see who was the strongest. Jesus lifted him high in the air and everyone clapped. Then the boy jumped down, but he followed closely. We all wanted to be as close as possible, and some tiny little ones were constantly pulling at the tassles on his cloak so that he could hardly move, but he took them by the hand and said things to them, whispered things which made them run to their parents and jump in their arms. I waited my moment, and it seemed like hours after we had set out. It was so hot that day, and we all stopped by a terebinth tree. There was water there, but he didn't rush down to drink, he turned, I think he was looking for his flask to fill it, and suddenly he saw me standing there.

He didn't say anything, he just held out one arm and I walked into it and he held me. His arm was all round me. I kept looking up at him and I was so happy I just started to cry. I felt stupid, but then I saw the tears in his eyes too. He held me so tight, then everyone moved on, someone brought him a drink, the disciples and the people came like waves carrying him down a great river. I stood and let the people push past me, and I didn't mind. I stood there by the old terebinth. I leant against it, and there was camomile all around my feet and deep purple sage, so dark and so rich. I bent down to pick some, and my father came towards me with the mule laden with all our pots and the dishes for Pesach. He said, 'Oh, there you are.' And I could not remember the last time I had heard him speak to me so casually.

When the sun was low in the sky, everyone began to sing together, the sound was so deep and mysterious because there were at least three thousand of us. You could hardly hear the words, it was more like water over stones or the wind humming. Perhaps the pilgrims were just playing with an old psalm, singing around it and making up new sounds, but the first torches were lit in the distance and I remember the strangeness of that night. I caught the words like leaves tumbling towards me: 'bless the lord', 'servants of the lord', 'all who stand by night'. Twilight was falling and we were setting up our camp near Beth-Shean. We were on our way to the house of the Lord.

Cleopas was beside my father and the old man had hardly spoken since the day of the miracle. Even his customary silence had descended into something far deeper. He was waving his hand across all the people pitching their tents, still singing, many of them, and in the far distance Jesus was standing beside some old, half-ruined caravanserai, and hundreds of people were gathering around him.

'I sometimes wonder . . .' My father was running his fingers through his hair.

'Yes,' said Cleopas, as if my father had nothing more to say, as if 'wondering' were all they would ever do now.

'Yes,' my father repeated. There was silence between the two men for a long time, but when my mother joined them, the singing started up again in some place nearby, from some cluster of tents in the haze, a wave of yearning, a lovely sighing kind of song.

'I wonder who they're singing to?' my father said suddenly.

'What do you mean?' My mother was uneasy whenever my father threw out such questions, which often seemed to come from nowhere, without warning, but were heralds of some new struggle in his spirit. He never seemed to settle. He was always moving on somewhere, and this had been a hard burden for her to bear. She, for the first time in years, was at peace.

My father was at peace too, but somehow he could hold questions in his mind at the same time, live and breathe in conflict and yet remain curiously at peace.

'Are they singing to the God of Israel or to . . ?'

Cleopas took advantage of my father's hesitation. 'The people are dreaming,' he said softly, as always without a hint of judgement, as if he too were a dreamer wandering among their tents and singing into the dusk, under the gathering stars. 'They dream of a Messiah to save them from the Romans.'

My mother sat down beside my father and spoke so quietly I could not hear for a moment. She was speaking of me. My father nodded.

'He saved her from death,' she said, 'don't you think that death is a harder enemy than Caesar?'

My father stood up. He walked to a rock, leant against it, bent down to it, then turned abruptly.

'Is he the . . . Messiah? Is he . . . the one?'

My mother turned round to me. She looked me in the eye. She knew I had heard. I walked up to her and she was looking up at me. I knelt down and I kissed her and we held each other. Was she depending on me, or was I depending on her? We no longer knew.

Cleopas was shifting slightly, rocking very gently. 'Only God,' he coughed and chafed his hands for a while, 'only God knows . . . who is the chosen one.'

High above the camp, Simon and Phineas were tethering their horses, looking down at the flickering lights of the pilgrim city. Songs rose in the clear air, as if they stood on the edge of a vast amphitheatre. Yacob and Lamech were there and, higher up still, Ben Azra and his retinue.

Phineas turned away from the spectacle, a sight which had once filled him with overwhelming joy. 'If there is an uprising in Jerusalem,' he said, 'we'll all be killed.'

'Gaius Velius Quintillus, your excellency', the old official bent down to Pilate, who sat surveying the newcomer at great leisure. 'Chief centurion of the twelfth legion, prefect of detachment of the nine legions and tribune of the thirteenth urban cohort.'

'Mm.'

The tribune stood there, the sun pounding on his helmet. He did not move, although the hinge on his backplate was digging into his shoulder. His dark skin and deep eyes were intriguing to the prefect of Judaea. A Carthaginian. The man looked hard and reliable, not some wretched fool who would get lost in the tangle of Jerusalem, not one of those mercenaries from Gaul or Bithynia.

Pilate nursed his hands. He hated the festive air in this little cramped city, the sweat and the stench of trouble, and he yearned desperately for his bath house in Caesarea. He dipped his hand in a scented bowl and splashed his face.

'I asked for an experienced commander. It appears I have one. Tribune!'

The tribune stepped forward and saluted, slapping his arm with unusual force across his breastplate. Pilate nodded with appreciation.

'Did the garrison commander brief you on the . . . curious customs of' – he made no effort to hide his contempt – 'the Jews?'

'Sir?'

' "Pass-Over", for example?'

' "Pass-Over"? No.'

'Ah. I'm surprised.' He coughed, and shifted in his chair. 'Well. The, er, Jewish passover . . . it's, it's a festival of . . . freedom.' He uttered a short laugh. 'They celebrate their day of freedom! Oh, it's some . . . it's something about Egyptians. Some old story.'

The tribune nodded uncertainly. 'Sir.'

Huge numbers of soldiers were assembling in the Antonia fortress, clattering up the granite steps. They ringed the colonnades below and stood along the porticoes of the temple. They positioned themselves by the shuttered windows on the four towers and along the battlements. A whole legion was dispersing itself in streaming patterns of men and glinting armour. Pilate looked up at his noisy militia, irritated by the constant interruptions, as if their boots were responsible for his headache. The permanent throb of Jerusalem. He emptied the bowl into his hands and rubbed the fragrance over his temples, and sighed.

He led the tribune up the steps, half way up the high tower, where they could observe the seething crowds in the city.

'Jews from all over the empire gathering here. Along with the whole of Judaea and all the disgusting pilgrims from the North. They're the worst. The Galileans.' He turned round suddenly, 'Oh, but I hear you've already put down a little revolt up there?'

'One hundred and seventeen crucified, sir.'

'Hm, and the ringleader?'

'Barabbas and the others. We thought . . .'

Pilate looked with surprise and admiration at his new commander. 'A public execution of rebels on the day of freedom. Very good, tribune.'

He turned to go and the tribune saluted.

'Hail Caesar, Son of the gods!'

'Hail Caesar,' Pilate replied quietly, 'but don't let them hear you talk of . . . the gods.'

The tribune looked down at the milling people, flowing into the temple. Pilate had gone. He adjusted his backplates, away from the bruise on his shoulder.

The next night, we stopped at Keruchim. Everyone was covered with dust. A storm had blown along the plain and tumbleweeds were hurtling over the cracked earth, bouncing like wild creatures. Children tried to catch them, but they were too fast, and they were made of thorns.

We settled in this ruined village, where there was a deep well and plenty of shelter. There were huge blocks of stone there, dark basalt, and there was white asphodel everywhere. It was growing in the sand and through the fallen columns of some old arch. It was so bright in the sun. I was glad because Andrew and Philip were there, shifting rocks and setting up camp. I knew we would be near Jesus. I would sit by the fire, as close as anyone, closer than I had dreamed, and hear the stories again.

He was a long way off, far back with Simon Peter and John. He was with Mary, his mother.

Miryam.

That was the first night I ever saw her, and she said nothing to me, but she looked at me. She caught my eye across the fire, and she smiled.

I have carried that smile with me, and that tenderness in the dark. I have treasured that gift to my heart, the eyes that stared at me without blinking and seemed to share some secret with me as the sparks fled into the blackness. She gazed at me as if I were her sister, a woman like her, and I was in awe of her beauty.

I have treasured all her smiles, her silences.

But her sorrow, I was ignorant of that. Now, in the night storms and the greyness that devours the horizons, the violent seas here, sorrow accompanies her smile. Her dark eyes look at me in a different way. They keep looking, as if she were begging for someone to have sat down beside her then, even a child like me, and put their arms around her. I did not know. No one knew, or guessed, where the road was leading. We were laughing and leaning forward into the glare, sometimes we were shocked by things he said, or delighted, but never saddened. No shadow fell across us as it had across her heart. As we all chattered and sang that evening, beneath her loveliness and her calm she was racked by some terrible anguish. She did not move from the same position all night, but huddled by the fire until it sank into white ash.

There were many things about that time. I remember so many because the stillness, the unreal stillness of that day and that evening was like a warning which no one could read. Everyone was being so ordinary, even those with questions and doubts, as if we could go on like this for ever, our lives would be a festival of firesides and songs, as if we could demand of him by right a lifetime of stories and signs and wisdom.

Earlier, the disciples had been shouting at each other. There was really quite a heated, stupid argument as they were setting up camp. It was hot, even though it was very late in the afternoon, and perhaps the sweat of the work was getting to them. I could just hear grunts and then shouts, and then some – I thought it was swearing. They were getting angry with each other. I kept away, playing with the tiny children who were running round and round to make themselves dizzy and then falling over shouting with laughter. We did that for ages. But Thaddaeus and Philip and even Andrew were arguing quite violently. Thaddaeus was putting up a post and he kept jabbing it into the earth, 'When I'm in charge – when—' and Philip was just laughing him to scorn, but he carried on spelling out the words with great deliberation,

'When I'm in charge – in God's kingdom—'

'You!' Philip hurled a stone on to the corner of the tent and almost ripped it. 'He'll never pick you. You couldn't run a market stall!'

Andrew barged in and shouted, 'I was the first to follow him, if anyone is—'

'Could you lead an army?' Judas jumped down from a broken wall and strode up to Andrew. He was shaking his head. I saw him do that so often, that week. He was half-smiling, a sort of bitter ironic smile, shaking and shaking. As if to say, 'You're all so ignorant!' He was losing patience with all his friends. They all seemed to madden him, and his anger was a strange kind of reluctant fury, as if he were forced to put all of them right.

'Will men follow *you* to glory?' he asked, and he just held out his hands. And he looked round, he even looked at us in the meadow beside them, as if we were his witnesses, as if all the children would bear him out.

'I was the *first*!' Andrew shouted, and he thumped his fist hard on a block of stone. He hurt himself, but he wouldn't show it.

They went on like this until Jesus came, and Judas and Philip both walked up to him, desperate to have the first word. They were talking to him in urgent whispers, like very important friends with secret business.

'Master—' that was all Judas said, and then Philip stepped in front of him.

'We've been waiting for you to come,' he said. Jesus stood very still and all the crowds held well back. 'Tell us, who will be greatest in the kingdom of heaven?'

He said nothing for a long time, and surveyed the line of the disciples as if he were about to select someone, but then his eyes travelled past them into the meadow, into the field of coriander where I was playing with this little boy. He was dancing around,

174

'Come down,' said Jesus, 'there's plenty of room.' (p. 91)

'You didn't anoint me with oil, but she has poured out this ointment, all over me, all this fragrance, all over me.' (p. 133)

'My father pulled me on, dusting me down all the time, as if the streets themselves were contaminated.' (p. 4)

'The entire shoal had risen to the surface as if it prayed for capture.' (p. 75)

'He thought I was a dream, a dancing dream that had
leapt into his garden.' (p. 149)

'You do not believe anything I say, so why should I tell you?' (p. 241)

'Father, I give you my spirit.' (p. 265)

'Mary,' he said. (p. 275)

spinning. He fell over and laughed. Jesus laughed softly too. He looked back at his disciples. 'All right,' he said, 'I'll tell you.' He stepped into the field and picked the little boy up in his arms. He was only about two, but he wasn't afraid. Jesus lifted him up and the boy looked back at me and then at his mother who was watching. Then he put one arm round Jesus' neck and with his other hand he stroked his beard. He ran his tiny fingers through his beard and then patted him on the head. It was so funny. I had never seen anyone do that, no child or adult, touch his beard or his hair like that. Jesus was so moved. That was the amazing thing. I could see the tears in his eyes, something about that little boy was reaching him and loving him so deeply. He couldn't speak for a long while, but then he lifted the boy down, he set him down in the middle of all those great, rough men. The boy stared up at them, spinning very slowly around, and then sat down.

'Unless you change utterly and become like little children,' Jesus said with such sorrow in his voice, 'you will never even enter the kingdom of heaven.'

They were just staring at him and then at the boy, who looked up at them. He wandered over to Jesus and held the tassles on his robe, like the little ones always did.

'Whoever humbles himself like this little child – he'll be the greatest in the kingdom of heaven!'

Jesus picked him up again and held him to his face, and the boy was wriggling and twisting round to look at the strange men who had been shouting. And Jesus took him over to his mother, she held out her arms, and the boy folded into her, vanishing into her embrace.

We all stood there, listening to the sound of crickets and the frogs by the trees. The sun had disappeared and there was a bird rustling in her nest, fussing around, and then silence again.

I saw this man in the shadows, a tall man, very richly dressed. He had a great white sash and jewels on the girdle. He was watching Jesus so intently, long after the disciples had got back to the tent and were hammering the pegs without saying a word. The man came forward, and I could see that he was thinking of something, some question, something was burning in that man's soul. I will never forget his gaze. It was as if he felt such hopelessness and yet such longing.

Longing that came with me, that took me here, that touched my life for ever, the traveller who could not stop. Who journeyed on when others fainted and others turned back. That man, one day, took hold of me. In his grief and his shame at what he had not been, he turned to me and begged me to go forward.

I see you in the shadows again, my friend, you who called me, you who dared to send me beyond the furthest horizon when the world was in ruins.

I see your weariness and your confusion, as you were then, as you always were, but hiding that courage, the madness that drove you further than anyone except Thomas. The glory that called you into mists, into the lost island, that took you beyond the reaches of your own dreams.

You were like me, you dreamed.

He stood in those shadows, as the fire was being lit, as we gathered and sat down, and he waited until long after Jesus had eaten and the children had sat down beside his feet.

He was always waiting on the edge, wondering if he should speak, ready to fall back into silence. 'Master,' he whispered. He looked at the children and then back to Jesus. Then he seemed to look at himself and his eyes lowered to the ground. He sat down.

'What must a man do to be saved?' he said.

'You must trust in the Lord your God with all your heart,' Jesus replied quickly, then he turned and looked at the man and said, 'and . . . ?'

'And . . . ?' the man echoed.

'You must love your neighbour as much as you love yourself.'

The man who was called Joseph, a rich merchant from Arimathea, was uncomfortable in the firelight, finding himself among the poorest children and the fishermen from Capernaum and some ragged women who had been singing loudly by their tents and now seemed brazenly to meet his gaze. He looked around for a moment, and said,

'Who is my neighbour?'

It was one finger. A finger in the dust. All the other stories I remember, he made so many movements, so many sounds and voices, but this one was so still, frighteningly still. We watched that finger walk through the dust as he said, 'There was a man going down from Jerusalem to Jericho.'

One or two children laughed, but I couldn't. It was the way he pushed it slowly through the earth, beside the fire. There was something so deep, almost ominous about the way he did it, and I saw a dread in Joseph's face, as if he were battling against himself. He was hiding his own reluctance to listen.

He was not a proud man, although he was rich, and he was not humiliated by sitting down and listening to a story. All the rabbis told stories, but this finger . . . the finger walking, shovelling dust until the nail was dark. There was pain in this tale.

'Down the steep gorge all alone.'

We watched him steadfastly cutting the ravine.

'Suddenly,' he said – and we caught our breath. His finger now lifted, high above the ravine, high into cliffs and the sheer walls of red sandstone – we were painting our own pictures, as he taught us that night to tell our own stories from now on, to learn from him, to take power from that finger trailing sand.

'Robbers appeared!'

Children beside me jumped back. The robbers were too real, they would leap from the black trees and savagely attack us all.

'They kicked him and beat him, they stripped him and left him for dead.'

His palm lay upwards. He held it there for a long time, and he was looking at us, challenging us to say what happened next.

'Now it so happened that a priest was coming along from Jerusalem.'

We saw him, in his fine clothes. We imagined the holy man approaching and we were relieved. The poor broken traveller would soon be saved.

'But the priest walked by on the other side.'

I saw Joseph arch his neck for a moment, feeling some pain or knot in his back. Jesus curved his fingers slowly, very deliberately and fastidiously, past the body. 'He didn't dare find out if the man were still alive, because he believed that it was wrong to touch a corpse.'

We watched the priest go, far into the darkness, far along the other side. As if that side of the road stretched for ever, deep into some tunnel.

That was all he told us about the priest, but then he lifted his hand high again, back towards Jerusalem. 'Then!' He said it with such power. 'Then!' We edged forward, to see how the man would be saved from death at last.

'Along came a rich and powerful Sadducee.'

He did not look at Joseph when he said this, but all the children gazed at the rich merchant who was on his way to the temple in Jerusalem. Someone like Joseph would surely save the man, there was no doubt at all.

'He walked right up to the man but, like the priest before him, he thought he should not touch the body – and he crossed right over to the other side.'

Joseph nodded faintly, hugging his knees. He was already writing this story in his own heart. Jesus stopped for a while, and stirred the fire with a stick. A log tumbled over and disintegrated. Flames leapt up, and in the brightness he suddenly seemed to be very tired. I thought he was going to get up and walk away and leave us to decide the ending. But he tossed the branch into the flames and swept his hand through the night one more time.

'But at last, along came a Samaritan.'

Someone laughed, or snorted. But he went on, 'He saw the poor man lying on the road dying! He took pity on him. He fetched ointment and poured it on the man's wounds. He took off his headdress and ripped it in two, and made bandages.'

I couldn't help myself, I was thinking out loud and just blurted, 'A Samaritan?' 'Yes,' he said softly, then this boy next to me stood up and said very loudly, 'Samaritans throw rocks at us!' Then his brother spat on the ground, 'I spit on them!' he shouted, 'I hate–'

The look that came over Jesus' face, the look he gave to that boy. I felt sorry for him, because he shrank down. He hid behind us, his hands over his eyes. He knew he had said the worst thing, and he thought he was just taking a good part in the story. Jesus looked and looked at him. And then Joseph buried his head in his hands. It was a strange sight, that tall man with his magnificent hat. I don't know what it was made of, but there was crimson and white silk and some kind of spotted fur, and there it was, tilted oddly, balanced against his hands.

The fire was burning and crackling, like something that would erupt into the night. Jesus moved his finger again, so slowly, both hands, two fingers travelling. 'The Samaritan took the man to an inn. He paid the innkeeper and he said, "Whatever it costs to look after this man, I'll pay you everything on my return!" '

Joseph felt the silence and the eyes of the master. He looked up and his hat fell into his hands. He held it there as if it were nothing, as if his dignity were like some chaff or bracken to be tossed on to the fire. He fingered it and I thought he was going to throw it into the flames.

'Which one of the three men proved to be the man's neighbour?'

'The one who showed him such . . . love.'

From the moment that Joseph said 'love' like that, I cared for him. I felt pity, because of the pain with which he said it. Why, I didn't know. Why was that word so full of anguish? He said 'love' as if he had never known it or given it to anyone in the world.

* * *

'You go then,' said Jesus, 'do the same.' And he held out his finger, covered in grime, as if pointing to an extraordinary distance beyond the hills. And Joseph just stared. He sat there and stared at the same spot, late into the night, long after we had all gone to our beds. Miryam sitting by the fire, huddling, half-waking, half-sleeping; the merchant from Arimathea shaking his head softly, then nodding; two dim shapes beneath the stars. And Jesus walking alone, way out into the desert.

He was lying down beside the yellow broom tree we had passed on the way. He was stretched out weeping.

My father could not sleep. He had not been beside the fire at all. He had eaten alone in the tent, and then walked off. He stood for a long time, half the night, by an old gate that was hanging from its hinges. Everywhere was the scent of lavender and the yellow coriander that had made the ruins their home, and beside him were the pink crowns of hyssop jutting from the rocks. They were dripping with dew. He was cupping his hand under the water, like a small boy, and tasting it, and then looking out across the huge steppes where the mist was coming at dawn.

He was puzzled at first, then troubled, by the figure who had left the fireside and was now pacing backwards and forwards in the meadow. Then the man turned, and as soon as my father saw the tall figure and the robes, and something about his restless manner, he walked briskly towards him. The man didn't move or turn round.

'Joseph,' he said.

Joseph turned and looked at him, half looked at him. 'Who

is it?' he said. My father laughed lightly.

'So many years,' he said. Joseph studied him again, scrutinised the face in the dusk.

'Jairus . . . ?'

They walked to the far edge of the meadow, beside the spring. The water was dark, gushing into a vault of stone. They studied it as if somehow the leaping brightness disappearing into its hole, and the music, would instruct them.

They were both travelling with Jesus and neither knew their destiny.

'I heard you were in Alexandria. Then in Spain,' my father said. 'You've even travelled to the White Island.'

'My merchant days . . .' said Joseph, as if they were a thing of the past, a reckless indulgence.

'Trading with the Britons. You're a brave man.'

Joseph breathed deeply. My father nodded, drawing their pleasantries to a close. 'You've done very well in your life.'

'Much too well.' Joseph turned and looked hard into his eyes.

'The Sanhedrin,' my father said, without a hint of disapproval. 'That's an honour.'

'I am on the ruling council and I would like to board the next ship I can find,' said Joseph.

They looked where the mist had been a few minutes earlier. Wisps rose and curled and vanished in the glare, like smoke, till there was nothing left but the tiny figure of Jesus walking towards them.

My father looked back to Joseph. 'Does he disturb you?'

'He disturbs . . . and he touches me.'

'All I know is that he has the power of God and that I cannot sleep at night any more.'

Joseph looked at him for a long while. He knew nothing of what had happened to my father or my mother, or to me. But he could see in my father's face, in the eyes of his old friend, a man who was pleading to know the truth.

'All good men in Israel should stay awake and pray,' he said.

10

I knew from his eyes that Jesus had been weeping all night. It was not the weariness or the heaviness, the bloodshot look that I knew so well from my mother when she had been exhausted with grief. There was none of that. He had washed himself over and over again, and his face and hair glistened with drops of water. His shoulders were soaking wet. That told me he had been in deep sorrow, that and the gaze he gave me when I ran up to him. It made me stop, just before I leapt into his arms. I felt such fear.

He had entered some dark place.

He smiled and held out his hands, and I walked to him reluctantly. I felt ashamed that I had disturbed his silence.

'Have you been out all night?' I said. He said nothing. I held him. 'You're cold,' I said.

'Yes, I am cold now,' he said.

I didn't dare ask him what was the matter. I knew something was terribly wrong, some great pain was in him, and it felt as if the dark was already taking him from me.

I can feel him now, holding my hand but not holding, looking out so far to the thin line of those cliffs. A camel is snorting in the byre, its nostrils flaming with breath which freezes and hangs. I know something, but I dare not say. I know he is in terror and rage somewhere, he is walking somewhere deep down or far away, and he is not with me.

Death was near. I knew the smell of it. I knew its presence, but I did not know why it was there. Light was slow in coming, light bleeding down from heaven through thick clouds, as if the dawn was struggling to be born. A horse came suddenly out of the blackness, a mad reckless galloping, and the animal reared up by the trees. The rider slid and almost fell to the ground but kept on running to us, stumbling, in one crazy desperate movement. He grabbed hold of Jesus.

'Teacher!'

Jesus looked at him in the gloom and shook his head.

'Reuben?'

'I've ridden . . . two days.'

'What's happened?'

'It's Lazarus,' he said.

'Lazarus?' He sank down, as if struck in the stomach. He let go of my hand and he fell down. I can see him now, he is falling and doubling up. I did not know what to think. Why was he so wounded? Why couldn't he do anything? Why was Lazarus, the very name, such torment to him?

'He's so sick,' said Reuben.

'Lazarus?' Jesus repeated it again, as if he did not want this to be. I knew then how much he loved him. He loved his clowning, laughing friend, his exuberant, happy friend and his two sisters who argued and cried and yearned to hear the sound of the teacher's footsteps at their door. Now death was their guest.

Reuben was on his knees. He was facing Jesus, holding on to him, and something made him more desperate than ever. Something about Jesus, the way he sat down there, made Reuben panic and shout.

'Please, you must come to us! Martha and Mary. They're

185

begging you! Please . . . if you don't come now . . .'

'Tell Martha and Mary . . . I will come . . . soon.'

Reuben was almost shaking him.

'Please!' he said. 'Oh, please!' And that poor baffled man just knelt there and the big tears fell off his beard. He kept looking at Jesus like a dog, like some animal with huge pleading eyes. He kept holding out his hands as if to say, 'I've come, what else can I do? What can I do?' Jesus got up slowly, he nodded, hardly a nod. He looked at Reuben once, then turned away and walked into the wood and leant against a tree. He was shaking.

Reuben rode away and I could hear his sobs in the darkness.

I waited a long time. Waited till some light cheated its way through the tangle of branches. The sun was on Jesus, but he hadn't moved.

'Why didn't you go? Why? If your friend . . .'

I couldn't say anything else. I was just holding out my hands to him. I wanted Lazarus to have what I had, I wanted Jesus to sit down beside him and touch him. I wanted Jesus to save that man from going down there, from going down into the deep place. I didn't want anyone to go there. The pain was flooding back to me. I felt that man's pain, in his bed and all the people round him in Bethany, although I did not know him.

Jesus looked at me at last, and he said,

'There is a purpose in all this grief.'

He was strong. He was standing tall. He was walking out into the sunlight, which was spreading through the grasses and down across the well.

I could see my father and Joseph standing there. They were bathed in light.

He took my hand again and I felt strong too. I felt such a

great strength in him and I knew that he was with me again. He was here on the earth, and he was walking. He was walking towards the pilgrims, who were washing and folding their tents. The disciples were pulling up pegs from the ground. A little boy and girl were chasing birds which fluttered over the ruined archway and the wisteria which was shaking in the breeze.

He stopped. He looked back to the hills where the darkness and the haze had lifted.

'All this will lead to the glory of God,' he said.

We travelled on but no further than Jericho, and we stayed there for three days. Finally, we climbed up through the ravine to the eastern side of the Mount of Olives. Many were singing, but Jesus walked in silence. He walked ahead of everyone in deep silence, never stopping to rest until he came to the outskirts of Bethany.

Martha came running to him. She was so angry.

She ran to him and he stood there, and she pummelled him with her fists and she shouted. 'If you had been here! If you had been here!'

'Lord,' she shouted, 'Lord,' and then she wept.

He did not hold her or try to soothe her at all. He just looked at her, looked straight at her.

'If . . .' she shouted again, and her words became all jumbled. 'If . . .' She just shook her head and held her arms up, half up in the air, her fingers were all tense as if she wanted to snatch something. She was wanting to rip some goodness, some power from the air. 'My brother would not have died,' she said.

We all watched. No one moved. The whole procession had come to a halt and no one dared utter a word. Those at the back could hear wailing and crying. They knew something was wrong and they stood in reverence. They did not run forward and peer, although the children looked out from behind their parents.

There was fear in the crowd.

Jesus stood very still. His hands were clenched. I could see that he was in great pain, and I looked at my mother. She looked back at me and she was very afraid.

Martha stood up straight, in front of Jesus. She had expended all her sorrow. Her voice was flat.

'But even now,' she said, 'I know whatever you ask from God . . . God will give you.'

Jesus said nothing. He did not nod or put a hand on her arm. It was so unlike him. He was alone again, and he was walking. He was far down. I knew where he was. I could see him down there. I could hear him calling, down there. I began to cry, but I didn't want to. It was so evil, so pressing, the darkness. I could feel it stifling me, gripping me.

He was absolutely rigid and still and he said to Martha, 'Your brother will rise again.'

She said – she nodded almost carelessly, as if she were shrugging this off, saying something only out of duty and respect, 'I know that he will rise again at the resurrection on the last day.'

Jesus said to her, 'I am the resurrection.'

My father stumbled. He fell back, I felt him. He went weak. Joseph grabbed his arm. And I saw Cleopas, his eyes were wide open.

I saw many, just staring, who could not believe what they had heard. Some seemed very angry and upset, others were just mouthing the words. The disciples were looking at each other.

Martha was crying again, silently, because she could not control her tears any more. She had hardly heard at all. She just nodded, cast her eyes down. And that was when he held her. He took her, for one moment, in both hands. She looked up to him and she could hardly see him.

'Whoever lives and believes in me, will never die. Do you believe this?'

'I believe,' she said, and she was turning away. She could not face him any more. 'You are the Christ from God, who has come into the world.'

She said it walking away from him, then she began to run. She ran all the way back to Mary. She called out, 'The Lord . . .'

Mary came out, very slowly. She came out into the light and Martha held her. It was so wistful and unreal. They were just rocking together as if they were one person. They were bound together in this terrible sadness. All the mourners came after her. They had flutes with them, but they didn't play. They were very respectful. Their faces were white because they had covered themselves in dust.

Mary walked to Jesus. She was very weak. She was almost like an old woman, she was so frail and lost. She had cried out all her strength. She wasn't angry. She just looked at Jesus and said, 'Lord . . . if . . . if you . . .' She kept repeating it. 'If you.'

Then she broke down in the most violent sobbing, but it was rasping because she had lost her voice. 'Oh,' she said, 'if you had been here!'

He was breathing deeply. He was drawing the air into him. He was standing still again and waiting, he was gathering

189

strength. Seeing Mary had made him stand so firm. He just held her as she collapsed into his arms, and he stroked her head. He curled his arms around her, then very gently he pushed her away.

'Where have you laid him?' he said.

Martha said, 'Lord, come and see.'

She led him to the tomb.

He is standing in front of the tomb. He turns to see everyone weeping. He looks at that great stone, the jagged, battered stone. The lump of rock that cuts out the world. He lifts his hands in the air. And he screams with rage. He howls.

'See how much he loved him.'

'See how much!'

'Couldn't he have stopped his own friend from dying?'

There are people talking about me, behind me. I can hear them.

'They say he raised Jairus' daughter!'

But then someone says, 'Raised her from a deep sleep!'

I want to turn, I want to tell them, but my father is holding me tight. He is listening to them in grim silence.

'The crowd believed it was a miracle.'

Then Cleopas speaks to the Sadducees, he speaks softly, with that dangerous tone in his voice. 'Can a father and mother be mistaken?' he says. 'Don't they know when their own daughter is dead?'

'The whole of Israel is deluded,' Ben Azra says. There is such a bitter anger in his voice.

'You make an exception of yourself?' says Cleopas. 'You see everything so clearly!'

Jesus is weeping and standing there. Weeping silently now. The rage is contained. He is holding himself so still and walking, walking somewhere. He is going so deep, he is beyond anywhere he has been.

'Jesus said himself that the child was merely asleep!'

'Asleep!'

'That's it!'

'And this is death.'

They say it so bluntly. 'This time, it is death.' Four days in the grave. Four long days and long nights. My father is squeezing my hand. He knows my pain, and my mother puts her arms around me, as we watch him standing there before the tomb.

My father says so gently, to save me, to save us all from sorrow, he says softly, 'No man can do . . . all things . . . no man . . . no man . . .'

It is the word 'man'. It is the question on the word 'man'. Joseph is standing beside him and on his face is a look of awe. He is looking round for comfort, because that traveller, that pilgrim from the outer edge, is feeling something so deep and so new. He is feeling the stirring of life in the grave of his heart.

He stands still, for one more minute.

He says, 'Take away the stone.'

Martha comes forward and says, 'Lord, there will be a stench – he has been in the grave for four days.'

He doesn't move. 'Did I not tell you that if you would believe, you would see the glory of God?'

'Glory.'

191

I feel the pain inside me, the pain of such longing. I look up to him, and he doesn't turn back to me. But he knows I am there. He has told me of the glory.

'I thank you, Father!'

He shouts it to the sky.

'I thank you because you have heard me! I know that you always hear me, but I have said this for all the people here – so that they will believe that you sent me!'

The joy. The joy in his voice. The happiness at the word 'father', and the thanking. The lifting of his hands. His way. His way. He lifts them so high, he thanks, he shouts,

'Lazarus! Come!'

The darkness is everywhere, we are all in it, we are all deep down.

The voice is ringing. It is echoing down. We cannot move because we are bound. We cannot move, but we can hear.

His hand is reaching. His hand, like dawn, is slicing the dark. He is stepping in. We are outside and inside the tomb. All of us, we are watching as if we are on the edge, but we are inside and we are bound.

We are bound by death.

His hand comes for us.

His hand comes down and we are held.

We breathe.

The breathing. That is the first thing. Silence and then breathing.

The wave of fear now, in the crowd. Is it breathing? Is it rustling feet?

Jesus is standing at the tomb and his friend Lazarus walks into the glare. There are screams.

'Unbind him and let him go.'

Mary is touching her hair and her face with trembling fingers, as if she does not know what is happening. She is falling into a dream. Martha is looking at Lazarus, then at Jesus, and Jesus nods to say, 'Let the man go!' She smiles. She is smiling. Jesus looks at her and keeps nodding.

She takes the headcloth and removes it.

It is Lazarus, yawning. His eyes wide open. He is puzzled at his costume. She unwinds more and he says nothing, he just sits down so meekly and lets her unwind it all. She covers him with her robe.

He looks at her, such a peculiar look, 'What are you doing, woman?' Mary is holding him, crying, sitting down beside him. And Lazarus shrugs his shoulders.

He looks so completely puzzled by everyone.

But Jesus stands in front of the tomb.

I can see his sorrow and I can feel his rage. He is still and he is standing alone, in the mouth of the darkness.

11

Ben Azra spurred his horse away from the cheering crowds, far from the festival that sounded from the rooftops of Bethany. The people were singing and dancing, hurling their cloaks in the air like the banners of a victorious army. Ben Azra's men followed him, down the steep track into the Kidron valley.

'The Messiah has come to the Holy City', he said.

No one spoke.

They rode on, in single file.

Caiaphas greeted him with a coldness amounting to disdain. Ben Azra's loyalty and zeal troubled him. There were too many champions of God's cause in Israel, and he did not wish to encourage any more righteous outrage than was necessary.

He hated displays of fervour. There were always men ready to stand up in the council and bang their fist and deliver some masterly little oration. He had come to despise many of the scribes and levites, many of the wealthy Sadducees with their frescos and their peristyles and their mikvaot of marble, their mosaic floors of fishes. They had ritual baths by the dozen but they were not interested in purity. They were interested in what they had to lose.

Caiaphas, since his elevation to high priest, had seen into the darkness. He had looked a little deeper into his own heart, courtesy of his righteous advisers, and he had seen a disquieting greed. He had reached the highest place, the most uncomfortable position in Jerusalem, and he did not want to lose it, nor did he particularly want to keep it.

Men like Ben Azra, with their ingenious schemes and their endless diplomacies – and their enthusiasm for bringing bad news, their relish for any kind of disaster blowing on the wind – such men were deeply menacing to him. They spoke of saving the people, of preserving the law, of placating the Romans and keeping everything in its rightful, precarious place. They were orderly, officious and even passionate men, but they were ignorant. Their restless controlling would lead to greater destruction than any false messiahs. Caiaphas did not fear miracle-makers from the hills. He was not concerned with itinerant magicians from the Galil, or with rebels chanting of holy war in their caves. He was happy to delegate God's judgement to the Romans, who were expert killers, who executed so efficiently and without emotion.

Caiaphas was troubled only by his Sanhedrin. He feared the wealth, influence and, above all, superstition of his fellow Sadducees. One day they would dispose of him, if he did not piously look to their own very special interests.

Zeal? What was it, but a tool? It was an instrument of policy and when Ben Azra stood before him, trembling and raging with his speeches about magicians and signs and wonders, Caiaphas felt a warm, stale breeze blowing, fanning him into indifference.

These men knew nothing of the fire that raged, the fire of God's holiness which he himself had to approach on the Day of Atonement, carrying the burning coals on the incense shovel, fingering aside the vast curtains and walking alone into that dreadful emptiness.

It was then that he knew the peril of his life. It was then that he sensed another path and did not take it.

Each day he sat in the council, he knew he had to oblige and pay heavily for his cowardice.

'Astonishing tricks.' Ben Azra was turning to the assembled elders. He was raising his voice and his hands, bringing down imaginary doom on their heads. 'Dark powers,' he cried, shaking his head in disbelief. 'I have seen him with my own eyes. I have seen the tomb broken, the body stride out into the sunlight. Fantastic illusions and the people falling down in wonder. Already, they dream, they sing, they arm themselves. They are preparing for their Messiah, they are coming in their thousands!'

Caiaphas shifted on his throne, beneath the lotus buds and curling leaves. He looked across the assembly as one priest after another rose and delivered their stirring appeals.

'What are we to do? This man performs great miracles. If we let him go on – everyone will believe in him.'

'He will give false hope to all the poor. They'll follow him anywhere – to war!'

'Pilate will destroy the temple and all that we have.'

'Pilate?' Ben Azra strode around the chamber, with his sarcastic smile. 'No, the crowd will burn our houses for themselves!'

An old, well-respected priest stood up shakily. There was silence.

'The Romans will come, at the last, and destroy everyone.'

He spoke a truth, a terrible searing truth, in his feeble voice.

But he did not know the time or the day.

When we stood in the fallen columns and the putrid smell of flesh, when the stucco peeled and the fluted plaster lay in crumbled heaps beside the smashed altar, we knelt down and wept, and we remembered all the sayings.

We remembered how the carpenter had looked at the towers of scaffolding and the white architrave, the huge acanthus leaves, how people were sighing and pointing in wonder all around, and he had said, 'Not one stone will be left standing on another', and he had wept.

He had wept for Yerushalayim.

We knelt down and there were animals grazing in the ruins. There was a goat, some sheep. A lark was twittering and burbling, ascending from the stones.

My old father wept in my arms. He held me. He held on to me.

That was the last day I saw him.

The last sight was his face and the stain of tears. The tears of Jesus were on his cheeks then. He prayed for me and laid his hands on me. He blessed me in the dereliction. He sent me out, far beyond, he robbed himself of me.

He was standing in the court of the Gentiles with the goats, and the blackness that seared the white limestone all around him. He said, 'Go.'

Caiaphas was long dead, deposed and killed a long time before. It was the time of Ananus and they were still building, almost to the last. Still cutting and hewing the stones, and still raising the house of the Lord, when the legions came.

The people rose up, but they did not rise up in the name of Jesus.

They rose up in their own name and killed each other.

The chamber echoed that day with shouts and with fury. One man after another demanded action, immediate action against the sorcerer from Nazareth. Caiaphas rose abruptly and shouted, 'You know nothing!'

The noise subsided. It was rare for the high priest to betray emotion.

'Nothing at all,' he said softly. 'Don't you realise that all the might and anger of Caesar can be aimed at one man? At this "magician" from Nazareth! Let one man die – and all the people will be saved.'

He knew the Romans well. He had come to know the cruel prefect of Judaea on first-name terms, in private.

Pilate was extremely concerned for his own welfare. So much so that, beside him, Caiaphas could feel almost righteous again.

Judas stood on the brow of the Mount of Olives. Before him was a sea of silver, the leaves turning in the wind, thousands of trees in the endless groves. They were like an army in full regalia, ranks of trees and bushes, a huge assembly of cohorts and chariots. He could hear the chanting crowds climbing up behind him. They were carrying palm branches and singing hosannas. Everyone, all of Bethany, all the Galilean pilgrims, the whole world descending from the north, was intoxicated with glory, with the scent of a great victory. Judas knew it. He knew the moment had come. As soon as he had seen Lazarus step from the dark and fallen back in shock like the other disciples, as soon as he had seen the faces of Ben Azra and Phineas and Simon the Pharisee, all those collaborators, all those who contaminated themselves, he had known. The body had stepped out like the standard bearer from heaven.

A sign. It was a sign to them all, a sure sign of victory. He clasped the dagger in his belt warmly, like a friend, felt the leather handle for its inspiration.

The shouts and the singing rose into the sky, psalms like waves, like an ocean tumbling and foaming and riding across the deep gorge. God's holy power raging over the rubbish tips and the crucifixes of Gehenna, the terrible wasted years of the occupation.

He could feel the force of people, the sheer mass of praise and courage. Ranks of ordinary, loving, righteous people, and he would lead. He would be one of the leaders, he would sing with them, he would rise up at the right hand of Jesus and he would be the most audacious. He would step first into the temple precincts and run up the ramps, up into the Antonia fortress, the hellish power, and Jesus would send his angels. He would send thunder. He would raise the martyred dead from the earth, he would drive out the demonic forces.

The sea of olive leaves flamed and spread through his mind to the citadel. He could see fire now on the vast limestone battlements. The looming sky sank down and cracked and boiled and emptied itself of bolts of lightning. Huge furnaces raged and soldiers screamed in the collapse of their pathetic palisades and barracks, which snapped like twigs. People poured down the hills and from every tiny house, out of every door and window in the city of Zion – they came shouting victory, shouting the name of the Lord.

He could see Jesus rearing and leaping on a white stallion, and Peter and John and James running beside him with their swords. Children and old men, women and fishermen and carpenters and labourers, they were all flowing towards the burning, crumbling walls of the city.

The vision overpowered him and he stood there on the brow, under the savage heat of the sun, entranced, happier than at any moment in his life.

They had gone to fetch a steed for his Lord, he had heard the orders. 'Fetch the one from the copse of trees, tethered down there, tell the owner, "The Lord has need of him".' They had gone and soon they would return with the horse and Jesus would ride high. He would call to them all. They would gather round and he would demonstrate his power at last. With one word he would call them all to battle, he would defeat the Romans with a single breath of his nostrils. He would strike them dead with plague. He would topple the Sadducees from their perches and break their necks. He would bestow his love and his healing on the poor beggars in the streets and he would make his disciples warriors and generals in the kingdom of God.

At last the people behind him spread out along the hills, a great thin line of singing pilgrims, waving their palm leaves in the shimmering sunlight, and Jesus rode forward. They shouted hosanna and spread their coats in front of him. They hurled their branches into the dust. He rode forward.

He rode forward and all around him were children.

That was strange.

About a hundred children. Singing and jumping all around him. They were patting and stroking the ears of a donkey.

Judas stood and watched in utter horror.

Jesus was on a donkey. He was riding some little grey donkey. The children were laughing and waving their branches before him, and he was coming, stumbling on the rocky path so slowly and so clumsily, the donkey was picking its stupid, deliberate way down the hill.

The donkey.

Judas shook his head. He shook his head again and again. He rubbed his eyes. He dreamed too often. This was another dream.

But it wasn't. It was real. It was desperately real. People were pushing past Judas, crowds of pilgrims, children, ignoring him, just tumbling past him, pushing him out of the way, hurling him to one side. They were coming past him in waves. He stood there, overwhelmed. What was this? What nightmare? He had accepted all the parables, all the wise teaching, yes, all the words about children. He had accepted the spirit, understood the essence, but he knew that this was the time. This was the kingdom time.

Why humiliate himself, his followers, why approach the holy mount of Zion on a mule, a beast of burden, like some poor villager carrying his pots and pans and craving room at Passover?

Joseph was watching from the height of the ridge. He stood there with my father and with Cleopas. They watched as we ran on, around him, holding the donkey, loving her, stroking her ears. She was so placid and so very strong. She was little and his feet scraped along the ground, but she put her head up in the air and snorted and sniffed the breeze.

I remember how we just tumbled all around him, there was so much laughing. All that singing. 'Lift up your heads, O gates', I remember. 'Lift up, O ancient doors.' Then great waves of sweeping, yearning music, someone had cymbals, someone had flutes, all that burbling music, and then 'The king of glory'. We sang of the king of glory.

Joseph turned to my father and said softly, 'Behold your king is coming to you, humble and riding a donkey', and my father said without turning, looking down into the great valley, 'on a colt, the foal of an ass'. He kept saying it with awe.

My mother was holding his hand and I kept waving to them to come down, to run down towards us, but they stood there watching. She lifted her hand to me. Then she held my father so close.

Cleopas said, 'It's just how the prophets foretold the Messiah would come.'

'Messiah,' my father said.

He hardly dared say the word. It was a moment, a moment in his life which seared into his heart. It made the days to come a terrible anguish. It made it all so agonising, it plunged him into the depths. My father, for one moment, saw his Messiah riding to the holy city.

My mother was holding him, and they were both there against the sun. She told me how they had stood until they were quite alone, until everyone had gone into the city, even me, and they had broken down in utter sorrow and confusion and joy. Because they had not known. They had not understood.

They let me go with him and all the children, gladly towards the temple.

The crowd were singing behind him, 'Blessed be the king who comes in the name of the Lord!' and Simon the Pharisee had run up to Jesus and begged him desperately, 'Tell your disciples . . . not to say "king", rabbi . . . rabbi!' Jesus turned to him and looked at all of us, all the people who were still moving and streaming around him; he was shaking his head with such force and there was a stern look on his face, but a look of radiant joy too.

'I'm telling you,' he said, 'if all these people were silent, even these stones would cry out!'

Simon sat down. He sat down by the track and gnawed at his fists. He sat there, all alone. I think he was somehow regretful, somehow deeply sorry, but in his own confusion. He kept looking over to Phineas and the Sadducees by the gates. He kept looking at the men going down into the ritual baths, and all the people who were dutiful and holy. He stood up, he turned round, and my father and mother were still there. He could see them. He shook his head, just lifted his hands up as if to say, 'What do I know?' and then he was lost in the crowd.

Judas stayed up on the hill. He hadn't moved. Simon Peter went back for him, he was always so loving like that. So careful. He noticed how other people felt, and he stormed back through all the people, running, because he knew Judas was troubled. He waved up to him, but Judas would not come.

He climbed up beside him. He put his hand on his shoulder.

'Blessed be the king ... they're singing ... blessed be the king!'

Simon Peter was so proud, so certain now. All would be well. He knew Judas had dreams and plans, but they would pass. All would come true in some way, in the way of the Lord. No one knew how. But it would all happen. There would be a new kingdom, a new way. It would all be all right. Perhaps there would be a victory, a battle, he didn't know, but he trusted. He was happy to wait. The Messiah had come.

'They're singing "blessed be the king",' he said.

'Yes, that's what they're singing . . . now.'

'Come on,' said Peter.

'They're singing that now . . . but if nothing ever changes . . .'

Judas sat down on the ground. Peter waited for a minute, but Judas would not speak. He just gazed up at the guards, pacing. There were hundreds of them stationed along the porticoes of the temple.

The temple. The soldiers were striding along the temple.

Peter left Judas alone and ran down the hill. My parents were coming down with Joseph and Cleopas and they saw him leaping, bounding over rocks, grabbing trees and spinning around like a child, shouting. He was in heaven.

Judas came last of all, slowly, alone, scraping his feet in the dust.

We had all run into the temple through the great tunnel. I can still hear the echoing shouts, it was like being in the roots of the earth, some vast cavern. The footsteps clattering, the sheer din. I was holding my ears.

Jesus went ahead of us. He was walking now, quite slowly, and we slowed up behind him. He was looking from side to side. Miryam was with us and she was looking too. Remembering.

He was twelve again, like me. He looked at me and some of the other children, as if we were mirrors of himself. He looked at our eyes and our wonder. But then I saw such an expression pass his face. As he came into the light, everywhere there were traders, pigeon stalls, people shouting. All along the colonnades of the courtyard of the gentiles, right up to the balustrade of the precinct, there were market stalls and sheep and turtle doves in wicker cages. It was like some frenzied nightmare of people shouting about 'knockdown prices' and 'good bargains'. They were jingling the Tyrian shekels in their palms as if they were shaking dice, to attract customers. 'Good rates,' they called, 'best rates.'

It was like Sepphoris in the midst of the holy place.

Jesus stopped and there was this expression, a look of pure amazement and then anger. It came across his whole body like a wind seizing him, wrapping him round.

'My father!' he kept shouting.

'My father's house!'

Everyone was looking at him. All the mad, furious noise seemed to slip into nothing.

'My father's house is a house of prayer.'

He ran forward. He grabbed a table in both hands. He tipped it right over and the money and all the pieces of clay and the tablets, they all hurled into the air. He was so strong. They couldn't stop him, he went from table to table, stall to stall, hurling things down. Birds fluttered up into the bright sunlight. Lambs were running around.

'You have made it a den of thieves!' he shouted. 'Thieves!'

He spun round and round. He was jumping across the scattered baskets and he kicked this barrel of money. It fell over. It poured on to the white pavement, thousands of little shining coins. None of us dared move. None of the children picked up a single coin.

Miryam was standing so still. She stood in the shadow of one of the columns, as still as a statue. I felt safe near her. She took my hand. She said nothing.

Men were shouting at us. There were some on the scaffolding, not very far up. 'Who is this?' a man called, and one of the masons said, 'It's Jesus, the prophet from Nazareth.'

'I recognise him . . . the carpenter!' The tall man climbed down. I knew I had seen him before – it was the architect from the building site of the synagogue in Sepphoris.

'It's the carpenter,' he said, 'has the man gone mad?'

Then one of the Sadducees who was with our party, I think it was Lamech, stepped forward right up to Jesus.

'What sign will you perform to show you have the right to do this?'

Jesus looked all round him and nodded. He gave a little flick of his hand.

'This temple,' he said.

It was the way he said it, with such casualness, as though it were a thought which had flitted across his mind. The huge, magnificent place that everyone prized so much and we had all travelled for many days to reach.

'Tear down this temple,' he said, 'and in three days I will build it again.'

The architect was mad with anger. It made him go red and puffed. He could hardly speak. 'It has taken us forty-six years to build this temple. And you want to destroy it?'

Some priest stood forward and said, very drily, 'Are you going to raise it all up again in three days?'

He didn't say anything. He didn't answer anyone.

Roman soldiers were clattering down the steps. They had heard the disturbance and they came at a furious pace through the archway. There was a huge line of them, and the tribune at their head. He put his hand up and they stopped dead.

They were facing all the Galileans now, a huge rough rabble who had come running and shouting through the tunnel with their palm leaves and their coats flailing above their heads. The tribune looked at the mob in front of him with great respect, a stillness and a quiet fear, as if he were staring into the eyes of a wild beast that could spring at any moment and tear him and his men into pieces. He would not let his soldiers flinch or make one false move, one stupid act of indiscipline, one finger on a sword, one twitch towards a weapon. He kept his hand in the air like a rod of iron. It was minutes before he lowered it, and he never took his eyes off the Galileans and their prophet.

He was so dark, a complete stranger in that courtyard, with such deep eyes, as if he had arrived from another world, not just Carthage, but another order of life. He had a dignity and a sorrow about him and, although he looked so powerful and the sun flaming on his helmet gave him a kind of lustrous presence in the middle of that huge throng, he seemed uninterested in himself. There was no arrogance like the others, like the men who strutted on the battlements and the legionaries who ordered the crowds back in the streets when the cohorts marched through, there was none of that nervousness and shouting, all the insecurity of power. He was more like a hunter, alone in the night, gazing at some creature he did not know, respecting the shadows. He was trying to predict in his mind what would happen next, and he watched Jesus as if he were the only other man in the temple.

I kept with Miryam, well back in the shadows. All the children were hiding behind the columns. We thought there was going to be a fight and we were afraid.

The tension held for a long time. No one, in all those

thousands, even coughed. Then one of the traders began to crawl, incredibly slowly, towards a coin. It was a single coin lying near one of the soldiers' feet. He managed to reach it, stretching his arm right out and grabbing it between his fingers, but then one of the Sadducees started whispering to this learned-looking man next to him, and the trader thought they were talking about him. He stopped, terrified, but they weren't interested in him. Nor was the tribune, who kept watching Jesus as if he were confronting mortal danger. He watched him like a lizard blending into a stone.

Then the scribe who had been talking to the Sadducee stepped forward very suddenly.

'Teacher . . . ?' he said.

Jesus groaned. He threw his hands up and let them down again hard against his side. I could see such pain in him, as if he knew exactly what was coming.

'Teacher?' the man persisted. The tribune held his hand up still and not one soldier moved, because it looked for one second as if Jesus would suddenly sweep around in furious anger and smash tables again, and shout and whip the people. But the tribune held fast. The crowd shifted, but the lawyer, the wealthy-looking scribe with his plumed hat, stood there with a tiny smile flickering. He looked at the tribune, who did not return his gaze at all. He looked across the line of soldiers, then back at the crowd.

'We know that what you say and do is right.'

There was a pause again, and he looked round at the nodding faces of the holy men in the temple. They were all so serious and so solemn, and they were behaving as if they were the friends of Jesus. All they wanted was some helpful advice on a little point they wanted to make.

Jesus bent his head and shook it.

The man was not deterred.

He shouted out, so all the crowd could hear, 'Is it right for us to pay taxes to Caesar or not?'

There was a gasp. The whole might of Rome was watching, as if Jesus were some slave or gladiator cast into the arena, some poor fool flung into the dust without net or sword. The lawyer was so pleased with his question, he kept looking round and then up to the turrets, hoping to invite Pilate down to this little demonstration.

The tribune, for the first time, took his eyes off Jesus and glanced at the lawyer. Then he looked straight back to Jesus.

'Show me a denarius,' said Jesus.

The lawyer was puzzled. He looked back to the Sadducee, who quickly snatched the coin from the trader on the floor.

'Come on,' he said, but the man was extremely reluctant to let go. 'The master,' said the Sadducee with such a harsh tone that the tribune seemed to raise an eyebrow, as if he were assessing everyone, every single detail and each breath, each word.

Everything that happened seemed to make him look more intently, more cannily, at the face of Jesus, who lifted up the coin into the air, where it flashed.

'Whose portrait?' he said.

The lawyer shrugged at the obviousness of the question. This was some stupid, childish diversion.

'Whose portrait and title are on it?' said Jesus.

'Caesar's,' said the lawyer.

'Well then,' and he turned and looked straight into the tribune's eyes, 'give to Caesar what belongs to Caesar.' He tossed the coin back into the lawyer's hand, then he raised his hands high, he spread them out as wide as he could, in a great arc across the temple and the whole of Jerusalem and up to the heavens, a huge everlasting slow embrace of every person in the courtyard, 'But give to God what belongs to God!'

He turned and walked away, back through the crowd. The lawyer and the Sadducee stood there. They didn't move, and the tribune looked at them, looked them up and down, and then he looked over to where Jesus was disappearing through the arch. He looked with fascination and with such wonder, almost as if he could have run after him. His soul was running but his body was absolutely still. He spoke one command, softly, and all the soldiers swept around in formation and, running by threes, disappeared up the steps into the fortress. He stood alone before the crowd, which no soldier ever did, none of the regulars would ever risk such a thing, and then he nodded at us all. As if he were paying some kind of tribute to everyone for following this man. Then he turned with a sharp movement, such power, and strode up the steps.

We all cheered, we began cheering again and singing. Jesus was out on the steps and people were gathering around him freely, the traders were angrily setting up their stalls and clearing up the mess, but no one cared. The Sadducees retreated into their booths beyond the court of the women and through the Nicanor gate. The lawyer hurled the little coin on to the stones; it bounced and sent the trader scampering after it, cursing under his breath.

I saw Judas saying 'Give to Caesar what belongs to Caesar!' and repeating it angrily, and Simon Peter and John talking to him. He was shaking his head and I thought he was in tears. He kept pointing up to the soldiers by the columns, way above the arches. All the soldiers looking down with their spears, and he was shaking his head. 'Caesar, Caesar', and he shook off Simon Peter and John, but John ran up to him. He stood in front of him and I could see him sweeping out his arms, like Jesus, as if he were trying to tell Judas what he had really said, but Judas would not listen.

Judas stayed around the temple long after we had all gone up to the Mount of Olives. He watched the priests and Sadducees gathering in the twilight beneath the huge flaring beacons on the colonnade, he watched their long shadows, heard their urgent conversations late into that night.

He watched alone, hardly hearing or seeing anything. He seemed to stumble from one pillar to another. He would wait for a while, his back against the cold stone, staring and staring at the soldiers pacing. The moon was up, and against the livid brightness the legionaries seemed like ghosts parading silently, as if they were stalking his own life.

He shook his head in disgust with himself, at his faithlessness, and climbed up the long track to the first ridge, where the tents were spread in the dusk like a besieging army. An army of singers and playing children and foraging dogs. There were shouts on the air and sparks flurrying and dying. He looked along the line of fires, the scattered disordered line of tents with their pale lanterns, then looked up higher to the garden. Just below, in an open field that was ridged and stepped, Judas saw Jesus kneeling among his disciples. Already he felt like a visitor, an interloper who was disturbing their peace, and he looked back at the city walls, so vast and yellow in the moonlight, and felt himself floating hopelessly between two worlds.

If only he could understand, find some path, some bright burning illumination in his confusion. He longed to sit down at the feet of Jesus one more time and listen to the master explain everything. He wanted everything to be all right. This was not how he had imagined or planned the outcome, but what did he know? Perhaps Peter was right, there were many kinds of glory, of triumph. If only the master could explain, take him through each step, take him patiently through everything like a child. He would listen. He agreed with himself, as he climbed, that he would listen. He would devote himself that night to prayer.

He crept across the soft grasses and stayed way out among the bushes. The others noticed him and were untroubled. He often lay far out, alone, like that. But something told him he should get up and go into the middle and lay down his fears, yet he could not move. He did not want to move just yet.

He lay in the damp grass and listened. Words seemed to float like fireflies, they were bright but they did not stay, they hurried off into the night. Words, so many words and stories, and so many things he did not understand.

'The son of man will suffer.'

He heard them again, those harsh meaningless words. The strange sayings. 'Suffer many things.'

He did not want to go forward into that firelight and sit like Simon Peter and James and John, sit listening any more. There was only confusion.

He could hear Peter protesting again, arguing, but he did not even want to argue, all his resolve to cry out and beg for answers had melted. He just hugged himself in the darkness until the madness seemed to overwhelm him . . .

'The son of man will be arrested. He will be killed!'

Peter was hurling a log into the fire with such anger, it scattered soot and embers and spat crazily.

'No, Lord, that will never happen to you! *Never!*'

Judas did not stand up and walk forward and kneel beside his master and say, 'Help me, help me to know', as he had promised himself, but instead he crawled into the shadows and rolled from sight down a bank and burst out weeping. He wept tears of violent anger. He got up, brushed aside the dirt and the scattering leaves and ran, half falling and rolling, down the steep side of the hill. He kept shouting to the air, 'Messiah, killed . . .' He kept blocking his ears, as if the words were vicious birds of prey eating into his head. 'Killed by the Romans!' He ran on, shaking and shaking his head, 'No!' He ran until he came to the city gates, where pilgrims slept in their rows beside the crumbling fires. He stumbled and trod over them as they groaned in their sleep, ignorant, fated people who were following a false Messiah, dreaming of heaven while the Romans kept the watches of the night above. They never went to sleep.

Judas ran blindly through the labyrinth of streets, with no plan, no thought, but to run and somehow cleanse his mind of terror.

But others were wakeful, they stood in the gloom of a vestibule high above the colonnade, where the wind picked lightly at the drapery. An oil lamp smoked and thickened the air.

'There is no way of arresting him in public without a riot. We'll have to take him secretly.' The priest looked down at the barracks of the temple guard, where the moonlight fell like bright pools drifting over the cobbles. A horse's hoof clanged in the stables.

'There is no one who can lead us to him.' The scribe, who was still smarting from his humiliation before the tribune, stared pointedly at Ben Azra.

'Jerusalem is ringing with the Galilean dialect,' he said, and spat on to the tiles.

'There's no one!'

'No one?' said Ben Azra lightly. 'Oh, there's always someone.'

Judas clung to the high walls and their consoling shadows. He walked on, round and round, the words ringing and mocking in his ears, 'The son of man came to give his life!' . . . 'to give it!'

'He came to seek and save the lost, he came to give his life freely!'

He beat his hands on his forehead, slapping the words away, and a soldier shifted at his watch high above and fingered his sword at the spectacle of the deranged figure below. Judas fled hurriedly into the darkest alley-ways. His mind would not co-operate, he could not extinguish the lies and the twisted promises that seemed to swarm around him. He sank down to the ground, calling out again, 'No, never, no!'

And a fist grabbed at his ankle.

'Judas!'

He leapt back. There was a hand stretching out of bars, two hands clutching. And from the darkness, a voice rasping.

'Judas!'

He looked down in utter horror, for there, pressed against the bars, was the bloodied face of Barabbas.

'You've got to—'

'No!' Judas screamed.

'Judas, Judas!' Joram came up behind his leader, and then Nadab.

They were disfigured. They had been tortured almost to death.

They cried after him like children, wailing as he ran. He ran hurtling into a beggar and then into a cold brazier, sending ashes clouding into the night as he pelted down the street. But he could still see their faces and he knew it was no vision, no nightmare of his own. They had been caught and condemned and now Judas faced the same. He would join them at the very last, their paths would intertwine in some hellish pattern, fate would press them together in death. Even though he had chosen the bright path, he had followed and he had obeyed and given up everything.

In the blackness of the sky, above the roofs, his mind threw phantoms. Terrible visions came now, as if the chains from Barabbas suddenly wrapped and clenched his wrists and feet and hurled him on to a floating cross. He was hanging in agony with every disciple, with his master, with his friends. They were suspended from the heavens.

He screamed and ran, the jumble of voices, real and unreal, tormented him and drove him onwards to the temple. In its huge silence and the pilasters of gold, the spreading acanthus leaves beneath the moon, he felt calm again. He felt overshadowed by the power of it, and that was what he needed, what he craved for now.

The weakness and the submission to death haunted him.

He could breathe again now and imagine other futures. He felt his purse, the purse where he kept all the money for the twelve, everything for their provisions, but it was empty. He had given the money to John and impatiently told him to buy everything for the Passover. He winced at his stupidity. He had left himself nothing at all.

He thought of what he could do with money, he dreamed again, leaning against the vast blocks of masonry and beneath the towers of scaffolding.

Money. There was money everywhere here.

If he had money . . .

He could see a horse. He could see himself riding down to the coast, the ships at Caesarea, the lighthouse and the broad quays in the harbour, the full sails, the wide welcoming sea, Cyprus, Sicily, a villa with servants, a white balustrade and a fountain with a mosaic floor.

If he had money.

Ben Azra was alone when he descended the stairs from the high priest's chamber. He was among the last of the delegations. He had been well satisfied by the silence of Caiaphas and the mood of inevitability.

The moon was still high and in the distance the Galilean camp was extinguishing its lamps. He breathed the cold air, drank it like a clear draught from a stream in the hills.

A man stepped from the shadows and startled him, but he did not show his surprise.

He recognised the man, not by name but by sight and by his speech, as one of the Galileans.

'How much would you give me . . . ?' said Judas. His mouth was very dry and he did not complete his sentence. Ben Azra gazed at him and nodded to reassure him.

'If I . . . if I lead you to Jesus?'

12

It is hard to remember the happiness. The happiness – as I walked up those cracked steps, carrying bundles of almond blossom – the joy is troubling. I am shocked by the singing.

We carried shoots of basil and the poppy anenomes we had found, all the children had been out for hours gathering whatever we could, and we decked the room together. We were so excited, we sang hallel by ourselves.

Mary Magdalene was there, she had her skirts full of corn marigolds as if she were one of us, as if she wanted to be six years old. She was laughing and helping a little boy reach up to the windows and lay down his little heap of grasses.

The whole room was so fragrant and she seemed to find blessing here. She sat down in one corner, nestling into the wall. I hadn't seen her for the whole journey. She had kept away from Jesus, all the vast pushing crowds around him, because they made her afraid. She found it easier to hold back and walk with the little children, as long as she could keep him just in view.

Now she was sitting in the corner, where she could see across to the table on the far side where the disciples would eat with their master. She wanted to watch.

I don't know if she was like the other adults, like Cleopas and my father who had become agitated after the incident in the temple. She didn't show any worries to us, and she laughed and threw flowers to me. We were all happy.

The haroset was on the table, and I had helped to make it with figs and raisins and nuts, I put spices in it and then my mother had poured the wine on to it and stirred it into a paste. I loved the sweet taste of it, but not the maror. We all screwed up our faces at the bitterness, and that year Miryam made it of parsley and dandelion and something very sharp. The room was prepared for the seder and every table was laid, it looked so beautiful. The cups on the long table among the white lilies. They were shining in the lamps, shining as if they were the moon in the darkness.

We were longing for sundown and so impatient. My mother came and told us to quieten down because Jesus was coming soon, and that's all we could think of. Him coming and then we would sing and cheer, like we had down on the hill, and wave branches or our hands, we would sing the great hallel. We would get together and sing and he would laugh and tell us that we had angels in heaven, every single one of us, angels constantly beholding the face of God. I remember him saying that once.

We were overwhelmed with joy, just for those few hours. It was as if the world had stopped and the sun would not go down. Passover would never come, but we hung out of the window and ran around the roof and chanted to the sun to go down.

We were calling, in our innocence, for the night to come.

Judas stood in the shadows by the huge velvet curtain, reluctant to look the high priest in the face. One of the levites beside him, a captain in the temple guard, looked at Caiaphas and then back at Judas.

'Can you take us to him by night?'

Judas breathed deeply. 'In secret. No one will see you. I know his place of prayer.'

'How can we trust you?' said one of the priests. Judas stepped into the torchlight and bowed slightly.

'I want to serve . . . my people.'

'And yourself?' Caiaphas leaned forward a little wearily. 'How much will your services . . . for your people . . . cost?'

Judas was silent.

'Thirty pieces of silver,' said Ben Azra.

I don't know whose house it was, who provided that room, the great upper room. I think it was a cousin of Joseph's, or an uncle, but whoever it was took risks. It became like the ark, riding over the floods, over the years. I went back there once, many years after this. It was just the same, the smell of cedar and the huge doors that bolted on the inside, and all the people.

It always felt safe in that room.

We sat in the corner and waited. I sat next to Mary Magdalene and she was happy, because she could hear Jesus coming up the steps. My mother had sat down and Cleopas too. He was tired and leant his head against the wall.

There were about forty of us along with the disciples, but I could hear all the pilgrims, hundreds and hundreds going down into the Kidron valley singing. The torches flickered as they went past, like an army of flames. They were happy, because the sun was sinking below the hills and they were returning to their tents for Pesach. They didn't even know we were sitting in this room and they thought Jesus was coming up to the mount with them, but he slipped in with the disciples through the lower door and then, shielded by the steps, climbed to the upper level.

'Why are we meeting in secret?' I said, and Mary said to me so gently, 'Because Jesus is safer here.' Mary needed him to be safe, to be near her, and this room was the best place she had been since leaving Capernaum.

'Safer?' I said.

'No one will arrest him in the middle of Passover.' Cleopas put his hand on mine, but I called out loudly, 'Arrest him?'

My mother put her hand to her lips, but I was gazing at Jesus as he came into the room. I could not imagine anyone touching him. No one would harm him. No one could possibly arrest him or take him away. I knew that for sure.

I knew his power.

He sat down at the table, reclining in the seder way. They were all reclining around him, leaning on their sides. The whole group of them were so relaxed and laughing. Not Jesus, he was very quiet, so still, and he seemed to look to the far end of the room, past all of us. I didn't know what he was thinking.

He was thinking. Something was going through his mind, and I saw him look round immediately when one of the disciples came in late. It was Andrew carrying some fruit, a huge basket, and people clapped him and he gave a bow. Then he chucked it on to the floorboards and a pomegranate rolled under the table.

Simon Peter was outside, looking out of the door, up the cobbled street, and people were still streaming past him. He grabbed Judas as he passed.

Judas swung round, as if ready with a knife, but Peter laughed at him. 'Come on, Judas, where have you been? We're all here.'

Judas tried to smile and climbed up hastily. He didn't know

about this place. Would they stay here? Would they go up to the garden later? His mind was in turmoil again, all the plans and the ideas, the fears, the nightmares. He stumbled in, and avoided the gaze of his friends.

Jesus looked at him.

He watched him as he passed, as he bent his head away. There was such a look of pity. He was shaking his head and we all thought it was because Judas was late. We mistook it for good humour. It seemed like part of the festival, the sort of thing anyone would do. 'Late again.' The disciples were patting him on the back and he was sitting down with his back to us. I remember that curved back, so low, as he bent over his food.

Jesus kept looking at him, then away, then back to him. I saw it several times, even when he said the b'rakhah over the wine, when he lifted the first cup and blessed the fruit of the vine, he was looking back to him.

Judas looked so vulnerable and so little and now it is easy to see that he was in torment. The happiness all around him was driving him to despair, to a deeper despair, one that he had not expected and had no weapon against.

We sang the psalms and he did not move.

'Praised are you, Adonai our God, King of the universe, Creator of the fruit of the vine.'

The first cup.

The table was a long way from us, and so I kept asking what was happening.

'He's blessing the bread,' my father said.

'He lifts it so high.'

'He always does that,' said Cleopas, 'it's his way.'

221

* * *

Raising the bread high, with both hands high above his head. Raising it slowly, as if it were a great weight, lifting it past his eyes. Looking at it closely, and then following it, gazing up at it, and breaking it.

His hands trembling and breaking it.

Blessing and breaking it.

I have seen him do that, again and again. I have seen him do that in the hands and in the eyes of others. I have seen the raising up and heard the blessing and watched the pieces divide and felt the pain. I have felt his pain.

I know it, even in the wastes and the forgotten places, even here in the dark. The trembling hands are high above me. Fragments are falling.

His way.

'Take, eat . . .' He gave some to each disciple. He gave some to Judas.

His voice was so soft. 'This is my body,' he said, 'which is broken for you.'

They were looking at him in astonishment. Thomas blurted out, 'Your body?' He was looking round at the others, but no one said anything. Thomas just shrugged. It was as if he couldn't understand a word, and he was smiling in that dreamy sort of way. 'Body,' he said.

Jesus gave him a piece, a large piece of the bread, and said directly to him, 'Do this in memory of me.'

Then he took the cup in his hands. He raised it up, and it

222

was dark. Almost into the darkness, above the lamplight, so the rim of the cup was lost in shadow. There was a shadow over his hands.

He held it there for such a long time. He was trembling again, shivering.

I didn't like it. I didn't understand.

Why was he holding it and shaking?

No one seemed to ask, or say anything, but I wanted to, so badly. I wanted to say to my father, 'Why is that happening? Why has he gone cold?'

I wanted to put my arms around him and keep him warm, as my mother had lain next to me when I was dying, when the cold descended and gripped me.

'Drink from this, all of you,' he said. 'This is my blood.'

'Blood?' I turned to my father but he would not look at me. He was watching every move and he was sitting so still.

'Poured out for many for the forgiveness of sins.' He gave them all the cup. He gave it to Judas, and Judas would not drink. He pretended to drink. He put the cup to his lips.

The cup.

It stood on the table, among the flowers and the marah, the shankbone, the haroset, the lamps. Jesus was turning away from it. He took it into his hands and set it down, and then turned away for one moment. He stood up in the shadows, away from us all. He was saying something to himself. His shoulders were moving and he was struggling, as if he were about to shout something or cry out with rage, but he turned and he was very calm.

He said to Simon Peter, 'This is the last time I will ever drink wine with you!'

Peter interrupted, banging his hand down impatiently.

'Master—'

'Until—'

'What are you saying? We won't let you die!' His hand was on his sword.

'Until I drink the new wine with you, in the kingdom of my father in heaven.'

'In heaven? No! No!'

Jesus looked at Peter, then at Thomas, then at Andrew, John, all of them one by one. They were looking astonished and frightened. Peter was lifting his sword out of his belt, and Jesus was shaking his head at him. Peter was so desperate and so angry with this talk, he was ready to dig the blade into the table, but Jesus looked up, above their heads and said:

'One of you sitting here is going to betray me tonight.'

John spoke up, he hardly ever spoke, but he almost shouted, 'We'll all stand by you! Every one of us!'

Peter leapt up and held his sword high, 'Even if everyone in the world deserts you, I will never – *never* – let you down!'

'Simon Peter.' Jesus lowered his eyes and looked at him with that look of pity again, and that dread. 'Satan wants to grind you into powder and scatter you to the wind! But I have prayed for you.'

'Master – you know me! I won't leave you!'

'Simon!'

'I'll go to prison with you – *execution!*'

'Simon Peter, by the time the cock crows today you will have denied three times that you know me!'

He sat down, his sword knocking clumsily against the table. He let it fall to the floor. He looked round him at all his friends, and beyond into the darkness where we were sitting. I saw Mary Magdalene next to me touch her face and her arms as if she felt this wind blowing. She looked suddenly so afraid and sad for Peter.

He was bereft, like the smallest child in the room. He held his hands out, once, appealing to the others to be reasonable. To agree with him, but no one spoke.

They were all wondering and they were all afraid then. They started talking busily, whispering and arguing. It went on for a long time.

I was glad my mother was next to me. She was troubled, but she shook her head and brushed her hand through the air as if to say to me, 'Don't worry about things you don't know.'

'Your singing was good,' she said, 'I heard you at the beginning. I heard you sing by yourself.' She handed me some food and I took it from her, but I didn't eat. I couldn't eat again that night.

Jesus was talking to each of his disciples one by one. He came to Judas and the others ignored him. They talked amongst themselves.

'Judas,' he said, 'go and do what you have to do.'

'Master . . . ?'

Judas was so startled, he laughed. He opened his hands to show he had nothing in them, but Jesus paid no attention. 'While you have the chance, go on, go and do it.'

He was shifting on the bench, badly frightened.

'Go and do it quickly!'

'Master . . . I . . .'

He got up and left very swiftly, saying nothing more and not looking back over his shoulder. He went straight out of the door.

James looked up and said, 'Where's Judas going?' and Andrew shook his head, 'Don't worry,' – he poured himself a drink, spilling some on the table – 'he'll be back.'

About an hour later, Jesus stood up and said, 'It's time.' He walked out of the room alone, without waiting for anyone, and the disciples had to scramble down the steps and run down the valley to catch up with him.

There was a long line of us, beneath the moon. We carried fire from the great room back to our camp. It was like a slow, twisting river of fire through the olive groves. Some children were asleep and riding on their fathers' shoulders, others ran through the lavender and the violets in the darkness. They chased each other around gnarled trees and through the bushes until their mothers shouted and scolded them. The moon was like a vast lantern hanging above the white ridge, but then it disappeared suddenly underneath ragged cloud that was sweeping in from the north. Thick cloud was coming and the stars were slowly vanishing.

My father walked urgently with Cleopas. I watched him striding ahead, the flames of his torch rising and falling with each step. Every now and then, he would stop for Cleopas and the old man would refuse his arm with an impatient wave, catch his breath, and shamble on up the steep track.

When they reached the top by the tents, they saw Jesus standing alone, near an old gateway which was cut in stone.

He was leaning forward with both hands against the wall, quite still.

The disciples were sitting and standing nearby, chattering in the darkness, waiting on his instructions. They often waited, sometimes for hours, like that.

My father walked up slowly and Jesus turned and looked at him. He still had one hand on the wall. He didn't speak and my father was suddenly unsure, bewildered, and he looked back to Cleopas for reassurance. Cleopas nodded.

I was walking beside him. I knew something was terribly wrong, something, I didn't know what. The garden. He was standing outside the garden. He had often been there on the other nights throughout the week, but it was the way he lingered. He kept looking back to us.

My father said, 'Teacher – come with us. Sit by our fire . . .'

And Cleopas rubbed his hands together and then pushed his fingers through his hair. I had never seen him so agitated. 'There are many things we don't understand,' he said.

Jesus reached out to them, but he didn't touch them. He just said softly, you could hardly hear his voice, 'I will come and talk to you, Cleopas. I promise, I will come to you . . . very soon.' He was struggling to finish. He said 'very soon' again, as if he were telling himself something too. 'We will talk about many things.'

My father and Cleopas kept looking at him. They didn't know what to say, they couldn't say anything else. They just sort of bowed their heads and then hesitated. And then turned. They walked away and I could see that they were so troubled that they didn't even speak to each other.

I ran to him then. I ran straight into his arms.

I said, 'Where are you going?' And he looked at me. 'Where?' he said. 'Where . . .'

I was holding his hand, holding it to me, I said, 'Where?' I was crying. I didn't know what else to say.

I couldn't do anything. I was trying to hold him. What was it? What was it about the gate and the silence? And his fear? He was in such deep dread and any moment I knew he was going to turn. I gripped him hard.

'Don't be upset,' he said. 'Don't be afraid.' His arms were cold, they were so cold, but they clung to me. He held me like he never had before. He knelt down to me. He said, 'In my father's house, there are so many rooms. So many! I'm going to find a wonderful place for you.' He said that into my ear, so gently. 'For you. One day, you'll always be with me.'

It's snowing. The snow is surging in the night, it hasn't stopped falling for days, it seems like weeks. And every day I see him.

The garden. The stone threshold. Gat-Sh'manim. The place of the wine press.

He is getting up, and I am almost lifted up with him, because he is still holding me. He takes my hands away from him very slowly. He kisses one of my hands and looks at me one more time. He touches my hair and then he pushes me, like he did when I awoke and I was sitting on the bed and everyone was staring at me. He pushes me into the world.

Into the night.

He is standing there, still, and looking at me, as I walk backwards away from him.

I walked into the crowd and I fell over. Miryam found me. I was lying on the rocks and I was crying.

She didn't say anything. She was looking, too. Oh, how she looked into that night. I couldn't bear to see her, just staring into the garden as he was turning. She was so still and so beautiful in the deep shadows. Someone's torch, passing by, lit up her face and there was one tear. Only one. But she shook and held herself, as if in a violent gale.

He turned round and looked once more over to her. He shook his head. He shook his head as if there was some question or thought, something he had been trying to find and he was telling her, 'Nothing, nothing.'

He called, 'Simon Peter, James, John . . . No one else.'

She stood there beside me as he turned with them into the blackness.

There was light on the step. Some torchlight for a minute, as others gathered up their things. The old step, so worn by the olive growers, and the leaves shifting. Even in the stillness they seemed to turn.

Miryam took my hand and we walked across westward to our camp, and that was when she took me into her own tent and let me stay up through the night beside the fire.

'We must watch,' she said.

I did not know what she meant.

'We must watch.'

He begged them to keep awake but they did not. They did not, not even Peter. They said they would keep guard and they stood around the trees for quite a long time, stood and did not say much, stood and then leant against the great twisted trunks, then slipped down to the ground, then sat hugging their knees in the cold air, keeping their eyes open, forcing them open. Then they slept, one by one.

They slept, curled up like babies, under the canopy of leaves, under the turning silver.

He fell down on the bare rock. He stretched himself out, but he didn't weep. He lay there still, his mouth against the stone, his eyes looking into the hard emptiness.

He did not speak or cry for many minutes.

He lay there and he could hardly utter the word, but when it came, it came like a torrent through him.

'Father, Father.' He cried 'Father' into the earth, into the stone.

He went back to Peter, James and John and they were snoring, clung together like drunken men.

He woke them and they stumbled up and stood upright for a long while among the trees. But when he came again, they were on the ground and their mouths were open.

He fell down again and prayed, prayed until the sweat poured and fell on the earth. He stood up and shouted into the night, 'Father, let there be some other way!'

'Let there be!'

He could not endure the silence, he kept crying and sobbing because there was nothing. He begged, 'Let there be another way, another way!' He smashed his hand down on to the rock, and he rolled and looked up into the thickness, the absolute blackness of that night without stars, under the cloud.

And he saw the cup.

It was coming. He saw the cup. It was lifting, his own hands were lifting it, it was raised so high. He saw the cup. It was huge. It was dark, darker than the night, but it shone from within with a terrible fire.

He screamed out, 'No! Take this cup away, take it away. Take it away.'

It hung there above him, and he pushed his hands into the still air. He waved his hands, clawed at the night, but it still came closer, it was close enough to kiss.

'Father . . . Father, dear Father,' he called out, whispered out, 'listen to me! Listen! If there is another way.'

He believed it. He believed it for one moment, 'A way – a way out!' He knew there was a way and his father would find it. He was certain, for that second, for that single second, that there was another way, and he stood and he looked. And he saw the path up the Mount of Olives, he saw the looming ridge and beyond it the desert. He saw the vast spaces and the night and the endless ways, the paths in the drifting sands.

A voice came to him, a sweet, kind voice, caressed him and told him to run.

The voice told him there was still time.

The shadow stretched over him, the one that came at the opportune times, came stalking and offering life. He raised his hand then, and said, 'Not my will.' He raised both his hands and called out to his father, 'Not my will, but yours be done.' The shadow sank into the groves and sped up the track into nothing.

There was nothing all around him, above him, no word and no comfort, as he lay down and said, 'Not my will, but your will, your will be done.' The sweat came from his head like blood.

He said 'Father' with such difficulty, as if he were learning the word. He said it again, and the third time he spoke it tenderly. And then he lay silent. After a long while, he said it one more time, he said 'Father' with deep longing.

The night was still for the last time, as a nightingale sang invisibly somewhere high up above the garden, higher than the olive trees, on a ledge of rock. Its song fell like a stream, came down around him, burbling and rising again and piercing the great darkness with its cries. It seemed to be weeping and performing a lament, which then turned to joy and then sadness, it rose and caught the air with its mysterious and deep desire.

He stood up, and the tears were on his face, new tears. He wiped them away. He took courage and stood silently by his sleeping friends. He stood there for many minutes and did not wake them.

By a cistern in the olive grove below, the temple guard waited with their shuttered lanterns. There were about a hundred men, who had climbed the hill with extreme care. They had kept far from the pilgrim tents and their fires and squeezed up a thorny and forgotten goat track. They were under orders not to alert the Galilean mob at any cost, and to abandon the raid if they were discovered. They would simply spread out into a night patrol in search of temple thieves.

Judas reassured the captain. 'He'll be here, I'll go up to him.'

'How will we know?'

'I'll greet him with a kiss. That's the signal.'

They moved up stealthily, in twos wherever it was possible,

and then a rearguard of fifty held back. The others assembled, crouching below the old wall of massive, heaped-up boulders.

Jesus knelt beside Simon Peter and tugged at his arm gently.

'Simon Peter, couldn't you watch with me for a single hour?' The fisherman woke up and rubbed his eyes and, in his embarrassment, pushed hard at his friends and angrily ordered them to wake up.

'Get up now,' said Jesus, 'the moment has come.'

A man was walking towards them and Simon Peter felt a rush of fear. He felt for his sword under his cloak, but the man waved. It was Judas, walking towards them alone. He was smiling and waving in the darkness.

'It's only Judas,' he said, turning to James and John, and he waved back.

Judas walked up to Peter and then past him, without speaking. He was still smiling as he approached Jesus and put his arms out towards him and kissed him.

'With a kiss?' said Jesus.

He held Judas close to his face, right there, and said, 'Judas, are you betraying me . . . with a kiss?' He touched the kiss on his cheek, ran a finger over it, as if he had dreamt it.

Suddenly, every tree was alive with fire, every bush became a man wielding a sword, the shutters snapped open and light spread from the lanterns over Peter and James and John, a flickering deadly glare banishing the soft night, iron scraped and spears gathered around them like a forest shaken by the wind. No one, in all the mass of men and shields and weapons, uttered a single shout or made any command. The manoeuvre was well-rehearsed and in strict silence.

Peter turned, he looked at Jesus, back at Judas – then at the circle of warriors and their lanterns. He rolled his eyes around, like a bull cornered in fear. He struck out in fear, not as he had dreamed and boasted but in terror and without direction. His sword swiped down a young man's head and cut off the ear. There were gouts of blood as the youth fell, clutching, and Jesus stepped in front of Peter, in front of the line of spears raised high to pin the fisherman to the ground.

'No!' he shouted. 'Don't you think my father could send twelve legions of angels to my rescue, if I asked?' He turned to Peter, who had lost his sword in the grass and was on his hands and knees in utter confusion. 'But that is not the way.'

He raised his arm and the soldiers fell back, ready for him, but he brought it down very gradually and touched the man's ear.

The man looked up, strangely. He sighed. He touched the place and there was no blood. He felt the ear and began to tremble. He kept touching it and looking at Jesus. The soldiers lowered their spears. They looked in fear at their companion and then at Jesus.

His hand lingered over the young man and no one moved.

Then, at a signal, they rushed upon him and bound him tightly, and Peter and James and John ran into the grove, through the trees and bushes, stumbling, scratching themselves and banging into stones, falling and leaping into the night. They ran, leaving everything, their food and their cloaks. They kept running.

No one pursued them, but the soldiers formed a tight circle around their captive, lashing his wrists with cords that made him bleed. He cried out.

'Why have you come with swords and clubs, as if I am a

criminal? Day after day I've been in the temple, and you didn't lay a finger on me.'

They hauled him silently, dragged him over the rough boundary of the garden and into the safe-keeping of the second contingent.

Judas was watching, left alone, watching from the empty garden beside the crooked trees. He heard his master's words on the air, as if they were travelling back to him.

'This is your time,' he said. 'The kingdom of darkness.'

The kingdom time.

He shuddered and looked up at the vast sky, without blemish. An unsullied darkness where there was no moon. He buried his face in his hands.

Joseph was standing alone on the roof of his kinsman's house. The whole city lay before him, the intricate pattern of streets, the houses muted, lost in shadow. Only the temple was sharp against the night, rearing up to the heavens with its continual burning against the whiteness and the gold.

To its side, the huge iron grate of the fortress beacon smoked on the tower. Soldiers and priests were always awake.

He gazed into the depths of Kidron and beyond, up the steppes of limestone to where the tents clustered like bats in a damp cave. He could make out the hint of a flap or a roof in the dull light of the surviving fires.

There were lights, hovering in the dark then extinguishing, and a tiny stream of almost imperceptible lights flowing into the deep thickets. He thought nothing of them at first. His mind roamed over the days and the nights.

He was sailing on some sea voyage of his own, on some wild

and lonely journey in his mind, the spray in his face. He was battered by thoughts and hopes.

The Messiah riding on a donkey and the children.

It was in the faces of the children that he had seen the glory of the Lord. He saw the light in our eyes, although we did not know what was happening, and he wept over his poverty on the steps of the temple. He had sat there for a long time, till nightfall.

Every day, every hour in Jerusalem, had brought him back to one place, the fire at Keruchim and the hand pointing in the night, into the far distant darkness.

'Go.'

He did not know what this meant. The meal had left him confused and afraid, and he had slept fitfully for an hour in the corner then woken up suddenly, jolted as if by an invisible force. He was sweating, dripping all over. He had walked out into the cool air and up on to the roof, and he was pacing, smoothing his brow, drying his hands on his cloak.

He saw the lights, the tiny specks of light shifting, snaking down the hill, then assembling into a cluster in the valley, like a tree of stars. He could not imagine what procession of pilgrims or night patrol would be scouring the valleys at this time. He grabbed the balustrade fiercely. There was a sudden, terrible realisation. He ran down the stairs and stood in the deserted street and looked around frantically. There was no one, only him. No disciples. No pilgrims, only him and the shuttered lanterns and the spears climbing into view. He walked forward and stood on the brow of the road and watched the detachment approaching him in silence, and he saw their prisoner.

He was being pulled and the ropes were tightening round his hands. His head was down and he did not look up at Joseph.

Joseph stepped up to the captain of the guard, a man he knew well, who halted his troop and looked into the face of the tall merchant from Arimathea with an awkward respect. He could not push such a rich and influential figure out of the way.

'By what authority do you arrest this man?'

The captain produced a warrant, scratchily written, with a heavy temple seal.

'At the command of the high priest – and the Sanhedrin.' He waved his hand and the troops marched on, streaming either side of Joseph, who turned.

'I have signed nothing! There are many elders who have not been consulted.' He ran after them, mumbling and repeating under his breath, 'This arrest is illegal!'

Simon Peter slipped up the road, keeping the column just within sight. He flattened himself against a wall, slipped out of the shadows, ran for a while, then stopped, picked up the line again. He pulled his cloak far down over his forehead.

He saw them turn, not towards the temple, but into the courtyard of Caiaphas' own home.

They led the prisoner into the great hall, where he stood in silence beneath the latticework of the magnificent ceiling. Small torches in brackets of twisted leaves burned along the fluted columns. He stood alone and the mosaic of crested waves at his feet stretched out towards Caiaphas. The waves and the pattern of rosettes and the motif of the thin-necked perfume bottles.

A gift for services rendered.

The high priest leant forward, his hands clasped together in front of his mouth.

* * *

In the courtyard it felt bitterly cold. The clouds had torn apart and the moon was edging into view. Peter drew his shawl down further and stepped nearer the brazier where a crowd of guards and servant women huddled. He reached nearer the flames than he was intending, as a young woman shifted and made way for him. He knelt down, his head low, looking deep into the blazing coals. A rush of fire made him lean back, slackening the shawl, and the glow burnished his face.

'Hey,' the servant girl peered at him, 'weren't you with him in the temple?'

'Me?'

She waved at the soldiers, 'We've got one of the followers of Jesus here!'

'You're mad! I don't know him.'

Peter laughed with incredulity and then stooped down to the warmth. She looked at him for a while, and then at her companions.

The councillors had assembled along the frescoed panels, deep in the recesses. They were reluctant to congregate around the blasphemer, who stood alone in the shadow of interlocking spears. There were twelve soldiers around him, all levites from the temple guard, and they stood anxiously around their charge.

They were not superstitious men, but they had heard the stories.

Caiaphas did not look up from the parchment scroll unfolded before him. 'There are many charges against you,' he said. His voice was soft and precise.

'Any one of these could lead to your death.'

The prisoner said nothing.

'But perhaps where you come from that causes no concern?' He handed the scroll back to a scribe and looked up. 'It is heaven you come from?'

There was silence. Caiaphas shouted suddenly, with fury, 'Or is it Nazareth?' He stood up and walked forward, and there was an uproar of shouting from the councillors, who moved forward to the columns. Joseph, who had slipped through the antechamber and into the hall unseen, ran out into the torchlight and called above the fury, 'This court is illegal! There must be fifty elders. And we cannot try a man by night!'

'Exactly,' an old man swung round to him, Annas, the father-in-law of the high priest. 'As it is the middle of the night, why disturb so many councillors when the man has already condemned himself?'

Joseph looked round and saw the familiar faces, the friends and relatives and powerful allies of the household, the inner chamber. They were all around him and suddenly they were more intrigued by his interruption than by the prisoner who stood still, dumb, without looking at Joseph or at anyone in the vast hall.

'The charge of blasphemy is self-evident,' said Caiaphas, looking directly at Joseph. 'But if you insist on hearing more witnesses!'

They were brought in, two of the moneychangers and the foreman from the building works.

'This man said he would destroy the temple of God!' said the traders, and elaborated at length. He had hurled the temple coinage into the dirt.

'He claimed to have the power to build it again,' the foreman said, 'in three days.'

Joseph stepped towards Caiaphas in desperation. He caught his eye and stopped, hesitated. He turned round, to all the councillors.

Joseph was known for his eloquence and his power of speech and respected throughout the land, in the highest court of all. He must speak.

'Does our court try a man without listening to him first?'

'Are you from Galilee too?'

Ben Azra stepped towards him, and then Annas, right up to him.

'Are you a disciple of Jesus?'

Joseph looked at the figure among the guards, circled by spears, and looked at the throng of men. He looked at the loneliness of Jesus. He lifted his hands to say something. He gestured vaguely into the emptiness.

'I . . . only . . . seek . . . to do what is right. I know nothing, I.'

'You know nothing?'

Caiaphas came down beside him, looking him full in the face. Joseph tried to meet his stare, but he could not. He looked down at the frozen patterns on the floor.

'I . . . I know nothing of this matter,' he said.

A man seized Peter by the shoulder, and twisted his face into view. 'You're one of his followers!' he shouted.

'I swear – on my mother's grave – I have never met Jesus!' Peter barged away from the fire and walked into the darkness, cursing.

Caiaphas circled Jesus slowly, with a malign curiosity. The matter had become more than inconvenient to him, more than one of those predictable crises he had artfully managed for so many years. It had become sinister.

'If you are the Messiah, tell us.'

Jesus looked him in the eyes. The high priest returned his gaze implacably. He mastered the strange fear that was rising in him, for the benefit of his council, and did not flinch even at the unexpected sound of the carpenter's voice.

'You do not believe anything I say, so why should I tell you?'

He seemed to be whispering to Caiaphas himself, but everyone heard the words throughout the chamber as if they were floating through the shadows towards them, towards every single member of the Sanhedrin.

'But soon the Son of Man will be seated beside the throne of God!'

There were shouts of 'blasphemy' and they rent their clothes. They screamed hatred and judgement at him and the guards clutched their spears, as if the whole chamber would turn into bloody riot, as if the elders would seize upon the prisoner themselves and smash his head on the floor.

Ben Azra spat in his face, 'So you are the son of God then?'

'It's you who are saying so!'

'Me?' He looked round at his jeering and shouting companions, eager to take the credit for this arrest, for saving the city of Zion.

Annas called across the confusion, roaring to Caiaphas, 'Why do we need any more evidence? He should die! He is condemned by his own words!'

Caiaphas nodded to the guards, who seized him where he stood meekly and pushed him from the chamber.

* * *

A crowd had gathered round Peter in the courtyard. A man from the high priest's household was walking up to him, inspecting his face thoroughly. 'You were definitely with Jesus,' he said. 'You're from Galilee! You *are* one of his men – you're a Galilean!' He shouted to the soldiers by the fire, 'He's one of them!'

'You're a filthy liar! *Liars! Liars!*,' he said, stumbling through them, raging, 'I never knew him – *in God's name, I never even met the man in my whole life!*'

The cock crew as Jesus entered the courtyard. The cry, from somewhere far away, rode on the dark and echoed.

It came again and then again. Jesus turned and looked at Peter, and as the soldiers shoved him forwards viciously, he kept looking. He did not turn his head away until he had passed through the arch.

When the soldiers and the priests had gone, and the long line had disappeared up the broad street to the governor's residence, Simon Peter walked out into the road alone. He could not see where he was going. His tears did not stop, even when he reached the garden again and climbed beyond it and kept climbing. He stood on the highest ridge of rock and he gazed down into the night, into the valley, and he could see no lights, no city, only the fog of his weeping. He stood there on the sharp rock and prepared to kill himself.

Joseph of Arimathea walked behind the councillors and the soldiers, behind the silent figure of Jesus, and he gazed at the earth passing under his feet, the dust and the shadows thrown by the lanterns. He stopped outside Pilate's house as the others went forward, and wiped the pouring sweat from his face. His whole body was soaking wet. He walked on in a dream, through the huge gates. He could hear the sound of his own heart beating, as if he were the only person on earth.

As Ben Azra turned into the doorway of the inner quadrangle, the Gabbatha where the judgements were pronounced, a man seized his arm.

'I have made a mistake,' he said.

'What's that to me?' said Ben Azra, shaking off his assailant and walking on. He did not hear the clattering of coins that fractured the air, spinning through the darkness, silver fire illuminated by the moon. He did not stop to see the figure lurching from the pedestals to the massive steps, shouting, 'I have betrayed an innocent man. Betrayed . . . a good man.'

To the soldiers on the watch, he was some drunk, best left alone.

Judas walked out into the fields where the mist was rising, although it was still quite dark. Very methodically, and without passion, he tied a rope around his neck, slung it over an elder tree, looped it round several times, and then hurled himself into the darkness.

Peter lay on the ridge high above, stretched out. There was blood on his face where he had beaten his forehead in his violent grief, but he had not jumped. He had fallen asleep.

We were all sleeping, every one of us, except Miryam. The other disciples sat hunched against the wall or strewn in the grass where they had set up their look-out high above the garden, and they had all slept through everything. The pilgrims were snoring in their tents. They were happy, they had been singing late into the night, and Miryam had listened to them with such compassion, as if they were all lost children, and said 'Let them sing, they should sing. It's Pesach.'

She was holding in her hands a bright casket, whose figures were almost worn smooth. She held it to her breast. She kept rubbing it with one finger, as if trying to read it. I did not know what it was, nor did I ask her, but she looked at me once as though I were a ghost or a dream, and she caught her breath. I thought she was going to weep, but she didn't, she just reached out and stroked my arm as I was staring into the heart of the fire.

There was such sorrow in her, such mysterious calm. I could not possibly break that silence. At last, my eyes became so heavy, I was drifting, and she laid me down so that I would not come near the fire, and she put my head on her cloak. The earth was cold and my feet were cold and I kept waking up, and all I could see was his figure on the threshold of the garden. He seemed to be calling. I remember him calling and going into the dark, turning. He was turning away from me and leaving me in silence, but in the way of dreams, he was calling.

I don't remember what he was saying. I think he was talking to Miryam, I think it was some word to her, I could hear it definitely. Or it was to both of us, but it was not possible for me to understand it because it was in a different language.

Some word, I will never know. I fell into a deep sleep at last.

Pilate strode down the steps, stumbling into the darkness and then into the flare of torches along the pavement. He stood on the massive slabs in his bare feet, furiously tying up the clasp on his robe. It eluded his fingers. He twisted his face round to look at the hideous black assembly of robes and officials and felt disgust.

'If I have been disturbed to hear some trivial point of Jewish law!'

Caiaphas stepped into the light. 'This man—'

'Some quibble about this wretched Passover!'

Pilate fumbled with the jewel, pointedly ignoring the high priest. Annas thrust a trembling finger at the prisoner, hidden by the ring of guards. They pushed him forward.

'This man is stirring up the people to rebel.'

Pilate put his face right up to the old man. 'I will charge you all with threatening the peace of Rome! *All of you!*' He walked back to his stone sedile with its discreet imperial inscription. There had been an agreement to avoid graven images, so the eagle had been chiselled off. He stood there, his hands on the smooth patch, utterly weary.

Caiaphas spoke again. His voice was tiresomely familiar to Pilate, grating and unsympathetic, the most despicable kind of ally. Always crawling for some further concession, some ridiculous little favour in return for co-operation.

'This man,' he said, 'is the enemy of Rome.' He said it with a ghastly finality, that flat dull way he had of making absolute pronouncements. Pilate sat down and arranged his tunic around his knees and sighed.

'Who is he and what has he done?'

Ben Azra led the prisoner forward. 'Jesus from Galilee.'

'Jesus . . . ?' Pilate had heard the name somehow, in some

half-finished briefing. Where had he heard it? And why did it have a disturbing ring to it? 'Oh . . .' He looked at Jesus, who seemed to be looking past him as if oblivious to him. 'Is this . . . the man . . . ?'

Pilate's voice trailed into silence. Annas stepped forward, 'He opposes paying taxes to Caesar.'

'In other words, he shares your opinion,' Pilate wheeled round to Annas with contempt. He glared at the throng, the huge unnecessary multitude of priests and clerks and scribes congregating on his judgement floor. He looked at the games of the soldiers etched into the limestone, the triangles and dials inscribed around the pillars for their pathetic wagers. He felt hatred for everyone, the legionaries, the temple guardsmen, the Sanhedrin.

And this prisoner. He felt nothing for him. 'Opposes paying taxes,' he muttered to himself. 'And?' he shouted to Caiaphas.

'And he says he is the Christ, the king of the Jews.'

That was interesting, the first spark of interest in the whole occasion. Pilate rose, walked to Jesus and took him on one side, into the cool darkness of the vault.

'The king of the Jews,' he said. 'Are you the king of the Jews?'

'These are your words.' Jesus spoke without looking at him.

'Have you nothing to say about the charges against you?' He felt inexplicably angry, suddenly violently angry with this Galilean peasant who stood there in his dusty robe in insolent silence.

Jesus looked up at Pilate and gazed into his small eyes.

Pilate felt an unaccountable sickness in his stomach. He was shocked. The man looked at him as if he were naked.

'I . . .' He rid himself of the figure with a clumsy gesture, a guard came and took him back to his captors. Pilate sat down uneasily. 'I find no case against this man.'

'If you do nothing about this man, you are no friend of Caesar!' The face of Caiaphas seemed to leer at him from the gloom and there seemed to be laughter somewhere. Roman laughter. Pilate closed his eyes and breathed deeply, as if in pain.

'He is a Galilean rebel. Take him to Herod.'

The delegation moved on and Joseph of Arimathea followed, as if sleepwalking down the empty streets of Jerusalem. There was nothing he could do and he knew he should go home. He knew he should accept what he had done and lie down for ever in the darkness.

They came to Herod's palace and were greeted like actors in a tragic spectacle. They were cheered and applauded. Pilate had thoughtfully sent his herald ahead of them. Caiaphas and Annas and their retinue awkwardly accompanied Jesus through waving servants and a line of curtseying soldiers.

For Joseph, who had travelled the world and seen the most desperate barbarities and follies, it was a horror beyond everything. In the royal chamber, where the pennants hung over the black marble dais, he felt the most terrible cold, as if strapped to his own corpse. A foul-smelling cold, yet the room was sweetly perfumed and frankincense burned from enamelled bowls.

Herod Antipas was in a state of wild enthusiasm. He made an impressive entrance, with a fanfare, wheeling around several times and falling at the feet of Jesus.

'Oh what a pleasure, what an honour! To be in the presence of the king! The king of the Jews,' he added, sharing an intimate secret with his courtiers. They laughed and clapped and called out like wheedling children, begging for more. Herod obliged.

'Look, I bow, I kiss your feet!' He prostrated himself and his courtiers gasped. 'I thought I was a king, but now I see before your majesty . . . how I lack all royal qualities, the secret of power on earth, for you have . . . great power.'

He stood up slowly before the prisoner, whose silence was becoming a little tiresome. 'Don't disappoint your servant, your worshipper! I would love to see . . . something, a little act, a little display, I don't ask for much. A sign. A small wonder. I've heard the stories, but there's a habit of exaggeration in Galilee. Your followers should never rely on second-hand reports, you see my problem?'

No one spoke. Even the chief priests were silenced by the antics of the Galilean ruler. They feared him, his stupidity and his rage. It was unlikely he would co-operate.

'Robes! Purple! The finest! A crown . . .'

He was shouting and clapping his hands, skipping up and down.

Then he stood very still in front of Jesus, who never looked or spoke to him once. Soldiers came from the darkness bearing a crown plaited from thorns. Herod took it carefully, winced mockingly as a thorn pricked his thumb, drew in his breath, held it out to the courtiers, lifted it high.

'A crown,' he shouted. He waved it slowly through the air. Then he dropped it very slowly and delicately on to his head.

'A crown,' he said, 'perhaps it will encourage you to perform as a king. As the king of the Jews.' He nodded at one of the soldiers, who suddenly pressed it hard into his scalp with both hands.

The blood ran down his face and on to his robe. There was a deep gash over his eye, but he did not move at all. Blood ran down on to his lips and fell on the tiles.

Herod looked down with sympathy. 'A miracle or two could still save you from something very unpleasant.'

A second soldier lifted the robe of purple on to his shoulder and tied it with a cord around his neck, hard, almost choking him. He coughed and tried to catch his breath several times.

'Perform,' said Herod.

He sighed theatrically with considerable pique, as if the top billing in the arena had been cancelled, and a few courtiers clapped dutifully. The rest were staring down.

Joseph of Arimathea was leaning against a huge porphyry vase, hiding his eyes.

Herod looked at Jesus again, this time with loathing and with horrible disquiet at the still, hauntingly still, figure bleeding profusely. He stepped back.

'Send his majesty back to Pilate,' he said. 'Let Rome decide the fate of this dumb prophet, this marvellous . . . mute king of the Jews!'

He made as if to pluck his beard but snatched at thin air.

Caiaphas and Annas were grateful for Herod's incompetence. They knew that Pilate had been forced to make a show of deference. He had made too many mistakes in the past, smuggling votive shields with their emblems into Jerusalem by night, murdering Galilean protesters, Herod's men. Mingling their blood with sacrificial lambs. He had to be careful, and there was the matter of the temple treasury funds which he had pilfered for the building of the aqueduct. The emperor had warned him. He had made far too many mistakes. It was time to make some friends.

Pilate surveyed the crowd, such a large crowd for so early in the morning. The traders, at least fifty of them, the builders, every mason and clerk, the scribes, merchants, officials from the treasury, every servant from the households of Caiaphas and Annas down to the footwashers and the laundry maids, everyone had been assembled and stood in the dusk, where the moon still hung low over the horizon and the sun was no more than a strip of light through the trees, touching the battlements of the Antonia tower with a faint pinkness. They gathered, shepherded and marshalled by levites and Sadducees. Ben Azra, Phineas, the duty priests and their assistants, wove through the throng and took up their positions below the balcony where Pilate was leaning.

High above, there was movement among the Galilean tents, a few carried water, a few doused fires. Tiny figures meandering through the groves. Time was short.

He rubbed his hands against his unshaven cheeks and cursed himself for his luck. One miscalculation and there'd be another Galilean massacre and he would be blamed, he would be recalled, there would be trials, there would be arraignments and depositions, and he would be lucky to escape with exile.

Death was on his mind unexpectedly, his own death. He had ordered Jesus to be whipped but the flagrum had failed in its vicious task, the lead balls and the bits of sheep's bone ripping off his flesh had not been a sufficient warning. The man had said nothing. He always said nothing. He looked to be near death, but then he would stand and somehow condemn them all. He felt an odd sympathy with Caiaphas, there was something deeply dangerous about the man.

But he had examined the case. There was no case. He did not like any of it, and even this could go so badly wrong, he could be accused of another heartless miscarriage of justice. Letters could be sent to Rome. His mind was in a torment and he hurled the scented water on to his face and shouted for more. Servants hurried off into the cool marble hall. If only he could hurry off with them, sleep, hide, if only he could delegate and rid himself of this decision.

Caiaphas was looking at him with that sneer, that hidden sneer, that holy nastiness that he had been forced to respect. The man was a snake, a reptile, like something out of the African night, so deadly still, so patient. He clearly knew what he wanted and he would not leave without it, nor would his eager henchmen.

'What do you want me to do with him?' he said, almost pathetically, despising himself for every word. Caiaphas said nothing but indicated the crowd. Pilate leant over the balcony again and asked them, 'What do you want me to do with him?'

'Crucify him.'

Their shout was orchestrated and their rage seemed artificial to Pilate, some concoction, some deadly beverage they had been handed.

'Crucify him?' he said with incredulity, but they roared back. They waved and shouted. They were happy with their mindless chanting, 'Crucify, crucify'. He looked down at them as if they

251

were vermin. He tried to control his sheer contempt, to master the violent wrath which had earned him one rebuke too many. He clutched the cold stone of the balustrade.

'I cannot,' he said to Annas and Caiaphas, hissing the words to them. 'I cannot execute an innocent man. Deal with him yourselves!'

'We do not have the power to condemn any man to death,' said Annas, coolly, as if he were in some senatorial chamber, alone before men in togas. A polite, thorough little legal point.

'But by our law', said Caiaphas, 'if he says he is the Son of God, he must die.'

'Son of God,' said Pilate.

He knew their obsession with blasphemy and he knew how close he had come to angering their god. How he was damned in their eyes already. He knew these were matters of deadly and inevitable importance. It was their whole world.

The world he hated and had to inhabit.

'Son of God?' he said, and he looked over to Jesus, who stood in the brightening porch, the sun falling across his ravaged face. The crowd continued their music, their drumming senseless chorus. 'Crucify him.'

Pilate went over to him and stood alone with him.

'Where do you come from?' he said.

The man was silent again. It was his weapon, his heavenly armoury. Pilate could see that. Silence. Gazing. This awful humility and stillness. This battalion in the shape of one man who would not move and would not speak.

'Why don't you answer me! Don't you realise, I have the power to release you or to crucify you?'

'You would have no power over me.'

His voice was so clear and strong, suddenly shocking. Pilate stared at him in disbelief.

'If it hadn't been given to you . . . from above.'

'From above?'

He looked at him, seeking clarification, looked at him, and the eyes stared back at him, open, open and deep and unblinking.

Pilate felt rage and misery, desperation. 'Who are you?'

Against the rising waves of hatred, the horrible banal repetition of death, death, death from the crowd, Pilate looked at the man alive before him. He looked at the living, breathing man and was overwhelmed by the presence of him. The man in the doorway, in front of the dark interior, who was bound and beaten and bleeding before him now. He looked at him, up and down, and found himself looking above him, looking high up into the pale sky.

'Here is your king,' he turned to the crowd. But they didn't hear him. They sang out for his death. They chorused all the more loudly, as if Pilate were some kind of dumb show waving useless arms and mouthing a worthless, meaningless speech.

'Your king,' he said.

Caiaphas was walking towards him and then Pilate struck the balustrade. He hit it twice, in fury, in inspiration.

'You have a custom,' he shouted, 'to release one prisoner at Passover – a tradition which I respect! Shall I release the king of the Jews for you?'

Ben Azra, Lamech, someone in the crowd, someone lost in the flurry of people and their shifting sea of faces, called out 'Barabbas'.

'We want Barabbas!'

The whole crowd screamed together, they seemed to delight in the word, the very name of the renegade they had despised until yesterday.

'The criminal, the murderer?' said Pilate. 'Barabbas?' He was curious, oddly curious, and dazed by the sudden absurdity, the reckless notion that he had unleashed.

'Barabbas? Don't you want your king?'

'The only king we want is Caesar.'

Caiaphas spoke the words quietly into Pilate's ear, as he stood there still reeling from the utter stupidity of it all.

'Caesar?' said Pilate, as if his voice were no longer his own. He looked over to Jesus standing in the doorway, and the shadow had fallen across him. He could not see his face. He was filled with terror, he whirled round to the crowd, but they threw back their chants and waved their fists. There was a riot coming, there was blood already in the streets. There would be murders in the temple precincts. He clutched his head again and rubbed his face violently, and then swept his hands aside in a huge arc, silencing the crowd.

There was a moment of sudden, urgent expectation. They all looked up at him and Caiaphas and Annas and others congregated around him, gazing, folding their hands.

'I . . .' said Pilate, 'I am innocent.'

The word had somehow migrated to his own soul. It was his own innocence that troubled him and he emphasised it very particularly. 'I am innocent of this man's blood.' He took the scented bowl and perched it on the balustrade, where every man and woman could see it.

'You see?' he said. 'I am washing my hands of this . . . of all of you.' He dipped in his fingers and pressed them down into the bowl, folded his hands into the lilac water. 'Of all of you!' he shouted, almost weeping in his rage.

He turned to Caiaphas. 'I am innocent,' he said, then he called to his soldiers.

'Deal with him according to Roman law.'

13

My father saw him first.

He had been up before the dawn, praying, walking through the groves, so lost in the darkness of the trees that he had seen no lights in the streets and heard nothing, no shouts or jeers drifting in the dusk. All he could hear was water, a stream pouring into a well. He had sat by it for a long time and thrown a stone down into the depths and listened. He was reciting the scriptures to himself and thinking of the lamps in the synagogue in Capernaum, he was standing there again and begging God. He did not know what for.

He did not know what he was doing, what he was praying or thinking. All his thoughts seemed to be circling in the darkness.

He was looking into the blackness of a well again, and he found himself singing of the Messiah. He turned back, deeply troubled with himself. It was not because he feared blasphemy, it was because he feared his own cowardice, he knew he was not ready. He could not speak, not in the synagogues or the temple, or to any of the Pharisees and doctors of the law, he could not imagine himself sitting down with Simon or Phineas and pleading from the scriptures, he could not even imagine himself leaving his home.

He had wanted Jesus to come and sit by his fire and talk. Talk through the night, tell him everything, how it was to be, but he had not wanted to follow. Something about that gateway and the tangle of branches, something there, some darkness or fear, something insisted to him now that he was unworthy, unfit for discipleship. He could not follow. Jesus had stood there and he had needed him and Cleopas and all the others, he had needed everyone to stand with him, to walk with him, but his whole manner at the gate said 'No'. There was no one.

Jesus had feared something, he was in terrible, mortal sorrow of some sort and even the twelve, even Peter, would not be able to go with him. The cup, he had raised it and it had been for all of them, but it shone alone.

He kept thinking of how it had shone alone, up there in his hands, still, beneath the shadow of the rafters.

The sun was piercing, tiny shafts of light through the layers of branches, as he abandoned the well and walked up slowly, heavily, towards the camp. He could see embers in the greyness, and smoke. He climbed out of the ocean of trees and their waving, caressing green, rippling into silver, but he did not notice the beauty of the dawn all around him or hear the turtle doves murmuring in the rocks where they brooded over their young.

He saw an arch filled with people.

Far down, he saw a door flung open and a man stagger into the light carrying what looked like a tree on his back, a rough dark beam so wide it smashed against the portals and he stumbled and fell.

A voice shouted '*Walk!*' and he staggered upward, swayed and then lurched into the bright sun. The tumult of people followed, held back by ranks of soldiers with their shields locked in formation.

My father was staring, horrified that some poor criminal was about to die at Passover and angry that the authorities were staging such a blasphemous ritual at the holy season. He clenched his fists and turned away, strode away towards our tent.

Then turned again. Something made him turn, drew him back.

He looked and saw in the rubble of the road far below the body of Jesus lying beneath the beam. He saw his face.

He saw him.

He called. I woke up to hear him calling. He was calling, he was howling like a wild animal. My father was howling and shouting and crying, 'They're taking him . . . they're taking him . . . they're *killing him!*'

We woke, I was with Miryam still, and I ran out of the tent. And I saw my father on the high ridge, he was pointing, he was stricken. He was holding himself as if he were being torn apart. He was shaking his head, again and again, shouting, 'No, no!'

My mother came out, she fell down, she got up and ran and stumbled to the edge. Mary Magdalene was running, she was falling and rolling, she ran down, all the way down, and my father followed. Everyone followed. We all began to run towards the procession, my father was screaming and shouting. He got to the soldier, right up to the tribune, and shouted in his face, 'What is the charge, what is the charge?'

The tribune said nothing. Not one of the soldiers spoke to him, he was going from one to another, grabbing at them. 'He is innocent. This man. This man!'

I saw Mary Magdalene run towards him, right up to him, but they grabbed her and hurled her from the crowd, she was screaming and lay in the dust. Someone kicked her out of the way, then she got up, she was shaking and calling and reaching out her hands. She was reaching them out and Miryam came to her and took her in her arms.

She took Mary and held her, and then she fell down herself.

She fell down when she saw Jesus coming and his face. It was his face all torn, his lovely face so ripped you could hardly recognise him. He was puffed and swollen from the beating, he was hardly able to see, one of his eyes had closed over. There was so much blood. The tribune came right behind him with his sword drawn. He wasn't looking to the right or the left, nothing could make him look anywhere, he was just staring, right up to the huge quarry where the filth was piled to the sky. Golgotha, he was looking at it over the head of the prisoner. My father kept calling, many many people were shouting, all the Galileans, lines and lines of pilgrims were coming, falling down the hills, some coming with clubs and weapons, some waving their palms still, like knives. Hundreds of people were crowding down, but the troops were being reinforced, there were streams and streams of legionaries lining the whole track. It was like a tunnel of spears. You could hardly see him.

I wanted to see him so badly, but my mother had got hold of me.

She was holding me back and I could see him going. I could see them taking him up to the hill. I cried and cried, 'Let me, let me'. She tightened her arms round me and my father came too, then she turned. She turned to look at him and I ran off.

I kept running although she screamed after me. She was so afraid for me, but I kept running. I ran high up the path. I could see him through the gaps in the shields, I could see him up there. I could see the plume of the tribune's helmet and I followed and ran alongside, until he fell. He fell down into the dirt again and the beam crashed on to his head. He stumbled up, they were kicking him up.

I ran in then and I saw him.

He looked right at me. He looked into me.

I saw him and the blood coming down over his eyes, until I couldn't see them.

He took my hand. He took it in his. For one second, he took it and squeezed it, so weakly. I said his name, and he said nothing.

They tore him away from me. They were tearing him away, pulling him, shoving me back, pulling him on. They were taking him away for ever. I knew they had him. They had him in their power.

I was standing by the rocks at the top, I was calling and calling, 'Jesus', when my mother found me. She burst out weeping and clutched me and I didn't move. I said, 'They've taken him from me. They've taken him from me.' I said, 'I want him, I want him, please get him. Father, go and get him Please get him away from them.'

He was looking at me and sobbing, 'Tamar,' he said, 'daughter.' He looked at me and then he looked up at the crosses.

They were banging. The groans. The cries.

It was darkness, it was a pit of blackness and banging and crying. I heard his voice, it was softer than the others. He just sighed out in pain, sighed out his breath and drew it in again. Then sighed, that deep searing long sigh.

Like the wind in the storm when it sucks at my door.

Like the wind here, when it comes in the heart of winter and when it brings desolation.

* * *

I hear him again. I hear him sighing, sighing out his life. I am calling to him, I am saying to my father, 'Go and get him. Get him back for me. Please get him.'

No one listens. There's no one who can move, only the soldiers. Only the soldiers banging and hauling.

They're raising him up, so high, so high above the foul waste. He falls on to the nails.

He screamed. That was the only time. The only moment. When the post went into the hole.

Joseph was sitting beside us, he had come up beside us, against my father. They sat there and watched. He said, 'I didn't . . .' He was weeping then so much. He kept saying, 'I didn't . . .' and my father took his hand. He said, 'I didn't . . . I could not . . . save him. I was . . . I was silent.'

Joseph of Arimathea. Joseph, in the spray and the loneliness, in the teeth of the gale. His journey was into night.

Silence.

There were so many. Peter was on the rocks above, not far, below a cave where the others were hiding. All except John. He was coming down, slowly, by himself, crawling down the rock face. Peter could see everything but he was hiding his face almost all the time. The others stayed in the darkness and the cold and did not move, for fear of being seen. But John came. He came up the filth, through the bones and the broken pots and the poisonous smell of rags, he waded up. I saw him, waist deep.

He walked up, at last, to the cross and he stood there, so

lonely, silent beneath Jesus, until the soldiers forced him away.

He walked back to where the women were, Miryam and Mary Magdalene and Mary the sister of Martha. Three of them against the fading sky. I don't know where all the others were in the crowd. Martha and Lazarus and Cleopas and so many, in the distance. Many had been stopped by the soldiers.

The exercise had been planned to the last intricate detail by the tribune. Even the choice of the nails, the style of the cross beams. The efficiency of the hammering and the rings of soldiers around every possible exit and entrance to the quarry.

There were cavalrymen stationed, about twenty, near the gates of the city, lines of infantrymen along the porticoes of the temple and along all the outside walls of the city, in every battlement and archway.

The tribune was absolutely still. He watched everything without any emotion, but was alone again. It was so clear that he was alone, even with all that vast army and with Pilate's garrison behind him. He just stood there, looking at Jesus, and once he looked up to the sky where the clouds were descending, they were rolling in from the north. The sun was being swallowed.

He looked back to the figure between the two thieves.

The Sadducees and the priests were standing far away, but they had a good view. One of them shouted, 'If he is the Messiah, let him come down now!'

No one said anything else.

Miryam was standing there, looking up at him, she never took her eyes off him for one moment. I never saw her look away. She never turned back, never hid her eyes. She was not weeping.

She was watching him.

She was talking to him, I was sure she was talking to him. It was as if she was saying something through that silence, as if she could penetrate the darkness or it was penetrating her. She was shivering and the other Marys held her, they all held each other as near to the cross as they were allowed. John was the only man standing with them.

John.

Jesus looked down at him, after a long time, and said, 'Son.'

John looked up and he was trying to say something, but he was choking it back.

'Son,' Jesus said. 'Your mother.'

And then he said to Miryam, 'Mother.'

He said, 'Mother.'

I heard him say it, and I can hear it. 'Mother.' The word that stays in the wind, the way he called her. So falteringly, and using so much breath. He had to stop for a long time, then he said, he lifted himself on the nails, wrenching his hands, he bit hard and said, 'Mother, your son.'

John stood beside Miryam and put his arm around her and the women fell down on their knees in the dust, weeping. We were all looking at them and the sight of them made sobs go through the crowd, waves of crying and lamenting. I could not cry any more.

I could not find my tears.

I kept looking at him.

Then the wind.

I saw the plume on the tribune's helmet lifting, like a horse's mane. He stood absolutely still, as if all order and all civilisation depended on him. His armour was so bright, as if it had been forged for the occasion. The sword and its winged creature with ruby eyes on the hilt, the muscled cuirass of silver and the leather greaves, the strapping, the shoes, the sash of his command.

And the plume riding, it was flapping furiously and madly and he reached up to his helmet and steadied it.

The clouds came, they fell down from the hills, huge billows of blackness, coursing through the Kidron valley and down upon Gehenna. The sun disappeared, flaming and struggling, with flashes and rays through the thick darkness, then nothing, engulfed in night. The tribune stood, holding himself against the violent storm. He would not move.

We were all bending down as the air, freezing and bringing pelting rain, tore at our cloaks and ripped my sleeves. I huddled into my father. My mother, father and I, and Joseph, all clung to each other. Jesus was up there, in the darkness. We could hardly see him, just the outline and then his face turning, his jaw out, he was looking somewhere. He was lifting himself so slowly in terrible agony to speak.

The gale howled and rubbish came flying, I saw pots and leaves and huge sodden strips of sacking whipping across the mound. Mary Magdalene was holding on to the cross itself and the soldiers did not shift her. They were holding on to the other crosses themselves, digging their heels into the soft, putrid earth.

The tribune was sweating, I could see him. Holding himself mightily, with every muscle stretched. He was leaning against the tempest, determined to stand and not to flinch. Huge gusts came hurling and took his helmet, but he caught it and put it back on and held it there.

Jesus lifted himself up at last, and he stayed there, his wrists pouring down blood, the nails had furrowed a deep gorge and it was dripping down his arms, down the wood. He looked out, far out, and then the cloud came down upon him. It came down as he cried out, 'Father!'

'Father!' He shouted into night and into the pit below, up into the heavens, the black heavens that were bursting down around him, 'Father, I give you my spirit.'

His body fell, and as it dropped he sighed out, 'It is finished.'

There was darkness, and no one could see anyone. I could not see my parents. I could feel them, but I couldn't see even their shapes.

The wind was all we knew, the wind that tore through the valley and into the city, through the narrow streets, screaming and wrenching every piece of material, every hanging and cloak, all doors smashing and banging, backwards and forwards, and the wind still travelling, stretching down through the deep tunnel into the court of the Gentiles, through the battlements, over the towers, around the columns and the long line of arches, into the court of the women. The wind ripping back bronze doors and scattering the incense bowls, descending from the white tower engulfed in blackness and seeking its entrance into the holy of holies, where it devoured the emptiness and filled it full of the howling and the force which rent the curtain down, down through the middle seam. The gold beading scattering in thousands, the threads hanging and the huge, unseen darkness melting into the invisible embrace.

'Father.'

We sat there and the word was in our minds, although he was dead upon the cross and hidden.

We could all hear it, as we had first heard it, whenever we had first heard him say it.

When he thanked his father or wept to his father.

Light was returning, a glimmer, some lost beams on the horizon battling with the sky and growing.

Enough light to see the dull shine on the tribune's helmet.

It was in his hands, and he held it there very still.

When the wind dropped down, he did not replace it. He said, 'It's true. This man was a son of God', and he turned to his soldiers. He looked at them, the long line holding the crowds and the men delegated to the crucifixions, with their pincers and awls, their bags with the tools of their trade.

He looked at them and then up at the figure of Jesus on the cross.

He walked slowly up to the body and took a lance from one of the legionaries. He was about to pierce him but then he stopped, he handed it back to his second in command, who stabbed the side. Blood flowed down the shaft, blood and water, all down the body. Down his legs.

I didn't watch. I was lying in my father's arms and my face was in his robe. He put his face next to mine, like he always did.

He put his face to mine and just held it there, held me.

I could hear the sound of the other victims, their legs were being broken. They had to kill them all before sundown.

'Don't break the legs of this one,' said the tribune, and he looked up again at Jesus and looked at his head, bruised and fallen down.

He turned swiftly on his heels, with great precision. He looked back at the crowd, who began to move off, slowly, under escort from the soldiers.

He waited until all the soldiers had gone and almost all the people. He looked at us sitting there, and at the women, and at John, as if he were questioning us, as if he wanted to say something to us but he couldn't.

He walked away alone and did not put back his helmet. It was raining and the water was streaming down his neck.

Pilate was sitting alone in his inner chamber when they brought Joseph of Arimathea to him.

He was sitting alone in the dark, beside a single lamp, and staring at the wall.

He did not speak to Joseph for a long time. He avoided interviews in his private chamber but had refused to come out and talk in the judgement hall. He was nestling in the dark, massaging his fingers, contemplating the cracks in the plaster.

'So,' he said, without turning, 'you want me to give you the body of your king?'

'Yes.'

'Why?'

'I would like to bury him in my own tomb.'

'Your own tomb. You're too generous.'

Pilate looked round slowly, his lip trembling with disgust.

'Your own tomb and you want to . . . accommodate a condemned man?'

'Yes. A decent burial . . . it must be done before the Sabbath.'

'You were with the council.'

Joseph did not reply, but looked down. He was sweating.

'What do you hope to gain?'

Pilate looked away again and Joseph took a pace forward.

'I . . . I did not have the courage to speak for him when he was alive.'

'So now he's dead, you're offering to defend him?'

Pilate resumed his task, rubbing each finger slowly in turn. He grimaced to himself, nodded. Then looked up at Joseph, surprised to see that he was still there.

'Take it.'

14

The casket and the figures riding.

She knelt down beside him and broke the seal. The fragrance was strong even before she opened the lid, but as she raised it the air filled with myrrh as if a torrent had broken its banks and flooded the desert.

We could not smell the blood or the filth of the quarry any more, and we did not speak or weep any more because the perfume demanded our silence. We folded the grave-clothes around him, allowing the linen to soak deeply in the ointment which seeped from the upturned chamber.

Beneath it there was the emblem of a sword, and I saw that it had never been touched, that Miryam had never touched it as she had the riders and their steeds, which had been worn into glass. The sword was fresh and sharp, and when she saw it pointing towards her, she groaned. She then closed the casket, with its strange clasp like a hand wrought in onyx stone, a dark hand. She knelt down and kissed it and wept.

She wept for a long time alone and it made the tears come again for all of us. We were all weeping and holding him, rocking, except Mary Magdalene. She had slid down in the soaking heaps of rubbish and curled up. She was lying far down there and streams of water were forging through the mud, flooding around her head, but she did not get up or move.

My mother took my hand and I looked up at her, and the desolation of her sorrow, her bitterness, her rage for me – her shaking her head at me and crying for me – made her look so old and so frail. I had never seen my mother old. I kept holding her close and she was leaning on me. My father came too, behind us. He said nothing. He had blood all over him and he had cut himself on the nails, trying to wrench them out so slowly and carefully, desperate not to deepen those terrible wounds.

The wounds.

I kept seeing them, that night. His wounds, I couldn't stop seeing them all. I had taken his hand in mine, when they were binding him, and the gash down his wrist was so vicious. I had held his hand to my cheek for a long time, his right hand, and then let it go and it seemed to fall for ever.

All the tents were waterlogged after the storm and the pilgrims sat by their choking fires. We sat together with Cleopas on the soaking earth and said nothing. I wanted to touch his arm, but I didn't dare. There was such a huge loneliness around him, even my father did not speak to him.

The twilight was gathering around us and we did not move.

Far below, Joseph and John, with all the other women, had taken him to the tomb.

They laid him there before sundown.

They laid him on the ledge in the cold, shifting the body into place, Joseph's place.

He was the last to leave. He thought of the hand pointing beyond him to the far darkness of the hills, and the fire burning in the night at Keruchim. He thought of the huge chamber in the house of Caiaphas and the faces that gathered around him, questioning him.

He stared into nothing. Gently, he led Mary Magdalene out of the way, where she had lain in the white dust at the entrance, and rolled the stone with John.

They watched it sink into its trench and seal the darkness. Branches cast shadows across the rough hatchings on the rock, the chisel marks and the hammerings, faint bent shadows that were vanishing into greyness.

Mary Magdalene knelt beside the rock, her face against it, her arm stretched out as if to embrace it and tear it down. They left her there for a few minutes, but as the last rays of the sun sank through the groves they urged her away.

'When the Sabbath is over, we'll come back,' Miryam said to her softly and took her hand. She pulled it back.

'My lord . . . my lord has gone! He's gone. He's gone.'

'I know. I know . . .' John knelt down and put both arms around her and lifted her, weeping with her.

'No, no,' she pleaded. She was whimpering and turning back all the way through the garden, suddenly stopping and turning, 'No, no.' They carried her, almost, down the slope, down the new steps cut into the rock and past wild roses that mingled their scent with the myrrh on their clothes.

She fell down on the last step and begged them to leave her there, but they would not.

'It's the Sabbath,' they said, 'we must all go home.'

'Home?'

'We must all go.' They began to weep again, all the women, because they knew they had no home. Their home was in the dark with him, their only home. They walked down through the dim groves and the last straggle of bushes before the sharp rocks descended into the steep pit.

They could see the outline of the crosses, and Joseph turned his face away. He kept walking, looking away, until he could see them no more.

She wandered in the night again. She was in the streets all through the night. They had taken her to the upper room and tried to feed her and give her some water to drink, but she would not take anything and suddenly burst away from them. She ran down the stairs and up the stepped street towards the temple mount, and John ran into the street after her, but he could see nothing, only hear her cries. He began to follow, then stopped, shook his head and looked up at Joseph. Joseph waved at him desperately. There was danger for them all and John returned, bolting the door.

She ran through the streets, howling her grief. She stumbled through archways and down steps, banged into doors, but no one looked out at some madwoman on the Sabbath evening.

She longed for madness again, one moment of relief from the terrible sanity that now tormented her. The clarity with which she saw the tomb, the finality of it, the courtyards where she longed to see him but knew it was some shadow, she longed for any illusion, craved voices and false comforts. She willed herself to go mad, but she could not, all she could see was the vast empty city, the dark hills and their lights, the fires where he was not sitting. She could see endless places, cobbled streets and docks, tethered boats, old familiar trees, she could see such an array of emptiness and she could hear nothing without his voice, without him, as if the whole world were churning slowly into silence.

She ran through the streets until dawn, fleeing into the

darkness under the implacable gaze of soldiers. The next day she lay among bones and scavenging dogs beneath the brow of Golgotha.

Early on the third day, before it was dawn, she scrambled up to the garden where the tomb was cut into the rock. She imagined that she would meet the other women there and they would comfort each other and perhaps prepare new spices for the body.

She thought of touching the body one more time. She climbed, stumbling hastily, scratching herself, rushing as fast as she could, because she could see pale light coming through the throng of branches. If she had missed the other women she would be overwhelmed with sorrow, if the rock had swung down into its groove for ever. She began to weep again and fall and pick herself up, sobbing and throwing her hair back wildly.

She had to find them. She had to go in there and touch him once more, hold him once more. She ran desperately into the wide clearing, but there was no one there. She looked around and could see very little, because the dawn had hardly penetrated the thicket of trees.

But then she saw that the tomb was open. In the faintest light falling on the channel of rocks and earth, she saw the great stone rolled up its slope and on to the level ground. She staggered back, looked behind her, around her. She could hear nothing in the trees or on the path below, no steps of people coming or going. She clutched her hair and looked again at the gaping darkness. Light was beginning to enter, very gradually, and push up towards the tall ledge where the body lay. She could see the whiteness of the grave-clothes and she began to walk towards them, looking over her shoulder once, then turning, crouching down. She reached in and her hand fell on the flat cloth. She stopped, and she could hear the sound of her own breathing. She was drawing rapid breaths and her hands were on her mouth. She could see where the strips of linen lay in the shape of a body. There was sunlight along the length of them, except for the feet, the place where the feet should have been, which was in deep shadow. She touched the place and it was cold, and her finger smelt of myrrh and cassia.

Her whole hand, where she had touched the cloths, was filled with fragrance, and she could hear the single note of a bird singing somewhere. It was echoing in the tomb.

She was afraid. She backed out of the darkness and fell against the first step cut into the rock. She twisted around, keeping her head low, terrified that soldiers were lining the bushes. They had come, they had taken him. They had taken him to some terrible secret place. 'They've taken the body,' she said. 'They've . . .' and then she crawled into the garden and began to weep, her face and her hands flooding with tears, 'Ohh . . . ohhh . . . my lord, my lord . . .'

Light was streaming through the branches, the first light in the garden, but she sat among the rocks and the long grasses, hunched and sobbing, moaning and calling. She called 'Lord', and shook her head and said, 'Where?' until she did not know what she was saying any more. She collapsed into the dust and lay there gasping and holding herself like a baby, rocking herself.

'Lord,' she said. 'Mine . . . mine . . . my . . . ohhh.'

At first she did not hear the voice beside her, because it was very soft and the birds were gathering in the trees. Their chorus was rising and she thought she heard some blackbird or doves rustling in the balsam tree which stood beside the tomb with its long weeping branches and its thorns.

'Why are you crying?'

She heard it then, but she did not move. It did not make her afraid and she knew it was no soldier, for it had asked 'Why are you crying?' She shifted herself a little, tried to sit up but could not. She knew it must be the gardener, because Joseph was a wealthy man and he had planted rare trees and flowers which she had never seen before.

'They have taken my lord away,' she said, 'and I don't know where they have put him.'

She began to shake and weep for a while again and the figure said nothing, but sat down beside her where she was lying. After many minutes he spoke again.

'Tell me who you're looking for.'

She shook her head, struggling for more words that would not come. The voice was gentle and persistent.

'I might know where he is.'

She turned to him and could not see that anything through her tears. 'Oh sir, if you're the gardener, please tell me where they've taken him.'

He looked at her. She could see that he was looking straight at her, but she couldn't see his face. He had some cloak, some robe around him, wrapped as if for a journey. She knew the cloak, but she couldn't think how.

He kept looking, and he was holding out one hand to her.

'Mary,' he said.

She was focusing. She could see something, she could hear a voice. It was saying . . . her name.

*   *   *

Mary.

She looked up. She looked right up into the brightness, and she could not see the face because of the brightness of the sun behind it, but she knew.

She knew then.

She reached out her fingers slowly, trembling, so slowly, to touch. The wounded hand. She took his hand, crying, and held it to her. She said, 'Lord?'

He nodded very carefully and slowly, in his particular way, as if he were talking to the children by Galilee and telling them something they had to remember.

He nodded. She reached out and fell into his arms. She folded into him, looked up at him, couldn't say anything, but just stared. She looked high up as if he were so far from her, but he was there. He was beside her, holding her whole body as he had on the rubbish tip of Capernaum. He was holding her again and saying 'Mary'.

She clung to him fiercely, as if the dawn would lift him away, as if some mist would rise and burn in the heat and he would be gone, the dream would melt into blue and leave her broken in the dust.

She looked up. High up into his eyes. Now she saw them. She saw his eyes for the first time as the sun filtered through the cypress trees and the rock roses that grew so wildly and chaotically from the ledges of the rock. All around him was light, light coming now, and he let her look. She looked deep and he returned her gaze until she was sure. Until she knew. He let her feel and stroke his hands and touch his forehead and sigh, and then cry, and then look down, close her eyes and open them again. And see the nail marks in his feet.

When she saw those she gave a cry and brushed her hair again, wet with tears, across them. He pushed her away gently, took her by the shoulders and eased her away.

'You don't need to hold on to me any more. Not now.'

She let go.

'Not now I am going to my father, and your father.'

She let go and sat back as he stood, and he was so tall in the sun, so different, but it was him. It was him, and she could see his footprints in the dust. Everything about him was the same and yet it was as if she had met him for the first time.

She was filled with fear and with love.

He lifted up his hands and she saw the marks, and she felt as if all her burden of grief had been lifted for ever from her heart.

Joy filled her. It kept coming, it kept rolling towards her and filling her, every single part, and she held her hands out to him as if she were receiving his joy. She did not know where to go, whether to stay or run, or what to do, except gaze on his face. All she wanted to do was to look up into his face for ever, for all her life, for all eternity, but he said 'Go'. He said it firmly. 'Go, tell everyone. Tell Simon Peter.'

'Peter,' she said.

She did not look back but ran stumbling down the steep path, where briars and tendrils snatched at her dress, and she kept running, sliding.

The women were climbing up the track to the garden, bent down in their grief. They saw a girl high up, tumbling and rolling into the dust and getting up. She jumped down the wall of one of the other tombs, clutched a branch to steady herself, then ran down towards them.

They could see that it was Mary, and they felt pity for the fragile creature who was dancing in the graveyards and singing.

She came right up to them but did not stop, just called 'Seen, I have seen' and turned back shouting, 'The Lord, I have seen the Lord.'

They stopped for a moment and laid down their spices. They stood and watched her careering down the path and looked at each other. They knew that this had been coming and that it was inevitable. They had all been broken but she had been crushed into a stupor. They began their slow procession up the hill towards the tomb.

Simon Peter had come back into the city at the dead of night. He was bitterly cold and hungry. He had found his way to the upper room, reluctantly, and had sat on the steps to the roof for a long time. Andrew had found him, huddled against the wall and refusing to talk, but he had led his brother into the chamber where they all sat in silence. John had put a hand on his shoulder and tried to mutter something, and others had followed, but Simon Peter had walked out of the room, banging the door so hard that the plaster had showered from the lintel and a stone had fallen.

He had picked up the stone and held it and stared at it for

hours as the dawn rose, then he had let it fall from his hand and kicked it.

He was standing on the roof, staring vacantly at the morning intruding with shafts of light among the roofs and the battlements, light which filled him with terrible foreboding, when he saw the wild figure. She was running down the streets, her hair streaming behind her. She was picking up her skirts like a five-year-old and racing towards him, as if he were the most important person in the world. She stopped at the first door, panting and shaking her head, and then leapt up the steps two at a time.

'What is it, Mary, what's the matter?'

He stood in front of her, afraid she would run crazily off the edge of the parapet. She was gulping the air, trying desperately to speak.

'Seen,' she said.

'What have you seen?'

'Seen . . . come.' She took his arm.

'What?'

'Come!' she shouted.

'Mary,' he took her hand firmly. The woman was out of her wits, in some pitiable confusion. He felt anguish at seeing her so deranged and he could see that she had not slept for nights.

'Come . . . the Lord!' she shouted.

'The Lord,' said Peter very softly to her face, 'is dead.' He nodded to reinforce the truth. 'He is dead, Mary.'

'No.' She was pulling wildly at him, tugging his sleeve with great force, leaning back and pulling. 'No . . . in the garden . . . I've seen . . .'

'Seen?'

'Jesus.'

'You've seen Jesus?'

Peter put his hands to his face. She had fallen right back into the madness and he felt rage and an overflowing sadness for her. 'Mary,' he tried to take her arm, 'we're all downstairs, comforting each other, trying to . . . face . . .'

But he had not faced what had happened and could not. He turned away from her sharply.

She grabbed him with both her hands and shouted at him as if he were a disobedient mule. 'Come on, *come on!*' She pushed him from behind. 'He's alive, I've seen him with my own eyes', and then she ran down the steps and turned at the doorway and waved furiously, 'Come on.'

He ran after her, protesting, calling to her, 'The grief has made you mad', but he kept running as she faltered ahead of him, exhausted, and he ran past her.

He kept on running until he came to the tomb.

He saw that the stone had been rolled away. He walked a few paces forward then stopped, his hands on the great rock. He turned round and there was no one behind him, although he could hear voices in the far distance, far down by the quarry.

He looked into the emptiness, where he could see the sunlight pouring across the abandoned grave-clothes. He dived down, entered the darkness and walked deep into the tomb and around, then came back to the ledge. He was breathing hard as he touched the moist linen, lifted the head cloth. He let it fall.

It was empty, the whole shroud, as if it had been wrapped around air.

'Who's done this?' he said.

Furious tears were pouring down his cheeks as he climbed back into the sunlight.

'Who . . . who?'

He had let him go. He had denied him even in the tomb, even as a cold corpse alone in the darkness, he had left him there. He had let him be taken.

He ran from the garden and he could see Mary below with the other women. They were talking loudly and holding each other. They were embracing. He could not hear what they were saying, but he thought he heard laughter. He climbed up high, he began to run up high, away from everything, from the madness. He ran, weeping and cursing himself, he ran into the dazzling light of the sun, where he saw a stranger blocking his path.

He tried to push past but the figure would not move.

He looked up. He looked up again.

The light was too strong and he could not see.

He could not see because he was blinded suddenly, and then a hand reached out, two hands towards him and they were holding him right round his shoulders, holding him close, closer than anyone ever held him.

'Oh Simon,' the voice came like the wind over Galilee, 'son of John.'

15

I fear telling you what I know, what I have seen with my own eyes. I stand and stare across the curtain of rain, turning to snow again, and I wonder if I will betray him.

Was there one who did not, in some way? Is there one who does not?

Only Miryam, perhaps only she who never spoke of his appearing. Never, in all the years, on the long days and nights in Jerusalem and the years at Antioch and then Ephesus, into her shadowed room, into the deathbed itself. She never spoke of how he came to her or when, but he came, and he came to her alone. I do not know if he came to her first or if he gave that gift, that jewel, to Mary, if he trusted it to Mary Magdalene. But Miryam was alone in a room by herself beside the upper room. Two nights she was alone without candles or lamps.

I saw his appearing in her eyes. I saw him there. When I saw him like that, after so many years, as if he were with me once again at Emmaus, I turned away because I could not bear the beauty. The agony of his being so close and seeing him in her, like that, as she lay dying. She told me everything she had promised, all she had stored up since the fire above the groves as I lay weeping on the night of the garden. But of the morning, of the day of his coming, the first day, she spoke not a word.

She did not have to speak.

I covet her silence, her simplicity and her intimate, fearful communion with heaven. It was her anointing, it was how the angel strengthened her to live, and to die.

I must pray that I do not deny him. I do not fear the end nor the sword, I fear only losing him.

I fear failing his love and his wonder.

I fear you, because you will look at me and say nothing and turn away, because I have not given you water. I have not given you bread and I have not covered your nakedness.

Pray for me.

I will tell you what I can and how I can.

It was the evening after the Sabbath, and we picked up our tents. My mother said nothing, she had not spoken for a whole day. She had held me and I had held her, and I desperately wanted her to say something, but she kept shaking her head.

I packed the tent up myself and squeezed out all the water I could. It ran down the stones where our fire had been, and the scar in the earth seemed to be our destiny. My father looked into the dark hollow and then covered it up with wet soil mixed with ash. He sat there for a while until everything was ready. Twilight was giving way to darkness and he told us to move on as silently as we could, not to alert anyone, not to break a twig, but to walk by night to the little village seven miles away where Cleopas had a nephew. We were to wait there, the women and children, in safety, until the men came the following day.

Pilgrims spread out, down into the groves, in case any soldiers were sent from the temple after sundown. They would act as decoy if they had to, to save us.

I begged my father not to go and told him that Cleopas was too old to fight soldiers, but he held me and said there would be no fighting, no more deaths.

'We are no threat to anyone,' he said, as if this were the worst thing to admit.

We travelled so slowly, it was almost pitch darkness and we were not allowed to carry lanterns. We found the paved road after about an hour, and that was a relief, although it was hard to my feet. I had lost my shoes somewhere, down in the quarry. They were in the mud somewhere, strewn like the rubbish. I kept thinking of him as I walked on that cold stone road, lying in the cold. So cold.

I couldn't stop seeing him in the dark, stretched out.

We reached Emmaus and then we found the place. We all slept together in a barn with a broken roof. There were stars.

My father set out with Cleopas the next day, and he said that they walked so slowly he thought they would never arrive. Cleopas kept stopping and sitting by the road. He would look up at my father. He would say, 'Now then'. But he would say it to himself, as if he were dreaming or dying, as if the words meant something else. He was in terrible anguish.

They put their arms around each other and walked on, and as they went on they began to talk about everything, to go through all that had happened to them. Cleopas would sometimes stop and raise his hands to heaven, and then walk on. My father kept shaking his head, shaking it and repeating things.

284

He kept saying scriptures, bits and pieces of scripture, and then asking Cleopas what he thought they meant. They talked of the Messiah and they talked of the donkey and the palms and the gates that seemed to lift up before him in the cascade of singing.

And as they talked, this stranger came down a path a little higher up, which joined the paved road. He waved to them with his staff and they stopped for a moment.

'Do you mind if I join you?' he said, and they said no, they didn't mind.

They didn't care about anything any more and the man seemed pleasant enough. He looked as if he'd travelled some way and he was keeping his head covered from the sun, so the shadow fell across his eyes.

'It sounds like an interesting conversation you're having,' he said.

Cleopas glanced at him because the words were an odd intrusion into their grief. 'Some things are too terrible to explain,' he said.

'What things?' the stranger said.

'What things?' My father looked at him amazed, surely he had been a visitor at the Passover festival? 'The terrible death of Jesus from Galilee.'

The man walked forward slowly with them, prodding his staff into the stones. 'Tell me about it,' he said.

'Tell you!' Cleopas shook his head, raised his hands. 'Where have you been?'

'We believed he was a great prophet, more than that . . .'

'That he was the chosen one who would save Israel!'

The stranger was curious. 'The Messiah?'

Cleopas hit his fist into his hand, 'But how can the Messiah die the death of a common criminal?'

The man stopped and held his staff in both hands. He shook his head very slightly and sighed, almost laughed, as he said, 'Oh foolish men . . . you're so learned! You talk of prophets, have you never read the prophets? You talk of the Messiah, don't you understand that he had to die? Don't you understand the scriptures at all?'

No one had ever spoken to my father like this. He was known throughout Capernaum and in the villages of the Galil as a scholar, a man who could interpret the mysteries of the writings and the laws. He was trusted and respected by so many, they knew how he studied, how he prayed in the nights, and how he stood in openness of heart before his God. And everyone knew that Cleopas was a man of the deepest wisdom, but the stranger led them like two lost children, two ignorant souls, through the deep forest of the scriptures. He led them by books, by stories and by sayings, by one word here and one word there, by a song and a dream, by visions and testimonies. He guided them from the law of Moses to the words of the prophet Malachi, until their hearts burned within them, until they were gazing at the descending sun over Emmaus and the whole earth seemed to be on fire.

They arrived at the house, and the stranger appeared to be going further. They begged him to stay, 'You must come in and eat with us.'

He hesitated, twirled the staff in his hands and looked at the long road ahead. He shifted the robe around his shoulders a little. 'Well . . .'

'No, no,' my father took his arm. 'It's too late . . . too late to travel on.'

'I'll stay . . . a little longer.'

'As long as you can!' said Cleopas, flinging open the door.

He came in, stood there in the entrance as they prepared a place for him.

I saw him, and the robe slipping from his head a little.

I saw him. He was standing there, but I did not trust my eyes and the sun was pouring in around his feet. There was dust floating in the haze and I couldn't see clearly, I said, 'Who is it, Mother?'

Her voice was far away, it was lost in the air, as if she could no longer say anything to me. She was leaning forward and she was straining to see but could not.

'It's someone they met on the road.'

'Who is it?'

Cleopas was leading him to his place and he was sitting down. The old man was mumbling. 'Sir, as our honoured friend . . . would you . . . bless the food for us?'

'I will have to be going soon.'

'We understand but um . . .'

He takes the loaf.

I am looking at him, and he raises it very slowly and then he stops. He looks up and he looks at me from under his hood. He pushes it back a little further and I can see the wound on his wrist.

I can see the wound.

I can see the long scar.

I am crying out, but I am not making any sound. I am

standing up, but no one sees me. My mother is staring too and I say, 'I know.'

She is shaking her head, struggling to see in the darkness, because there is only one candle and there are shadows across the table, deep shadows across the bread.

But he is lifting the bread out of the shadow and the light falls on it, on every curve and dent. There is light spreading across his hands, but my father and Cleopas are sitting there quietly, politely, waiting for the stranger to give the blessing.

They do not see, they do not see.

He lifts again and stops and looks at me.

His eyes, into me. He is gazing deep down, forever down into me, way down into the depths.

Further than ever.

He is showing me something. Showing me himself in a second, in a fraction of one second.

Who he is.

He raises the bread to the height, up into the shadows beyond the light, and breaks it in the darkness, breaks it so that crumbs fall.

Broken and falling and rising. The bread still rising in his hands as it breaks.

'Blessed are you, O Lord our God, who brings forth bread from the earth.'

He says the blessing, but his voice is already an echo.

He hands the bread to my father and to Cleopas, but his hands are already a dream.

As they see the marks of the nails, as they leap up from their chairs and burst out weeping, he is gone.

They weep, they turn around, the people are standing. They are running to the table. My mother has fallen down beside my father and she is touching a footprint. She is looking up to him and she is shaking her head, she is . . .

She is smiling and the tears are running down her face. She is clinging to my father and he is clinging to Cleopas.

The old man is leaning back up to the rafters. He stretches out his hand to trace the air. He paints with his fingers dancing in the shadow.

He is crying with laughter. He is looking at all the dumbstruck people and the children who cluster like frightened creatures in a storm and he is saying, 'The Lord.'

He is singing out, 'The Lord.'

My father is standing up and he is looking for me.

The look on his face, the look of craziness and wonder, the confusion and the stammering.

He is walking towards me and he is lifting me up, my head to his head, he is gazing at me and his whole face is flooding. He just swings me around and around and he cannot stop laughing. He is drunk, jibbering with laughter, stupid, reckless, ridiculous laughter, more than on the day I was born, when he danced in the street and people stared.

More than ever, in his life, in the world. He is on fire with ecstasy.

I have never seen such joy in such a solemn man, such a

pious, kind man, such a reasonable, sad man crying with laughter, my father.

My father, who comes to me now.

Who kneels beside me in the night and reminds me of his joy. Of the joy he knows for ever. Who comes to me, once in a while, when I am forgetting.

When I am in the greatest fear, he holds my hand. I dream that, I imagine it, I sense it, I pray with him there, I know he is there, somehow impossibly. I can hear, when the wind tears at the shutters and smashes them into the tentacles of ice and they break, I can hear him whisper softly, 'Little one'.

I feel his great joy once again, and mine.

I can see him running, first of all around the room in that old tumbledown barn in Emmaus, beside the house where we had all gathered, and then out of the door – and Cleopas hopping over a bench like a ten-year-old, and falling and laughing.

'Come on!'

They were running into the night, before my mother could stop them.

'Where are you going?'

They were down the paved road, leaning on each other like two drunken revellers and hugging each other.

And we watched them stumbling off into the warm night, and the frogs singing in the bushes, jesting with their little croaks and calls, as if the whole world were waking up to laughter.

* * *

'The Lord', Simon Peter held out his hands to the other disciples in the upper room. Every eye was on him except Thomas. Thomas was leaning against the door and his eyes were closed as he dredged up the last reserves of his patience. He shook his head.

Peter threw his hands up, 'I . . . he was . . .' He sighed, paced the room. He took Andrew by the arm, 'I thought they'd taken the body—'

'Who?' said Andrew.

'Who would—' James was staring at him helplessly.

'Priests, Romans . . . but . . . he was . . . he was there right in front of my eyes. In front of me. This near!' He pressed his face to James, 'Right here, like—'

Then Thomas slapped his hands together, ordering a halt to everything. He opened his eyes, pained and deeply burdened for them. 'I cannot,' he repeated, '*cannot . . . believe . . .* what I am hearing!'

Peter swung round to him. 'Thomas!' he banged his fist against his chest. 'I . . . I saw him. I saw him.'

Thomas shook his head, half-smiling at their stupidity, incredulous, saddened, angered, 'You're all crazy! All of you!' He pointed into thin air, waved his finger around, 'Dreams and visions. Everyone is going mad.' He turned and took the handle of the door firmly.

'I'm leaving,' he said.

The door smacked open suddenly, striking him on the face and hurling him to the ground.

'The Lord!' Cleopas ran in followed by my father.

'We have seen . . .'

'What we have seen . . .'

They were looking to each other, breathless. They had been running, staggering as fast as the old man could go. He had found new strength and run all the way up the street, up the steps, and now he had burst into the room he was just smiling and looking slightly idiotic.

'The Lord,' he said, and looked to my father.

My father looked around the whole room and said, as quietly and as sensibly as he could, but he was trembling and still confused, 'We have seen . . .'

He looked back to Cleopas.

'We've seen him,' said the old man.

Thomas shook his head, without getting up from the floor.

My father looked down at him with pity. 'On the road from Jerusalem, on the road, right beside us!'

'He was with us. We didn't realise.' Cleopas moved into the throng, where Joseph of Arimathea was staring at him fearfully.

'With you? In what way?'

'With us!' Cleopas waved his hands furiously. 'But we didn't recognise him!'

'That's because he's in your imagination, Cleopas,' said Thomas. The old man sighed, looked at my father, sighed again, 'On the road!' he shouted, 'Thomas!'

'Then he was gone, vanished.' They completed their tale, the long tale of their mysterious visitor on the road to Emmaus. My father looked at Thomas, at Peter and the others, and said, 'He just went.'

'No one there,' said Cleopas.

'No one . . . there,' said Thomas, nodding as if he had finally appreciated the extent of their sickness.

'No one,' said Cleopas, 'an empty place. Two pieces of broken bread . . . a cup . . . and everyone was crying! And laughing . . . and crying.'

My father looked round at his silent friends, and at Peter who was nodding and smiling, shrugging his shoulders at Thomas. Laughing.

'It was chaos! We ran! We ran and ran to you . . .'

Thomas opened the door carefully and looked down the stairs, to make sure there was no further procession of imbeciles. He sighed gratefully and then slammed the door hard.

'Well,' he said, 'I'm sick of this . . . I'm sorry but . . .' He groaned, as if making a huge effort to talk to any of them. A look of desperation and rage came over him and he paced slowly, with great deliberation, across the length of the room.

He stopped.

'Unless I see him – right here!' he shouted. 'Right here! Before me. Like that. In front of me . . . right here, and unless I see the mark of the nails and put my finger in those wounds,' he stabbed the air with his finger repeatedly, 'I *will* not believe.'

'Thomas.'

A voice spoke right behind him.

He shook his head and shouted, 'What?'

'Thomas.'

He turned, angrily, 'I've got nothing to say on this matter to any . . . any . . .'

His voice fell into a whisper as he saw the face of his lord looking directly at him.

'I . . . anyone at . . . all,' he mumbled, and he began to shake with a dreadful violence as if he were about to collapse and die.

Terror had overwhelmed him, an inexpressible horror, and he turned to the other disciples and then turned back, wondering if he should run or fall down on the floor or scream, but he could think of nothing. He could not think. He began to touch his own face, as if he did not believe in his own existence and had burnt up suddenly, melting into the air. He sank to his knees.

'Go on.' He looked up and the Lord was gazing at him without reproach. 'Put your finger here . . . and touch the marks. Don't be a doubter any more. Believe.'

It was the love, the love which came surging through him on the word 'believe' that shattered him and broke him down, so that he began to sob, saying, 'My Lord . . . and my God.'

And it was the love that drove him, drove him on in the pitiless storms, the dust and through the furthest boundaries, beyond all the known world. 'You believe because you've seen me, Thomas, but even happier are those who will believe without ever seeing me at all.' Edessa in Mesopotamia, then Parthia, then the years in strange lands where he had to learn everything again, all customs and language, where he had to be reborn every day. Travelling alone, hungry and without protection, without a sword, without money, without anything but the word 'Believe'.

And the love that had pierced his soul.

He came to India, to Kerala, where the people received him, and they sat beneath the mango trees and listened to him as if he were an angel of God, and in the nights he would wander alone and grieve over the children's faces, their rapt attention and their faithfulness, and repent again of his pride, the blinding pride.

Love held him until he died, somewhere in the southern region in a place without a name, and they say he sang for joy on the day of his death and it became a sign to them all, and many believed in the risen one because of his singing.

Joseph of Arimathea, too, had watched in the upper chamber. He had watched every moment and every word, all that happened to Thomas and all the chatter with the disciples, because Jesus had stayed long into the night. He had eaten a meal with them. He had talked to every single one of them, each in turn. Each one alone.

Joseph had sat in the far corner and stared down whenever his lord happened to look in his direction.

In the small hours of the morning, just before he left them, Jesus came to him.

He sat down beside him and Joseph looked up and was about to break down in sorrow for his silence, for all that he had not done, for the long list of his sins, when Jesus lifted up his hand.

He pointed with his finger, and Joseph looked up and out of the window into the furthest night, beyond all the roofs of the city. He heard the word 'Go' but when he turned around, Jesus had gone.

16

It was Joseph who brought me here.

He brought me on his last journey, as far as Caerleon on the west side of the White Island. He was never buried in his own tomb, but laid to earth by the first few followers of the Way, who wept over his lonely grave for twelve days. The wind was violent and there were leaves like mountains. The whole forest was stripped bare in a single night.

He had never stopped travelling, never for one day of his life had he stopped carrying the treasure and the burning love. He spoke many languages and yet he did not speak of his master, so much as become him.

They called him 'Iachawdwr', the one who binds the wounds.

There is a guard here who remembers him, one of the legionaries who is a secret follower. He does not dare to speak. He is silent, but he has come to me with parchment. He has given me quills and just enough oil to burn low and I have written for you in the nights, in the endless winter. I have written what I can and the time is short.

We dream of endless time.

They say that the governor will return in the spring and the blasphemers will be brought to justice, those who have brought the emperor into disrepute. Those who will not worship at least with token sacrifices, a votive of flowers. All they ask is for our denial of Chrestus the troublemaker, and we can go free. As a Jew, I may be taken to Rome and tried before the emperor.

I pray to be worthy. I am ready to die here or in Rome. There are many gateways and nothing matters now, the snow buries everything and if it buries me I shall be glad. I have kept my promise. I have written to you what I know, I have told you what a girl knows.

I have lived long enough. It is your time. No one knows the day or the hour and you must live not knowing.

Even on that day, his last day, we did not know. We were blinded.

The cloud.

It came invisibly. None of us saw anything or felt anything, not even the wind, although the trees were bending far down the slopes, as far as Bethany. My hair was in my eyes and my mother's robe was flapping wildly. She put her hand to it, dreamily, as if she were smoothing out a crease. She was not aware of the gale that was coming around us, because all of us were looking at him. There must have been about five hundred of us, gathered all along the ridge. He was standing very still and there were anemones around his feet, bright spots of colour in the long grass, which was bending and flattening. The wind turned the grasses into an ocean of light.

The cloud. It was coming and we did not know. He was still so clear, and laughing with a little boy who had run up to him and jumped into his arms. He set the boy down and his mother took his hand, and there were little children calling

297

to him and he answered them by name.

He said my name.

I walked out but I did not run to him, I just came out of the
crowd a little, enough for him to see me. I felt so shy of him and
I felt afraid, but he said 'Tamar'.

He said it very quietly and looked at me, one more time.

It was a brilliant hot day and the olive groves were almost white
in the haze. People were asking him questions, daring to speak
to him, becoming confident because he had appeared many
times and we had become familiar with the veil.

The veil that fluttered to one side at will.

We had begun to expect him, and we did not know that the
cloud was coming . . .

Someone asked him, 'Is this the time when you will restore
the kingdom to Israel?'

He said, 'It is not for you to know the times or seasons or the day.'

He did not move from where he stood in the still sunlight,
and the raging wind that came sweeping down valleys, over
the hills, through the darkness of the groves, the wind that
came without sound made us hold each other. I stood between
my mother and father and they had their hands tight around
me, but because he was in the stillness and in the bright, the
dazzling sunlight, we imagined we were in the calm too. We
took no account at all of the storm of brightness that was
enveloping us all. He spoke so softly and every word was like a

clear note sounded in an empty chamber.

It seemed to echo in emptiness, in calm and cool shadow, like a song in a ruin.

'Go,' he said, and we did not know that he was going.

'Go through all the earth and make disciples of every nation. Baptise in the name of the father.'

The father.

The sweetness of his voice and the strength and the passion that urged us, that drove into us. The shout in our souls, 'Father!'

His tenderness fell on us like fire.

'And of the Son and of the Holy Spirit. For the Spirit will come upon you.'

We could not see him for a moment as he said 'spirit', as if the sun had shone down into blackness and stung our eyes, as if we could not tolerate the vision and so our eyes were dimmed into nothing. Then we saw him again, quite still. Just standing there, standing in the sunlight, his feet among the anemones, and the scars.

We saw the marks of the nails and they were crimson like flowers.

'I will be with you always, even to the end of the world.'

The cloud. It came invisibly, it had been coming and cloaking the sun, burying the brightness of that still day beneath the wild fire of light, unendurable light which we saw only for one second, for less than a second, the blink of an eye.

The wind was all, the wind that swept around us, carrying twigs into the sky, leaves and birds sailing.

The fathomless silence of that place.

I saw one of the little boys, one I had played with at Keruchim, and he was walking round and round the place where Jesus had been standing. He touched the dust, the print of his feet, and he began to weep so bitterly, as if the poor boy had realised suddenly that he would never see him again.

He was leaving him, he was going, turning and going, taken up, going, and the little one sat on the grass and wept and held out his arms to the air.

I ran to him and took his hand. I wiped his tears and I kissed him and held him. I said, 'Don't be worried, don't be upset. In my father's house are many rooms.'

He looked up at me with a frown.

'In Capernaum?' he said.

I began to laugh, I said, 'Yes! In Capernaum, in Jerusalem, in the whole world. The kingdom of God has come and now he is with us for ever.'

He looked at me, with such a look, and he gripped my hand because he felt safe with me. He was calm, like me.

We walked down through the fields together, all of us. I led him, and the other children ran with us, and Simon Peter came with his arm around Matthew. Cleopas walked with Thomas. My father and mother walked with Joseph and Mary Magdalene, and she was at peace too. I saw her stop and stand on one of the ridges, and she didn't look back. No one looked back.

Only Miryam and John stayed at the top, looking over Jerusalem until the sun went down.

EPILOGUE

It was two years later that I came back and there was snow. I walked through Kidron and it was falling, it had been falling for some time. I saw my own footprints. I had never seen them like that before, marks in the whiteness which were vanishing even as I looked at them. I walked through the groves until I came to the old cistern, the place where they had gathered to arrest him, and there was ice hanging there and drifting snow.

I can see now that it was nothing, those flakes falling and the little banks and ridges of snow where the wind had carried it, but to me it was a miracle of purity. The whiteness came like healing, came across the dread and the sight of the quarry below, the filth and the dreams, the many dreams I had been having.

I had dreamed of him so often and I had longed to see him one more time, but I did not admit this to the others, I did not even tell my father. I told no one where I was going that day, and I knew in my heart that I would not see him. I had to tell him, though, I had to stand on the meadow where he had been taken from me and I had to whisper his name, into the wind if need be, into nothing. I would expect nothing and see nothing, but I would talk with him and if I had to cry he would not mind. It had come to seem wrong to mourn after all the glory and all we had been given, after all the fire.

I did not entrust my forbidden sorrow to anyone, foolishly perhaps, for now I know they would have understood, but on that day I was still clinging on to my childhood by a hairsbreadth. I was fourteen. I walked alone under the mysterious brightness of the olive trees that bore the fruit of snow, little burdens falling on my shoulder, flurries of white, of dampness running down me. I did not reach the ridge but came once more to the threshold, the stone gate of Gat-Sh'manim.

It was there I stayed. I could not walk further, something took hold of me and it was as if a voice said 'Stay'.

I could not go in. I wanted to, but I knew it was not asked of me at that time. All I had to do was stay there in the falling snow, and watch the curtain of flakes sweeping all across Jerusalem.

I stood there until my footprints were obliterated. I did not need to whisper his name, for he was there.

WATTS

Watts, Murray

The miracle maker

$ 11.95

DUE DATE
